Anglesey and Gwynedd
the War Years
1939–45

Reg Chambers Jones

Anglesey and Gwynedd, the War Years, 1939–45
First published in Wales in 2008
by
BRIDGE BOOKS
61 Park Avenue
Wrexham, LL12 7AW

This is an enhanced and expanded edition of the book
Bless 'Em All
Aspects of the War in North West Wales, 1939–45
published in 1995

Reprinted 2009

© 2008 Reg Chambers Jones
© 2008 Design, typesetting and layout Bridge Books

All Rights Reserved.
No part of this publication may be reproduced,
stored in a retrieval system, or transmitted
in any form or by any means, electronic,
mechanical, photocopying, recording or
otherwise, without the prior permission
of the Copyright holder.

A CIP entry for this book is available from the British Library

ISBN 978-1-84494-051-6

Printed and bound by
Cromwell Press Group
Trowbridge

In memory of
my beloved wife

Maureen

Contents

	Abbreviations and Currency	6
	Preface	7
1.	On a War Footing	9
2.	Civil Defence	15
3.	Defences	35
4.	Evacuation	41
5.	Home Guard and Police	59
6.	The Nation's Treasure	86
7.	Agriculture and PoWs	95
8.	Industry	128
9.	The Armed Forces	157
10.	Social Life	227
11.	Mulberry Harbour	235
12.	Peace	243
	Select Bibliography	247

Abbreviations:

AAS	Anglesey Archives Service, Llangefni
AC	Author's collection
BP	Bangor Papers (Bangor University)
C&DH	*Caernarfon & Denbigh Herald*
GAS	Gwynedd Archives Service
ICE	The Institution of Civil Engineers
NWWN	*North Wales Weekly News*
PNP	Plas Newydd Papers (Bangor University)
PPP	Paget Private Papers (Plas Newydd, Isle of Anglesey)
BUA	Bangor University Archives

Currency

All references to money are in pre-decimalisation currency:
- 2.4d = 1p
- 12d = 1 shilling (1/-) = 5p
- 240d = 20 shillings (£1) = £1

Preface

For the greater part of the last fifty years or so, many wartime records have been hidden from public scrutiny but now, some of the secrets of the Second World War are gradually revealed to those who have the patience to delve amongst the historic documents. Most of these papers are with the National Archives but others are in private hands or in local archives. My task in researching and collating details of wartime activities in Anglesey, Caernarfonshire and Merionethshire, as the counties were known at that time, has been a fascinating one. Unfortunately, it cannot possibly be a complete account because of difficulties in gaining access to some records. There are many excellent books written on various aspects of the war; mine is merely an attempt to collate and record extracts from accounts of wartime incidents and activities together with personal recollections.

I am indebted to the Marquess of Anglesey for his time and guidance and for allowing me to delve into private documents and papers at Plas Newydd from where much of the interesting detail concerning the work of the War Agricultural Executive Committee was gleaned.

The Archivist and staff at Gwynedd Archives Service have once again been most helpful and patient as indeed has the staff of the Manuscript Department in the library of the University of Wales, Bangor. Mrs Carol Morgan, Archivist, Institution of Civil Engineers, London, very kindly provided me with information about the Mulberry Harbour. My thanks also to Miss Jacqueline McComish, Research Assistant, National Gallery, London, for allowing me access to material relating to the transfer and storing of pictures in Wales.

The late R. E. Roberts of Penmaenmawr was most generous in providing many documents relating to the Royal Air Force, the Royal Observer Corps and the RAF Mountain Rescue Service; also photographs and newspaper cuttings that he had systematically collected over the years.

I also wish to acknowledge the assistance that I have received from the following: the curator and staff of the Holyhead Maritime Museum; J. C. Davies; Mrs Hilary Date; Mrs Dorothy Dickie; Mr and Mrs Tecwyn Evans; Peter Hansford; Mrs Rosemary Hughes; W. L. Hughes; C. Norman Kneale; Michael Lewis; John W. Morris; Royal Air Force Museum; Roy Sloan; John Stops; Dafydd Whiteside Thomas; Mrs Bethan Williams and Len Williams.

My thanks also to Alister Williams, Sue Williams and Gwynne Belton of Bridge Books for editing the manuscript, and for their advice and guidance.

Reg Chambers Jones
August, 2008

Chapter 1
On a War Footing

In the years leading up to the Second World War, opinions varied as to Hitler's intentions and eventual ambitions. His ability to frustrate the people of Germany seemingly extended to politicians of other countries. Following a meeting with David Lloyd George, at his country residence at Berchtesgaden in Germany in September 1936, Hitler stated, 'The idea of a Germany intimidating Europe with a threat that its irresistible army might march across frontiers form no part in the new vision ...' Even though Germany's intentions had became obvious by 1938, and preparations for the inevitable war were already in hand, pleas for peace continued to be made by many countries, including Britain, with visits to Munich by the Prime Minister, Neville Chamberlain. These visits came to nothing and the German war machine started to roll across Europe. Parliament voted in favour of conscription, compulsory military service, men aged between twenty and twenty-one (with certain exceptions) had to register on 3 June 1939 at a Ministry of Labour Employment Exchange under the Military Training Act, 1939. At the same time, the Government's rearmament programme got underway and evacuation schemes and air-raid precautions were prepared. Nevertheless, even though twenty years had elapsed, the colossal waste of life and the horror inflicted on mind and body during the First World War were still indelibly printed on the memories of those who had survived the carnage and it was little wonder that pacifism and nationalism were advocated in the late 1930s.

There were many demonstrations against conscription throughout

The former Prime Minister, the Rt Hon David Lloyd George, MP for Caernarfon Boroughs, addressing an audience at Llandrindod Wells, c.1939. [GAS]

Wales. In Pwllheli, a crowd of about 1,000 attended an anti-conscription meeting conducted by a number of Free Church ministers. The audience adopted, without dissent, a resolution declaring opposition to compulsory military training. The Revd J. W. Jones, Criccieth, said that the conscription measure 'undermined the freedom of individuals and was a denial of the spirit of the Gospel'. He also protested against displays of air-raid precautions and recruiting parades on Sundays.

A similar rally was announced in the *Caernarvon & Denbigh Herald*, 26 May 1939,

> Anti-Conscription ... Mr W. D. Oliver Brown of Glasgow will be among the speakers at the anti-conscription rally at the Caernarvon Eisteddfod Pavilion tomorrow. Mr Brown represents the Scottish Neutrality League, a movement working for Scotland's neutrality in all wars ... Also attending at the above meeting will be Richard Bishop of Dolgellau (Welsh Pacifist Society).

The fact that an air-gunnery school was to be established in the area in May 1939 and training could take place on any day of the week, including Sundays, did nothing to ease the situation. Despite opposition from a number of organisations, including the Lleyn Rural District Council, it went ahead as did similar training courses in other parts of north-west Wales.[1]

However, not everyone was in agreement with pacifism as the following letter made clear,

> Conscription has come and is long overdue. It is meeting with strong opposition from religious bodies in North Wales. The same thing happened on the eve of the last war ... our cheery little band of Nationalists naturally object. They look forward to the day when Herr Hitler "delivers them from the brutal English yoke". But it would be well to remember that Herr Hitler has a poor sense of humour ...'[2]

The first indication of the seriousness of the situation, especially to the youngsters who had not experienced the tragedy of the First World War, were the posters distributed around towns and villages in August 1939. One of the first to be issued was from the Ministry of Information with the prosaic words 'KEEP CALM and CARRY ON.' Another was more ominous advising the population when and where gas masks were to be issued. These hideous items were intended to be carried on the person from the start of hostilities. At the same time, villages and towns in north Wales were told to prepare for an influx of evacuees from Merseyside and other areas that were liable to be affected by bombing raids. When the 'mothers and babies' evacuee contingent arrived in the first few days of September, they were given temporary accommodation in local community halls, schools and chapel vestries until more permanent arrangements could be made. Centralised facilities, including feeding and bedding, (which had been in place since early 1939 in anticipation of such an eventuality) were organised by the Women's Voluntary Service.[3]

Even after war had been declared, the editorial in the *Caernarvon & Denbigh Herald* on 8 September 1939 stated,

> Our leaders have stated that Great Britain has no quarrel with the German people. That is the truth. The British people have sought peace and friendly relations with the great nation but Hitler would not listen to appeals for conciliation. The Archbishop of Canterbury … says of Hitler that he is 'the last man to listen to peaceful persuasion'… This war is now called 'Hitler's War' …

Details of every individual in the United Kingdom, except those in the armed forces, were compiled by enumerators on Friday, 29 September 1939, and were used for the eventual National Register and the issue of ration books and identity cards. Registration was compulsory and penalties were inflicted for non-compliance or for giving false information.

It would appear that during the first few weeks of the war, not everyone had abandoned the possibility of peace and on 3 October Lloyd George made a most stirring speech in the House of Commons, warning the Government not to come to a hasty decision when considering peace offers. As expected, the speech was subjected to a great deal of criticism from some quarters. When, less than three weeks later, the former Prime Minister addressed an unexpectedly large audience of between six and eight thousand, at the Caernarfon Pavilion on the subject of peace aims, he started his speech in Welsh and went on to deal with Munich and Chamberlain's approaches to Hitler. He said that he had been falsely accused of proposing surrender, 'I simply proposed a conference now, before the great slaughter began, and not years hence when millions of young men have been killed, perhaps also many women and children … A conference now to save the world from the miseries and uncertainties of a prolonged war and before the nations become exhausted and impoverished and civilisation had been thrown back decades. That was my proposal …'

Such was Lloyd George's reputation that, with Neville Chamberlain as Prime Minister and Winston Churchill as First Lord of the Admiralty, many of his admirers wondered why he had not been included in the War Cabinet, '[He] is still full of vigour and a man possessing his outstanding abilities would be of invaluable help to the Government in the present situation … At 76 he may be too old for a strenuous executive post but his experience, his genius for disengaging essentials from "red tape" and his superb confidence in a crisis would be invaluable in some advisory capacity …'[4]

Chamberlain, however, was determined not to have Lloyd George in his cabinet although it is doubtful if the latter would have any desire to serve, such was the contempt that he had for the Prime Minister, whom he felt was the last person to lead the country through the war. Lloyd George was still a great orator when he appeared on a public platform, but such occasions were by then infrequent and appearances in the House of Commons left him in a tired state. Leo Amery, when he made his speech in the House of Commons in May 1940 attacking Neville Chamberlain, quoted Oliver Cromwell's remarks to the Rump Parliament in 1653, 'You have sat here too long for any good you have been doing. Depart, I say, and let us have done with you! In the name of God, go!' Lloyd George, who was in his room behind the Speaker's Chair at the time, hurried to the Chamber when he was advised of the observations being made. There, in a grave voice and with a warning, upraised finger, he set forth the peril of the issues raised by Britain's defeat in the Norway campaign, which he described as 'half-baked', and lacking in naval cooperation. Then, after warning Churchill 'not to allow himself to be converted into an air-raid shelter to keep the splinters from hitting his colleagues', Lloyd George struck at Chamberlain, with all the fury of his greatest days, 'It is not a question of who are the Prime Minister's friends. It is a far bigger issue … He has appealed for sacrifice. The nation is prepared for every sacrifice so long as it has leadership … I say solemnly that the Prime Minister should give an example of sacrifice, because there is nothing which can contribute more to victory than that he should sacrifice the seals of office.'

Chamberlain resigned on 10 May and Churchill formed a new government with a war cabinet on the model formed by Lloyd George in the First World War. On 11 May, Lloyd George told Churchill that it suited him not to be included in the Cabinet. 'It would be an impossible position to be in a Cabinet like that. They would be fighting me.' On 12 May, he wrote, 'I do not think Winston will approach me. I think it will be a coalition of the parties and their nominees. In that I would not have a place … I would simply be there fretting and fuming, and having no real authority, and then that would do me no good … Neville would have infinitely more authority that I would have, and he would oppose everything that I proposed.'

On 28 May, Churchill offered him a position in the War Cabinet, subject to the approval of Chamberlain. Lloyd George replied,

> You were good enough yesterday to ask me if I would be prepared to enter the War Cabinet if you secured the adhesion of Mr Chamberlain to the proposal. It is the first time you have approached me personally on the subject and I can well understand the reason for your hesitancy, for in the course of our interview, you made it quite clear that if Chamberlain interposed his veto on the grounds of personal resentment over past differences, you could not proceed with the offer. This is not a firm offer. Until it is definite, I cannot consider it.

Chamberlain resigned on 30 September and died six weeks later. On 12 December, Lord Lothian, British Ambassador to the United States of

America, also died. Churchill invited Lloyd George to London to offer him the post in Washington, but his doctor said he should decline the job. Lloyd George replied stating that he had no intention of accepting.

Meanwhile, in Wales, attempts at procuring peace continued and a resolution was passed calling upon the Government to acquiesce to a truce and an international conference. It also stated that, 'Professor J. E. Daniel, President of the Welsh Nationalist Party ... [is] to appeal to the Government immediately to take the initiative in securing an armistice and calling a conference to discuss a new European order ... '[5]

At a conference in Caernarfon the Revd Lewis Valentine (the first president of the Welsh Nationalist Party) said that, 'these days of war were of great danger to Wales. The Party's duty he said was to see that Wales did not cease to exist as a nation when England was supposed to be fighting for the justice of other small nations'. The conference's attitude to the war was reflected in two resolutions which were unanimously passed namely:

> That this conference of the Welsh Nationalist Party, firmly believing that nothing but evil can come to Wales through this war, requests the Government to call an Armistice and peace conference without delay, and by accepting Welsh Nationality as sufficient grounds for conscience objections to military service ...[6]

In an attempt to appease those opposed to conscription, the Secretary of State for War, Mr Hore-Belisha, stated that the War Office was very conscious of the feeling in Wales and that those who governed such matters would be in favour of keeping a man in the unit of his choice.

The inconvenience of the rationing of food, petrol, clothing and other material, was grudgingly accepted with periodic dissension. Perhaps the least inconvenienced by these wartime conditions were the poorer families whose ability to purchase was governed, not by rationing, but by affordability. Increased wartime production and labour demands transformed the Welsh economy and virtually eliminated unemployment that had been a notable feature of life in the 1920s and 1930s. Similarly, a turnaround also occurred in Welsh agriculture which had been very much in the doldrums prior to the war. Cars, still regarded as luxury items at the beginning of the war, were available to very few. Due to the shortage of petrol, and the difficulty in maintaining the vehicles, most were taken off the road and placed in storage for the duration of hostilities. Petrol was only available to very few essential users such as doctors, but even then it was severely rationed and became progressively more difficult to obtain. All new roads and improvements were postponed indefinitely, but existing roadworks were required to be completed as soon as possible.[7]

As part of anti-invasion measures being taken, the Divisional Road Engineer for Wales was ordered by the Government on the 29 May 1940 to remove at once, 'all direction signs on Public Highways throughout the

County. Precedence should be given in the first instance to Trunk Roads and Classified Roads, attention to the Unclassified Roads following in due course. Action in the first instance should be confined to roads outside built-up areas ... I should emphasise that the posts can remain for the ultimate replacement of the signs.'

By the summer of 1940, with the German Army poised on the coast of northern France, and the threat of invasion imminent, the Local Defence Volunteers (LDV) – later to be called the Home Guard – were organised so that any men who had not been enlisted into the armed forces, were coerced into joining a motley crowd of defenders. The force was dependent in its early days, during a critical part of the war, on using whatever weapon that came to hand to repel invaders, and members wore a uniform that consisted of civilian clothing and an armband with the initials 'LDV'. Many of those who joined the Home Guard were veterans of the First World War or possibly even the Boer War.

The threat of bombing and invasion, emphasised in many government leaflets and pamphlets, was sufficient to ensure that everyone involved with Air Raid Precautions, the Auxiliary Fire Service, the Red Cross, St John's Ambulance, the Women's Voluntary Service and other organisations, took their duties very seriously. However, an element of discontent was apparent as far as some ARP wardens was concerned. A letter, written on 3 July 1941, advised the Senior Warden that the wardens stationed at the kiosk at the end of Bangor pier intended resigning, 'those who had the experience of standing for hours in a draughty kiosk on cold winter nights know better than to wait for another winter to arrive.' Since matters had not been resolved by the autumn and they were facing another winter with no form of heating in the kiosk, nor any refreshments whilst they were on duty, they eventually went on strike. The wardens in the Penrhosgarnedd sector of Bangor were equally as disgruntled according to a letter written on the 8 September 1941, '... our sector extends along Penrhos Road from Penchwintan Terrace to Beulah Chapel. The road is very exposed ... and we have to patrol on some occasions for as long as five or six hours ...' Their main grievance was that there was no ARP post on their beat where they could shelter, rest or have refreshments during adverse weather.

Notes

1. GAS, XC2-3-7.
2. *C&DH*, 2 June 1939.
3. GAS, DI/689.
4. *C&DH*, Notes of the Week, 15 September 1939.
5. *C&DH*, 13 October 1939.
6. *C&DH*, 27 October 1939.
7. GAS, XC2-6-242.

Chapter 2
Civil Defence

Following the Munich crisis of 1938, the Government decided to enrol over a million men and women in various roles in the Civil Defence (or Air Raid Precautions as it was generally known). The estimated number of wardens required in Caernarfonshire had, by March 1939, been exceeded by 500, each applicant being vetted by the police. Amongst the variety of tasks expected of this multi-role army of civilians was that of digging trenches in the larger towns and cities, to provide protection for the public in the event of an air raid where specially built shelters were not available. The numbers required for the regular Caernarfonshire Fire Brigade was short of ten men and the Auxiliary Fire Service by 280. However, 760 had enrolled as special constables against the establishment of 734 in the first quarter of 1939.[1]

The police started ARP and anti-gas drill training classes at the Barracks in Caernarfon as early as 1938.[2] Similar classes were started in Port Dinorwic in June 1939, with tuition being given by Mr W. Pritchard of Vaynol House. The gas mask, which was issued to every civilian, was made of rubber, with an eye-piece and filter, which covered the face completely and was retained in position by means of adjustable straps placed over the back of the head. Babies were protected from a gas by being placed in a special container with air being made available by means of a hand pump located on its side. An official leaflet distributed from house-to-house stated, 'If the gas rattles sound, put on your gas-masks at once wherever you are, even in bed.' Caernarfon residents received their allocation of gas masks at the Pavilion over a period of three days from 8 September 1939. Even though the carrying of respirators (in the standard cardboard container) was compulsory, and dire warnings were given about the danger of a possible gas attack, there was a tendency for the 'little brown boxes' to be left at home or to be used for holding sandwiches.

Very few private houses had a telephone installed when war broke out. When a call had to be made, it was a case of walking to the nearest telephone kiosk, irrespective of the distance. When an air raid was imminent, it was imperative that the public was warned to take shelter quickly. It was for this reason that Senior Warden John Rogers, 3 Fron Dirion, Dolgellau had a telephone installed at his home.[3] A similar situation arose in October 1940 in Caeathro, near Caernarfon. The ARP warden's post consisted of a couple of rooms at a property called Bryn Eglwys. However, because the remainder of the house was unoccupied, discussion took place as to who would be responsible for installing electricity for heating and lighting, and also a telephone – more importantly, who would be responsible for the costs.

One of many Civil Defence leaflets published by the government in 1939.

During a Civil Defence exercise in Port Dinorwic, held between 7 p.m. and 9 p.m. on 3 June 1942, the ARP Controller for the county decided to release tear gas to ensure that people appreciated the importance of carrying their respirators. To create a more realistic situation, it was announced: 'General situation – Hostile troops have occupied Anglesey from bases in Eire. Air attack preliminary to a coastal assault by sea borne troops is in progress from Port Dinorwic, north-westwards as far as Conway.' The eventual report on the exercise stated that there was 'no sign of panic' and 'the gas test was most instructive.' Other Civil Defence exercises were held at Port Dinorwic from time to time and in Exercise Pippin, held on 25 April 1942, an incident was supposed to have taken place at the four-storey Arvonia shop in the village. Part of the building was stated to have been demolished and one person was trapped upstairs. The person in charge was asked, 'Can you stage a good scene for this to exercise rescue party ... I should welcome the laying of a booby trap or two for the rescue party to test their capability.'[4]

The National Fire Service (NFS) was also involved with Exercise Pippin and the report on their activities later stated, 'The hydrants had not been painted yellow and would therefore be difficult to locate in the dark. The NFS connected up to the road hydrant although there was no pressure in the mains due to the fractured water main ... [however] a local warden, who is a plumber by occupation, pointed out an alternative water supply by pipe under the roadway and this was used ... The NFS displayed excellent technique and alacrity.'[5]

Llanfairisgaer Local Committee decided, like many other communities, to form a fire-fighting unit at Port Dinorwic and appointed six members 'who would be trained for this special duty in connection with air raids.' A further thirty-four members registered for the ARP classes held at the Church House, Port Dinorwic on Wednesday, 25 October.[6] Later, a public meeting was held in the village to 'acquaint the public with the various means of notifying an air raid and what

Two groups of firemen in Holyhead. Above, members of the Auxiliary Fire Service, wearing wartime issue helmets and overalls. with a mobile pump. Right, members of the town's regular fire service in full uniform — crested helmets and thick fire-retardant jackets. [Holyhead Maritime Museum]

Left and below, two groups of Auxiliary Fire Service members from Port Dinorwic, including three lady members. [Alun Jones]

was required of the public.'[7] If an air raid had occurred whilst children were attending school, it was naively thought, 'on the question of dispersal of children from schools in the event of an air raid … it would be better for the children to remain in the school under the control of the teacher rather than be allowed to run wild outside … '

Even though the church house at Port Dinorwic was being used as the main ARP post and also by the British Red Cross and St John's Ambulance, a request made to the ARP Controller at the County Council offices in Caernarfon for a telephone to be installed which was dealt with 'in a non-urgent manner.'

One of the first tasks of the Government on the outbreak of war was to protect the general public as much as possible from the expected aerial bombing attacks, by creating a blanket of darkness over the whole country which involved switching off all forms of illumination that could aid hostile aircraft to find their way to a target, including the extinguishing of all street lights and the prohibition of any light emanating from houses, shops, etc. The Minister of Home Security, the Rt Hon. Sir John Anderson, who had arranged the distribution and testing of civilian gas masks, was also responsible (in conjunction with the police) for the enforcement of the Lighting (Regulations) Order, 1940, generally known as the 'Blackout' (this Order was to remain in force until September 1944 when, 'Restricted street lighting was restored in Caernarfon and other towns'). These regulations declared that no light whatsoever was to be emitted from any building during the hours of darkness. Some over-zealous individuals resorted to extreme measures as shown in a newspaper report in April 1940: 'Police Sergeant D. M. Hughes told the magistrates [at Caernarfon] that he had to extinguish an unobscured light in an office building by shooting it with a .22 rifle …'

A letter, dated 19 March 1941, sent by the Clerk of the Gwyrfai Rural District Council to the County ARP Controller, complained of lights being shown at RAF Llanberis when the village was attacked by 'hostile planes.' The reply from the Chief Constable stated that the RAF Station had a Certificate of Exemption from the provisions of the Lighting (Regulations) Order 1940, due to work of national importance. Any such lights however had to be extinguished when purple and red warnings were issued.[8]

All vehicles had to limit the size of side and rear lights to two inches in diameter and also by masking headlights, to regulate the amount of light shown. As an additional precaution, front and rear bumpers were supposed to be painted white. Buses and trains had blue-painted lamps inside and windows were covered up at night. Since shops were not allowed to show any light, boards were placed at the entrance which shoppers had to negotiate in a zigzag course during the hours of darkness. Pedestrians who were out at night wore a white band on their clothing to make themselves more visible, particularly by vehicle drivers (bands of white paint were painted on lamp-posts and the edges of pavements as an aid to pedestrians at night). As a means of extending daylight hours and counteracting the effect of the blackout, the end of British Summer Time was extended to 19 November in 1940. Even so, figures released by the Government showed that as a consequence of the blackout, 4,130 persons were killed in Britain by road accidents in the first four months of the war, twice as many as normal, and with 1,155 being killed in December.[9]

In April 1941, the Pwllheli and Lleyn Joint Ambulance Committee were given the opportunity of acquiring a new ambulance (a Chevrolet – JC 6892) from the British American Ambulance Corps to replace their existing Red Cross ambulance. To offset some of the maintenance costs, the committee decided that a patient using the ambulance as the result of illness or accident would be charged 1s. per mile for residents, and 1s. 6d. per mile for non-residents. If, however, the service of the ambulance was required for air-raid casualties, then no charge would be made. During the war, county councils held bulk supplies of petrol for their own vehicles (including ambulances) and no coupons were therefore issued or required. However, if the ambulance was involved in a long journey, which required replenishing the vehicle with fuel for the return journey, then fuel would be acquired by arrangement with the nearest county council bulk petrol supplier against suitable authorisation issued by the owner of the ambulance.

In January 1945, the Pwllheli and Lleyn Joint Ambulance Committee decided that their ambulance would not be able to convey two patients to the Naval Hospital at Bryn Beryl near Pwllheli, because of

British Red Cross Society and St John's Ambulance shared the use of this ambulance at Coed-y-Celyn in Betws-y-Coed. [Beti R. Matthews]

snowy conditions and the vehicle was not fitted with chains, a request was made for the RAF ambulance based at Penrhos airfield to be used instead. This resulted in a letter being sent by Group Captain Hembley, OC RAF Penrhos, to the committee stating that, 'even though the RAF ambulance was not fitted with chains, it nevertheless succeeded in negotiating the two journeys to Sarn Bach and return.' He also added, 'had there been flying in progress on the aerodrome the ambulance could not have been used.'

To reduce the number of casualties from bombing, it was decided that, in the first few weeks of the war, over two million shelters would be distributed to householders by local authorities. For those earning less than £250 a year, they were provided free-of-charge, but if the income was in excess of that figure, then householders were expected to pay £7 towards the cost. Anderson Shelters, as they were known (after Sir John Anderson), were being manufactured by the John Summers steel works in Shotton, Flintshire, from early in 1939 at the rate of 50,000 per week. They consisted of pre-fabricated, galvanised corrugated sheets that were bolted together on site to an eventual size that would accommodate an average-sized family reasonably safely and comfortably during an air-raid. The shelter was erected in a shallow hole dug in the garden, with the earth replaced so as to cover it to a depth of fifteen inches on top and thirty inches on sides and back. This work was expected to be completed by 11 June 1940, otherwise householders were liable to 'substantial penalties'. These shelters were supplemented by Morrison Shelters[10] which took the form of a reinforced table for indoor protection. As an alternative to the Anderson shelter, a brick structure with a nine-inches-thick reinforced concrete roof was built in some gardens, which not only acted as a shelter but also as a garden shed. Irrespective of the type of shelter in use, many recall enjoying a cup of hot cocoa and a biscuit and, at the same time, listening to the sounds of planes overhead and wondering, 'Is it one of ours or one of theirs?' When possible, a shelter was lit by a single bare electric bulb or, failing that, one or two smelly paraffin lamps which would provide a flickering light whilst patiently waiting for the 'All Clear' to sound.[11]

As soon as an air-raid warning had been given, day or night, householders who did not have the benefit of their own shelter, would proceed to purpose-built public shelters. The maximum number that could be accommodated in each shelter was specified above the entrance. People would bring whatever bedding that time and circumstances allowed, to try and get some sleep in order that life during the day could have some semblance of normality.

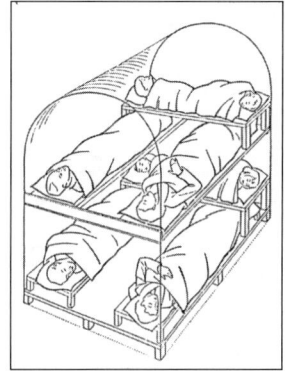

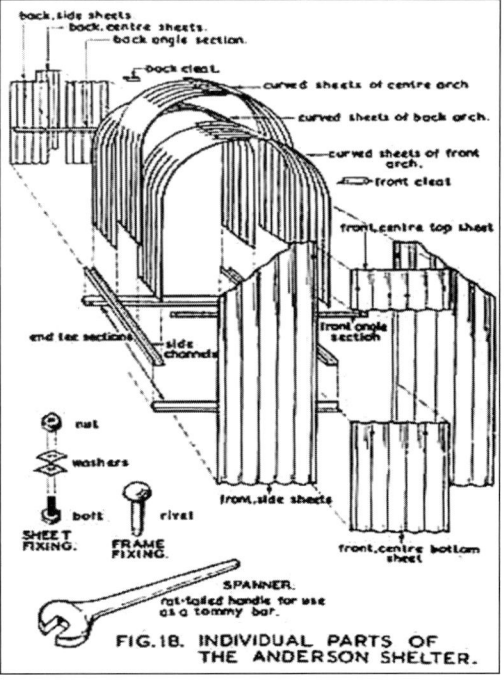

Two diagrams showing the component parts of an Anderson Shelter and how it was assembled and the arrangement for people to sleep inside it.

In Llandudno, a cave on the Great Orme, reputed to hold 'thousands of people', had been prepared for use as an air-raid shelter. Details as to how people would have been conveyed from the town to such a shelter were not given.[12]

In Caernarfon, 100,000 bricks were ordered by the County Council from the local brickworks for Communal Air Raid Shelters which were built at Pool Side (subsequent to the demolition of six derelict houses) and at Evans' Court in Pool Street.[13] In addition, the Civil Defence also took over the cellar of the R & I Jones stores in Bank Quay, no doubt considered totally safe as a communal shelter as it had been built as the strong-room for the original premises of Lloyds Bank. Those living in the vicinity of Castle Square would have had a similar air-raid shelter in the basement of the Prudential Assurance.[14] In August 1945, after the end of the war, it was decided that German prisoners-of-war would be employed in the demolition and clearance of bomb sites and the removal of air-raid shelters.[15]

Messages concerning possible air raids were classified by colours. A yellow message was an initial warning to wardens only to assemble at their posts. A red warning was an instruction that, 'wardens will immediately dash out to their respective sectors and blow short blasts on their whistles' as a warning to the public that an air raid was imminent and, where air-raid shelters were available, that everyone should take cover. A green message resulted in long blasts on their whistles and was an indication to the public that the raiders had departed. A white message indicated an 'all-clear' situation. The strident sound of a siren announcing an imminent air-raid conveyed a greater sense of urgency than the whistles which tended to be ignored. At a time when Liverpool, Manchester and other towns and cities in the north-west of England were subjected to heavy bombing, north Walians listening to the distinctive drone of the German aeroplanes passing overhead were reminded of their vulnerability. Although many thousands of lives were lost throughout Britain as the result of air-raids, thankfully, few were lost in north west Wales and bomb damage was minimal.

The threat of aerial attacks caused the Government to issue a number of leaflets in an attempt to educate the population about the dangers of aerial attacks, whether by high explosives or incendiary bombs, and how individuals should react:

What Might Happen In War

It is probable that in an air attack on this country, it is quite possible an enemy would make use of fire bombs. The object would be not only to destroy property but also to create panic. A large number of these bombs might be dropped in a small space. A large proportion of them would fall in gardens, streets and open spaces where they would burn out without doing much damage. But in a built-up area, some would fall on the roofs of houses. One of those houses might be YOURS.

Home Fire Fighters – however strong the Fire Brigade may be, an outbreak of many fires all close together and beginning at the same time would be more than it could successfully deal with unless the householder himself and his family took the first steps in defending their home.

In Civil Defence, EVERYBODY has a part to play. This is specially true of fire-fighting. In every house there should be one or more people ready to tackle a fire bomb. So read what follows: read it again and again, make the preparations which are advised and see that everyone in your house knows exactly what to do. Then you will be able to protect your own home and the homes of your neighbours. For once a fire gets out of control, you cannot tell how fast it may spread. All large fires start as small ones.

What You Should Do Now
1. Clear your roof space and attics of any old 'junk' that you have collected there. See that you have nothing there that will easily catch fire and nothing that would prevent you getting at the burning bomb.
2. Make sure that you can easily get into your attic or roof space.
3. Have ready at least four large buckets, a shovel or scoop, preferable with a long handle, and a fair quantity of sand or dry earth. Provide also what appliances you can; if possible, a stirrup hand-pump with the special nozzle giving either a jet of water for playing on a fire, or spray for dealing with the bomb itself. Failing this, a garden syringe would be useful, or even old blankets soaked in water. MAKE SURE THAT YOU KNOW THE EMERGENCY FIRE BRIGADE ARRANGEMENTS IN YOUR NEIGHBOURHOOD so that you can send for help if you want it. Your air-raid warden or a member of the Fire Brigade or the Auxiliary Fire Service will give you all the information you want.

How To Deal With A Fire
There will be two things to deal with – the bomb itself and the fire or fires that it has started. Each of these may have to be tackled in different ways, but the main thing is to stop the fire from spreading. A fire started by a bomb is just like an ordinary fire and water is the best means of putting it out. ACT QUICKLY. Every minute you lose makes the job more difficult.[16]

As the result of an increase in the number of air-raids in the latter part of 1941, employers were compelled to organise fire-watching duties. Employees who failed to comply with such a duty were liable to be prosecuted and gaoled as was the case with William Morgan of Llysfaen Road, Old Colwyn who was charged in May 1942 with 'Failing to perform Fire Watching duties at Ratcliffe Ltd, Llandudno Junction'. His appeal against a sentence of three months imprisonment was dismissed. In addition, the Ministry of Labour was empowered to direct men and women into Civil Defence and other services as an alternative to industrial employment. First aid, the medical services, rescue and demolition services, decontamination service (in the event of a gas attack), air-raid

Wounded servicemen at Coed-y-Celyn Auxiliary Hospital, Betws-y-Coed.
[Beti R. Matthews]

wardens and gas detection officers all formed part of the Civil Defence services. At first, all ages volunteered but, as the young joined the armed forces, an appeal in June 1940 asked for volunteers from amongst the over-50s.

Following the Home Office decision to issue 25,000 sandbags in March 1939 for the 'Protection of Police Buildings' in the three counties, it was reported in the local newspaper that, 'R. T. Jones [of Caernarfon] thought the provision was an unnecessary expense. 'Caernarvonshire', he said, 'had been classified as a receiving area and he could not imagine a stray aeroplane bombing village police stations like Llanberis …'[17]

Additional hospitals, such as the Gadlys Red Cross Auxiliary Hospital at Cemaes Bay, Anglesey were established for possible military casualties that civilian hospitals could not cater for. Gadlys was owned by three sisters who acted as matron, cook and general factotum. An article in the *North Wales Chronicle*, which stated that patients were appreciative of the kindness shown by the staff, seemed at variance with a report, written on 15 May 1944, which suggested that all was not well at the hospital. Three ATS and eight WAAF patients were of the opinion that,

> Matron is continually snooping and intruding into their [the patients'] private pursuits; instead of the place proving a happy restful interlude between hospital treatment and the resumption of service duties it has become a very disagreeable place. Gadlys Hospital is apparently generally known by its patients and by service people outside as 'The Concentration Camp'.[18]

When the hospital closed on 15 May 1945, notice was given that, 'The patients will be transferred to the Gors Auxiliary Hospital, Holyhead … all Polish patients will for the time being be accommodated at the Parciau Auxiliary Hospital, Marian Glas … '[19]

Lord Anglesey reported on 20 November 1941, at the time when Plas Newydd was being considered for use as a hospital,

> There is a great fight going on between Ministry of Health and Army Medical on the one hand, and the War Department on the other, because both want this house; the one to make a hospital for the whole island, which now has 70,000 inhabitants and 16 hospital beds, and the other for accommodation for either Searchlight or Anti-Aircraft Batteries ...[20]

Even as late as October 1944, part of Plas Newydd was offered by Lord Anglesey to the Joint War Committee of the British Red Cross and St John's Ambulance as a convalescent home.

When the 29th British General Hospital, Royal Army Medical Corps (RAMC) arrived back from Egypt on 11 December 1943, it established a base at Vaynol Park, near Bangor. In Betws-y-Coed, the RAMC also had its 11th Casualty Clearing Station at the requisitioned Bluebird Café and Waterloo Hotel and the nearby Coed-y-Celyn was also requisitioned for use as a Red Cross auxiliary hospital and rehabilitation centre.

Although the towns and villages of north-west Wales were subjected to aerial attacks, the reporting of these events in local papers lacked details as to the actual location because of water-time censorship. In one incident, bombs dropped offshore at Red Wharf Bay resulted in a number of fish being washed ashore. One individual, who found dead fish in the shallow water, phoned a local doctor to ask if it would be in order for these to be eaten, was told, 'Well the one that I am eating at the moment tastes alright!'

As the result of a Spitfire developing engine trouble over Beaumaris on 13 March 1941, the Royal Canadian Air Force pilot had no option but to bale out, landing uninjured in a tree. The plane, after damaging the roof of the Gwalia Stores in Beaumaris, crashed into 17 New Street. The occupant of the house, Mrs Louie Parry, who was on the first floor when the aircraft struck, suddenly realised that she was on the ground floor, from where she was rescued by neighbours and taken to hospital. At least, the local fire brigade and ARP wardens had the opportunity to demonstrate their prowess and expertise.

Aerial Attacks
As the result of a parachute mine being dropped at the top end of Penrhyn Avenue on the Maesgeirchen housing estate outside Bangor at 8.44 p.m. on 24 October 1941, one man and one woman were killed and fourteen injured. The bomb made a large crater in the roadway which measured twenty-six feet in diameter and was ten feet deep. Two houses were demolished and twenty-nine houses were damaged to such an extent that they could not be occupied, and a further 170 were damaged to a lesser extent. Furniture from these houses was stored in the old Woolworth's building and various chapel vestries in town until the houses had been repaired. Those rendered homeless were found temporary accommodation and food was provided at Robert Roberts' Café and by the WVS at the Rest Centre. A second parachute mine, dropped near the fifteenth tee of Bangor

Beaumaris, 13 March 1941, after a Spitfire had crashed into 17 New Street. [AC]

Golf Club, caused little damage apart from creating another bunker.[21] A raider that flew over Conwy on 13 March 1941 dropped bombs causing 'slight damage to twenty-eight houses (costing £15 to repair) and injuring three persons who were taken to hospital.'[22]

German aircraft dropped a stick of nine bombs on the mountain between Llanfairfechan and Aber on 8 September 1940 which resulted in a series of craters. A further visit by enemy aircraft was made to the Llanfairfechan district on 19 October 1940 when sixty-five incendiary bombs were dropped in a twenty-minute raid, but caused no significant damage. In another incident, a member of the public reported to the police that a parachute had been discovered on Llanfairfechan beach. On examination, it was found to be of German origin and with a number of ropes attached from which it was deduced that if a bomb or land-mine had been attached, then it had buried itself in the sand![23]

On Tuesday, 24 September 1940, as the result of a bombing raid on Llanllechid near Bethesda, the bakery in the High Street was damaged and the property, Llwyn Derw, in Water Street was demolished. Of the four occupants in the house at the time, one woman was killed and three people were admitted to the Caernarvonshire & Anglesey Infirmary in Bangor at 10. 30 p.m. – Mary Davies (aged 35) and Dilys Davies (aged 12), who both suffered scalp wounds, and Ronald Davies (aged 11) who had abrasions – one of the children subsequently died. On the same evening, incendiary bombs were dropped in the garden of 69 Carneddi Road, Bethesda, but caused little damage.

Of the six flares dropped on Llanberis, one landed on the Snowdon Mountain Railway platform and the others on the mountainside (it was decided on 1 March 1941 that in the event of an emergency occurring at Llanberis, the Dinorwic Quarry Hospital would be taken over by the County Council).[24]

A parachute mine was dropped near the railway station at Efa Lwyd Fawr on the outskirts of Penygroes on 20 December 1940, but the force of the resulting explosion was nullified to a certain extent by the soft ground and nearby hill absorbing most of the energy. Nevertheless, it still had sufficient force to destroy a number of windows in the area including those of Calfaria Chapel and the bungalow Penbrynglas.[25]

The incidents that were recorded for the month of October 1940 in the Register of Air Raids and Alarms were:

2 October 1940. 0715 hrs.	Enemy aircraft returned after releasing bombs and machine-gunned aerodrome – RAF Station Penrhos.
4 October 1940. 0645 hrs.	Train from Pwllheli to Afonwen also four farms machine-gunned. 5 HE Bombs dropped RAF Station, Penrhos and surrounding farms.
9 October 1940. 1810 & 1850 hrs.	16 HEs dropped at RAF Station Penrhos and Rhydyclafdy. Hangar and aerodrome buildings and Maes Pwllheli machine-gunned.
10 October 1940. 1910–1940 hrs.	30 HEs, 68 incendiaries 16 unexploded, Pwllheli machine-gunned 10 on RAF Station Penrhos, 10 field at Efailnewydd, 6

Clearing some of the bomb damage at the Wesleyan Chapel in Holyhead.
[G. W. Brown]

field at Llanbedrog, incendiary bombs in various parts of Pwllheli, Abersoch & Llanbedrog.[26] The raid on Penrhos and Pwllheli also resulted in an aerial machine-gun attack on The Maes, where some shops were damaged.

On the 11 October 1940 at 18.30 hours, incendiaries were dropped at Waenfawr, Llanberis and Llanrug.[27] Whether these were intended for NECACO at Llanberis, as on previous and subsequent raids, is not known. There were also reports of bombs being dropped between Nantlle and Drws-y-Coed.

A Heinkel He111 (F8LW-3962) of 12KG40, was shot down by Wing-Commander Wolfe and Pilot Officer Ashcroft (navigator) flying a Beaufighter (X8291) of N[o.] 456 Squadron based at RAF Valley. The German aircraft crashed in flames on the near the West End beach at Pwllheli at 01.15 hours on 30 July 1942. The report on the incident, stated that the fire and casualty service could not approach the burning aircraft because of exploding machine-gun bullets. Two crewmen survived and were taken prisoner – the pilot, Dirk Hofkes, and the wireless operator, Johann Hehser. The crewmen who were killed were Horst Vogt (observer), Fritz Graser (engineer) and Georg Hefferle (air-gunner). They were buried with military honours at Deneio Cemetery, Pwllheli on 1 August.[28] [29]

As the result of an air battle over Denbighshire on 21 September 1940, between Pilot Officer D. A. Adams flying a Spitfire of N[o.] 611 Squadron, based at Tern Hill, and the crew of a Dornier bomber of the 2nd *Staffel* of the Headquarters Reconnaissance Squadron, the German aircraft crashed besides Tyddyn Sais Farm, Trawsfynydd, where three of the crew were taken prisoner. The fourth member of the crew, *Unteroffizier* Gustav Pelzer, died and was buried in Pwllheli.

The wreckage of a Heinkel III on the beach at Pwllheli. Wg-Cmdr Wolfe and P/O Ashcroft, the men who shot it down, photographing the scene. [Edward Doylerush]

As a result of N⁰· 312 (Czech) Squadron and N⁰· 611 (West Lancs) Squadron being scrambled from Speke and Tern Hill respectively at 19.15 hours on 11 October 1940, to meet an incoming raid from the Irish Sea, Dornier 17z-3 (2772 7T+EH) was attacked and shot down into the sea off Bardsey Island. One member of the crew, *Feldwebel* Josef Vetterl, was killed and the remaining crew, *Leutnant zur See* (Pilot Officer) Jurgen Von Krause, *Obergefreiter* (Leading Aircraftman) Helmut Sundermann & *Feldwebel* (Sergeant) Heinrich Arpert (German Coastal Unit: *Küstenflieger Gruppe 606, Staffels* 1, 2 & 3) were picked up by a Royal Navy trawler and made prisoners. During the engagement the Hurricane L1807 flown by P/O J. A. Jaske was damaged but the pilot was unhurt.[30] (37. GAS XM/5849)

Wg-Cmdr Wolfe and P/O Ashcroft at Bryn Beryl Hospital, visiting the pilot of the Heinkel III shot down at Pwllheli on 30 July 1942. [Bryn Beryl Hospital via W. Alister Williams Collection]

Between 9 July 1940 and 24 July 1941, 131 high-explosives bombs were dropped on Caernarfonshire, of which, twenty-four failed to explode. In the same period, one parachute mine and approximately 271 incendiary bombs were also dropped.

Holyhead was subjected to a number of bombing attacks, including one when there was a Canadian ammunition ship at Salt Island unloading onto a train standing in the station. Had either the ship or the train been hit, the resulting explosion would have been catastrophic.

Other recorded incidents in Anglesey were:[31]

Date	Location	Nature of Explosives
22.07.40	Holyhead	2 parachute mines. Ship sunk. 11 dead, 3 seriously hurt
24.09.40	Llanfachraeth	Incendiary bombs
25.09.40	Llandegfan	Incendiary bombs
05.10.40	Holyhead	6 high explosives, 20 incendiary bombs. 3 seriously and 3 slightly injured. Church house demolished. 90 houses slightly damaged
10.10.40	Llangadwaladr	Incendiary bombs
06.11.40	Llanfachraeth	Incendiary bombs
08.11.40	Holyhead	4 high explosives (3 in harbour) 1 unexploded 1100lb bomb dug up
11.11.40	Penmon Quarry	3 high explosives
02.01.41	Holland Arms	2 parachute mines, 1 unexploded parachute mine. 3 slightly injured. 10 houses badly damaged
12.01.41	Amlwch	Machine-gun bullets
13.01.41	Holyhead	Machine-gunned

25.02.41	Holyhead	2 parachute mines, Salt Island. 11 slightly injured. 17 houses badly damaged. 250 houses slightly damaged
11.03.41	Mynydd Bodafon	1 high explosive bomb
	Llanfihangel	1 high explosive bomb
12.03.41	Llanfair PG	6 high explosive bombs. 2 light casualties. 1 house demolished and 1 badly damaged
12.03.41	Holyhead	2 parachute mines outside harbour
14.03.41	Plas Newydd Llanfair PG	2 high explosive bombs
06.04.41	Holyhead	2 parachute mines outside harbour
07.04.41	Dalar Crossroads	Incendiary bombs
09.04.41	Holyhead	8 high explosive and incendiary bombs, 2 in harbour, 1 unexploded bomb. Wesleyan Chapel damaged. 11 houses badly damaged. 144 houses slightly damaged
06.05.41	Holyhead	3 high explosive, outer harbour
07.05.41	Holyhead	4 parachute mines, harbour closed
09.05.41	Holyhead	Machine-gun attack. Bomber brought down in sea beyond Porthdafarch, Holyhead
10.05.41	Holyhead	3 high explosive bombs. 2 slightly injured. F.A. Post (Sailors Home), 25 houses damaged, 50 slightly damaged
31.05.41	Llandegfan	1 high explosive, shore of Menai Straits
24.07.41	Aberffraw	2 high explosive bombs, 4 sheep killed
	Bodedern	1 high explosive bomb
	Llanfaethlu	1 high explosive bomb
24.10.41	Pen-yr-Argae (?)	2 parachute mines
	Llanfachraeth	4 houses slightly damaged
01.11.41	Heneglwys	1 high explosive bomb. 2 unexploded high explosive bombs. Enemy bomber shot down

The Royal Observer Corps (ROC)

The Royal Observer Corps had been formed before the start of the war for the purpose of reporting not only the movement of all aircraft within a zone, both friendly and enemy, but also aircraft crashes and any changes in the weather pattern such as 'the lowering of cloud base over hills, ground mist forming which would obscure the ground, electrical storms, heavy rainstorms, sea mists, snowstorms, sudden gales, strong winds.' In the days when flying instruments tended to be unreliable, accurate weather reports were of great importance to novice air crews, especially when flying over mountainous terrain.

ROC posts were usually sited approximately ten miles apart, so that any air activity would be detected by at least one. The men and women who manned these posts, both full-time and part-time, were trained to identify

ROC, Penygroes. The members are only partially equipped with the ROC beret and an overall. Some are still wearing their civilian clothes.
[Aled Jones]

most types of aircraft and were expected to keep up-to-date with changes in aircraft design and the style of camouflage. Training in identification was provided in various ways, including model aircraft which they were supposed to identify blindfolded, simply by touch. Members of the ROC were allowed to visit RAF airfields in the area to see types of aircraft and to visit the Flying Control Room and the station cinema where they were shown 35mm Testcraft training films.[38] Their observations, with details of an aircraft's height, direction of travel and speed, were relayed back to headquarters but their findings were not always regarded as reliable, 'The Height Finder methods of some posts are still very uncertain. Head Observers must see to it that their posts' crews are able to work their instruments efficiently and quickly. This is a most important part of an Observer's duties and is indispensable to Fighter Command ...'[32]

When the ROC was first formed, members were not issued with a uniform and identification was by means of a striped arm-band and lapel badge. They were on duty for a minimum of twenty-four hours each week, but all members could be called upon to perform up to forty-eight hours a week if necessary.[33]

For a Leading Observer Class 'A', the scale of pay was £4 3s. 6d. for a forty-eight hour week, of which not less than forty hours was spent on watch-keeping duties and the remainder on administration or instructional work.[34] When a certain standard in identification of planes had been achieved, members were rewarded with a certificate, as was the case with O. Pritchard of Post B2, Group 282 (headquarters at 31 Bangor Street, Caernarfon), who was able to identify not less than twenty-five out of thirty-one different aircraft and was subsequently rewarded with a promotion in his rank. Some reports on the observations made were not always complimentary,

ROC parade at Caernarfon Castle. [Doris Rogers]

Air Raid Warnings – The Plotting and identification of aircraft by day has greatly improved though the one lone high aircraft in crowded areas still remains a problem. Plotting and identification by night is becoming more difficult. On October 24 [1941] a small force of enemy aircraft were engaged in mine laying between North Wales and the Isle of Man and occasionally came inland. One of these, Raid 145, crossed the track of a fighter in Caernarfon apparently J. 28 square and the fighter was tracked hostile to Shrewsbury giving 9 yellow and 14 purple warnings. The enemy losing height, passed out to sea near Llandudno to lay mines, apparently not tracked. Controllers should always bear in mind the possibility of this happening and make every enquiry about the position of fighters not only from their own neighbouring RAF sector but also from other sectors ... In this particular case Atcham and Shrewsbury knew that a Beaufort was in this area at the time. Caernarfon did not. The ROC is not always informed where friendly fighters are operating.[35]

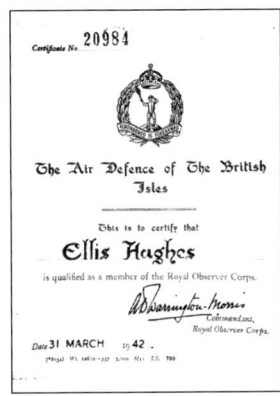

Membership Certificate of the ROC. [Ellis Hughes]

The Observers did, however, sometimes receive compliments:

Valley sector have destroyed several enemy raiders in the last two weeks and a letter has been received thanking Caernarvon for their accurate plotting. In particular a report of flares at sea sent out by an enemy raider proved of real value and established the enemy's position. The enemy was intercepted and shot down ... '
28. 8. 44 Sea Rescues – I wish you to personally convey my congratulations and thanks to the member concerned with the reporting of raid A45-N dropping red flares and the tracking of dinghy out to sea in the early hours of Saturday morning 26 August 44. You will be pleased to know that seven airmen were rescued and brought safely to Llandwrog and are recovering in the sick bay at this airfield ... The aircraft was a Wellington ... Group Commandant, 28. 2 Group ROC.[36]

Similar congratulatory messages were passed on in Anglesey:

Members of the Caernarfonshire ROC, Caernarfon Castle. [Doris Rogers]

Members of the Meirionethshire ROC, photographed outside their sand-bagged post. Note the theodolyte in the background which was used to calculate the height of passing aircraft. The post commander is proudly wearing his medals from the Great War.
[Y Tabernacl. Machynlleth]

1 September 1942: ... Headquarters Royal Observer Corps, 26 Bank Quay (relocated from 31 Bangor Street), Caernarfon. Recognition – Owing to the quick recognition of a Ju88 by A3 Post Rhosneigr the RAF were able to carry out an interception. Congratulations to this post and the Observers concerned. The Observers of this group as a whole are showing great keenness and are studying to keep themselves up to date as efficient Observers.[37]

26.8.43. Post 2/A.1 Amlwch is to be congratulated on their vigilance and reporting of aircraft down in sea at night on August 21/22 all crew of five being saved.[38]

ROC members were expected to report anything of a suspicious nature as they did on 21 October 1940:

... whilst out on patrol at 1245am suspicious winking or signalling lights were observed [by Four Crosses Observation Post] in an easterly direction from the square at Four Crosses. The attention of four members of the Home Guard who were on duty under Corporal D. G. Jones was drawn to the lights. From observations made these lights seemed to be Morse signalling and came from the vicinity of Braich y Saint, Criccieth or its near vicinity ... It is also known that the Observers then on duty at the Observers Post at Chwilog observed these lights.[39]

Often, messages, although describing an obvious tragedy, tended to be very matter-of-fact:

ARP Warden's Post Four Crosses (TN Chwilog 250): Report sent to the centre at Pwllheli: 17 October 1940 aircraft crashed at Llanaelhaearn, Caernarvonshire half a mile north-west from the Parish Church, machine completely smashed, British plane. Time of crash 11.45am. Occupants, two, both dead. J. T. Williams, Senior Warden, Four Crosses Sector.

Initially, the ROC headquarters was installed in the Chamberlain's Tower of Caernarfon Castle before moving to the Eagle Tower (which had the benefit of canteen facilities). Within the average twenty-four hours of actual watching that was required per week, eight-hour day shifts were worked from 8 a.m. to 4 p.m. followed by four-hour night shifts. At the headquarters, indicators on a large plotting table would show the movement of both British and German planes, together with the direction and height of flight. This information was relayed to them by telephone from observers at posts in various parts of the surrounding area. Senior officers, seated in an elevated position, were then able to see the type of aircraft that were in their area and take the necessary action. Whenever German aircraft were observed, the information was passed on to Ground Interception Control, from where instructions were given for Allied aircraft to deal with the intruders. All aircraft movements were recorded on paper so that the complete course would be shown from where the aeroplane had entered the zone to where it had exited.

Discipline was usually quite strict as shown in a letter dated 9 January 1942 from Captain J. W. Sanders, HQ Caernarvon, 'Welsh is still being used over operational lines at times causing confusion to brother posts ... This must cease forthwith.'

On 1 May 1945, members were informed that the stand-down of the ROC would begin simultaneously with the disbanding of the Civil Defence General Services on 4 May 1945, when all reporting would cease. Perhaps the final accolade for a body of men and women whose accurate and diligent observations had saved many lives, was expressed in the final report:

Members of the Royal Family played a great part in morale-boosting visits to all branches of the armed and volunteer forces throughout the war. Here, the Duchess of Kent is inspecting ROC members in Caernarfon Castle, October 1944. [Doris Rogers]

> Future of the ROC: ... while it is not possible yet to foresee what changes the future may bring in the aircraft reporting system of this country, it is certain that at present there is no substitute for the skill and experience of Observers and it is still conceivable that a satisfactory substitute may not be found.[40]

Notes

1. *C&DH*, 10 March 1939.
2. GAS, XJ1234/10.
3. GAS, Z-DAM-1814.
4. GAS, XC12-2-54.
5. GAS, XC12-1-103.
6. *C&DH*, 27 October 1939.
7. *C&DH*, 1 November 1939.
8. GAS, XC12-1-63).
9. GAS, XC2-6-243.
10. Named after The Rt. Hon. Herbert Morrison, who took over the post of Minister of Home Security on 3 October 1940.
11. NLW Ms 23073D.

12. GAS, M/1566/111.
13. *C&DH*, 15 November 1940.
14. GAS, XC12-1-54.
15. GAS, XC2-6-248.
16. Civil Defence leaflet N[o.] 5 *Fire Precautions in War Time*, August 1939.
17. *C&DH*, 31 March 1939.
18. PPP 187.
19. PPP 187.
20. PPP 459 and 469.
21. GAS, XM/797/4 & XC12-10.
22. GAS, XB2/79.
23. GAS, XJ2363.
24. GAS, XC12/1/6 *Notification of Air Raids (Method)* & XC12/1/168 *Notification of Air Raids (actual)*.
25. GAS, XC12-10.
26. GAS, XC12-10.
27. GAS, XC12-10.
28. Their bodies were exhumed in the 1960s and moved to the German Military Cemetery on Cannock Chase, Staffordshire. Their graves are located at Block 7, Grave 183 and Block 7 Grave 184.
29. GAS, XC12/1/1031 & XB6-247.
30. Courtesy G. W. Brown via Llangefni: WDAG/1
31. BUA, BP31733.
32. BUA, BGP 31695-742, Royal Observer Corps.
33. BUA, BGP 31699/31701.
34. BUA BP 31705.
35. BUA, Bangor Papers 31698.
36. BUA, Bangor Papers 31708.
37. BUA, BP 31904.
38. BUA, BP 31707.
39. GAS, XM 806/2.
40. BUA, BP 31741.

Chapter 3
Defences

With the threat of war looming, a number of warnings were issued early in 1939 regarding supplying details unintentionally that could be of potential benefit to the enemy at a time of hostilities. A letter dated 2 March 1939 from the Ministry of Transport, reminded harbour authorities of the danger of disclosing information about the workings of British dock and harbour systems which might assist a hostile power. If an enquiry was received for general information, that was readily available, i.e. published information, then it could be given out but, in all other cases, requests were to be sent to the Ministry of Transport to be dealt with through the Foreign Office.[1]

Even as early as 1938, air raid precautions were being discussed at the Caernarfon Harbour Trust office and, since this was listed as a Special Action Station by the Admiralty, air raid warning exercises were carried out periodically in the time leading up to the war. In May 1939, the Harbour Superintendent reported that 'inspection of the port and facilities had been made by an Inspector of the Air Defence Motor Patrol, Royal Arsenal, Woolwich for the purpose of making arrangements to base one of the motor patrol boats to be stationed in Caernarvon Bay. It was expected that the boat would arrive in Caernarvon towards the end of the month ...'[2] As soon as war was declared, harbour authorities were obliged to carry out instructions issued by the Admiralty, including the extinguishing of all navigation lights and, in Caernarfon's case, the cessation of night traffic in and out of the port. A list of boat permits, with the names of boats and owners permitted to operate on the Menai Strait, was displayed at the Harbour Office.

In February 1939, personnel attached to *Waterguard Surveyor* (under the supervision of HM Customs & Excise) had been asked, when boarding

Pill Box built adjacent to the Caernarfon Sailing Club. [AC]

Fort Belan. [AC]

foreign vessels in the course of their normal duties, to look for signs of 'strengthening [of steel decks] that would allow for the [future] mounting of guns.'[3] Within a fortnight of war being declared, Customs & Excise records stated that wireless equipment was being brought into the country in suitcases by German Intelligence Section and that 'people [were] attempting to hire boats in order to leave the country for Eire.' The following week, an observation was recorded that, 'It is strongly suspected that enemy submarines may operate off Bardsey Island and that they may obtain stores such as food, tobacco and perhaps lubricating oil from neutral vessels.' Whether these comments were based on fact, or hearsay, is impossible to say.

When the danger of invasion was at its greatest in 1940–1, exercises were carried out by locally-based armed forces and Home Guard units along certain sections of the coast that were considered the most vulnerable. Rocket stations were established on beaches that watched or patrolled, and a supply of light signal rockets was issued by Kinmel Depot for use along the north Wales coast. Instructions with regard to the use of the rockets stated, 'Rockets are not to be fired except when it is certain that the enemy are [sic] actually landing, and orders must be so framed that an Officer or selected Senior NCO is responsible for deciding if or when to fire. 20 May 1941.'[4]

A letter from Western Command in September 1940 gave notice of the formation of a Coast Artillery School on the Great Orme at Llandudno and that '... firing practice will be carried out at frequent intervals in the direction of the Menai Straits and Anglesey. Local sailing clubs in particular to be informed and others who could be affected.'[5]

Abermenai, considered the most vulnerable entrance to the Menai Strait, was guarded by a flotilla of six motor patrol boats which arrived at their base at Belan Point on 6 July 1940. The boats patrolled the coast as far south as Bardsey Island during the hours of darkness. With the additional activity both at sea and in the air, the Royal Navy requisitioned Fort Belan to accommodate their motor yacht, *St Joan*, and armed motor launch, *Whim*, used for inspecting ships entering the Menai Strait and for rescuing crews of aircraft that crashed into the sea. They were joined in 1941 by two high-speed launches HSL *135* and HSL *136* of N$^{o.}$ 63 Air Sea Rescue unit of the RAF.

The Admiralty appointed Vice-Admiral Hubert Lynes, RN (Retired) to be their Resident Naval Officer at the Port of Caernarfon, with the rank of Commander, based at Bryn Gwyn, St David's Road. An order which he issued on 2 July 1941 stated,

> ... south-western entrance to Menai Strait is closed to all Merchant Vessels, deep-sea trawlers etc. For all ports in the Menai Strait all such vessels must enter and leave the Strait by the north-eastern entrance only and obey the orders of the Examination Service Vessel there. The south western entrance is open only as follows – The Men of War who for every entry and exit will follow the procedure ordered for minor ports with Port War Signal stations (at Fort Belan). Llanddwyn light is temporarily extinguished and the tower and building are grey camouflaged. All the harbour lights at Caernarfon and Port Dinorwic are temporarily extinguished. The passage through the Strait is available for vessels up to about 260 feet long. But even for small craft local knowledge is essential and only very small ones should attempt the passage except towards High Water Slacks ... Passage beneath the Suspension Bridge or the Railway Tubular Bridge (by day or night) is prohibited until permission has been received from the Menai Patrol who will warn the military guard on the bridges. Failure to obtain permission to proceed will cause the offending vessel to be fired on ...'[6]

Under the Resident Naval Officer's command, guarding the approaches to the Menai Strait were two flotillas, each of six motor launches, which operate from Caernarfon and Menai Bridge. The launches were of small cruiser-yacht type, painted white and armed with a .303 machine-gun. The instructions added, 'these two Flotillas are to reinforce, inshore, the seaward watch and guard against invasion which is being kept off this part of our coast.' The Caernarfon flotilla patrolled the area from Llanddwyn Buoy towards Bardsey Island, a distance of two miles, while the Menai Bridge flotilla patrolled between the Great Orme and Lynas Point. In both cases, their role was to examine all craft approaching their respective entrances and, ' ... ensure that they have no enemy troops, tanks, guns, or other war materials, or spies aboard them'.

The night patrol was expected to give 'early information of the approach

Dinas Dinlle coastal defences. [AC]

of enemy invaders' and this was to be effected by means of 'Firework Signals.' Three or more light rockets, which would have a bright light lasting seven seconds in the air, would indicate when an 'enemy ship or other surface craft had been sighted.' If a large number of enemy aircraft were detected flying towards the shore, then one flash and sound rocket was to be fired. These rather vague instructions gave no indication as to how an enemy ship or enemy aircraft were to be identified, especially in the dark.

The launches had no means of communication, except at close range with voice or megaphone and semaphore hand-flags. It was expected that whenever the rocket signal from the Caernarfon flotilla was detected by the sentry post at Coed Helen army camp, the LDV or the Police, would inform their respective headquarters immediately. The Coastguard Stations and Coast Watch posts were expected to report any sightings to the Naval Centre and to the Royal Naval Officer at Caernarfon. Any signals seen emanating from the Menai Bridge flotilla by the LDV on the summit of Penmaenmawr mountain, or the Observer Corps on the Great Orme, were similarly to be reported to their superiors. The Menai Bridge end of the Strait was covered by the LDV at Red Wharf Bay, Police, Coastguard Stations and Coast Watch posts of the Royal Navy.

The Royal Navy's authority impinged upon anyone with an involvement with the sea, even local fishermen: 'Night Fishing – registered vessels granted permits to fish may do so at night anywhere within the three-mile limit.'[7]

According to a War Office letter to the Anglesey County Council, dated 27 July 1939, the matter of establishing an anti-aircraft artillery training camp (described as 'occupied all the year round by troops varying in number between 1000 and 1400' (AAS-WCM6)) at Tŷ Croes, Anglesey had been under discussion as far back as 1937. Even though the letter had stated 'firing from there [Tŷ Croes] would cause little or no interference to fishing or shipping', the Caernarfon Harbour Trust was informed by the commandant of the camp in November 1939 that, as the camp was due to be opened shortly, it was requested that the lighthouse-keepers be allowed to hoist and/or lower a red flag at Llanddwyn on receipt of instructions from the camp and also report the presence of shipping in the danger area.[8] A subsequent Harbour Trust minute of 2 January 1940 stated:

> On the 11 December the Anti-Aircraft Artillery range at Tŷ Croes was opened and firing is taking place from Monday to Saturdays inclusive commencing at 9am for the present and continuing until dusk. The pilots are instructed to hoist a red flag on the staff at Llanddwyn while firing is in practice during which time the bay is closed to fishing vessels.
>
> Arrangements have been made for merchant vessels to proceed on their course and firing is suspended while such vessels are proceeding within the firing area.[9]

Drifting mines were a constant hazard during the war and one was observed by the coastguard on duty at Llanddwyn at 10 a.m. on 17 October 1941. The mine was driven on to nearby rocks by the tide and the resulting explosion at 4.30 p.m. damaged the door and roof of the lighthouse and smashed four windows. On the 6 January 1942, several drifting mines were observed, some of which were driven ashore at Llanddwyn and Abermenai beach, and one drifted into the Strait, but they were all rendered ineffective by the Admiralty mine disposal officer.

In a secret document headed *Menai Bridges Broken Down*, dated July 1941, plans were made as to the type and number of boats required to be available for transporting people across the Strait if for any reason either, or both, of the bridges became inoperative. In addition to the military guard on duty on the bridges, further protection against sabotage was provided by posting one police officer (on duty between 7.30 a.m. and 4 p.m.) and two officers (from 4 p.m. to 7.30 a.m.) on the centre spans of the Menai Bridge.[10]

As far as the Conwy bridges were concerned, the army became responsible for the guarding of the railway tubular bridge, but the question of responsibility for the suspension bridge resulted in a great number of letters passing between local officials, Western Command Headquarters at Chester and Whitehall. Every endeavour was made for the army to guard both bridges, but the Under-Secretary of State at the Home Office stated that the police should be responsible for the suspension bridge.[11]

Having been advised in September 1939 that 1,000 square yards of the timber yard at the Victoria Dock had to be reserved for the Mines Department, it came as no surprise when the Harbour Master was eventually told that the Admiralty had decided to lay a mine-field off Belan Point, at the entrance of the Strait, and that the mines would be of the ground type, each weighing two tons, which could be detonated from the

Remains of an anti-invasion gun base at Llanberis Pass. [AC]

shore. It was intended that the mine-field would be laid on 5 November 1940 at the Belan Narrows by HMS *Vernon* but the work was postponed until 3 March, when HMS *Ben Nevis* called to ratify the area to be mined and the work was carried out on 20 March by HMS *M4*.

Similar mines were placed alongside the sea wall from a position off the Old Battery to the oil wharf at Caernarfon and buried below the surface of the sea bed. Additional precautions were taken with the military erecting two pill-boxes – one alongside the old battery and the other abreast of the timber yard at the Victoria Dock. Once the mine-field had been laid, the flotilla of patrol boats was withdrawn.[12]

In addition to being the base for the RAF Air–Sea Rescue boats, naval guns had been installed at Belan Fort as an additional precaution against unauthorised entry into the Menai Strait.

Penygwryd Defence Point. [AC]

Notes

1. GAS, XD15/30/94.
2. *C&DH*, 5 May 1939.
3. GAS XA1-6.
4. GAS XM1301-6.
5. GAS XC12-1-1.
6. GAS XD15/30/95 and XD 15/21/4.
7. GAS XD2 3703.
8. GAS, XD/15/3/6.
9. GAS XD15-21-4.
10. GAS XJ1234/11.
11. GAS XB2 511.
12. GAS XD 15/21/4.

Chapter 4
Evacuation

With the inevitability of war looming on the horizon, plans for the evacuation of children from the zones considered to be most at risk had been prepared well before the actual operation was put in hand. Nevertheless, the task of moving approximately 3,000,000 schoolchildren from one place to another, within a relatively short space of time, was, to say the least, formidable.

The Government Evacuation Scheme gave details of moving children below school-age (accompanied by their mothers), children of school-age, expectant mothers and blind persons from 'evacuable' areas to 'evacuation' areas. As the scheme was entirely voluntary, it was necessary to issue a Civil Defence leaflet in July 1939 to convince parents of the need to evacuate children and it was pointed out that, 'It will not be possible to let you know in advance the place where your child will be going, but you will be notified as soon as the movement is over ... Of course it means heartache to be separated from your children, but you can be sure that they will be well looked after. They will relieve you of one anxiety at any rate.' Many mothers had to make an agonising decision as to whether to stay at home with their husbands and risk their very young children being maimed, or even killed, or to leave for the comparative safety of the countryside. Others, in preference to participating in the official evacuation scheme, preferred to make their own arrangements and stay with friends or relatives in the country, but were warned that the government scheme would take priority and that there could be curtailment of both rail and road transport.

The areas nearest to north Wales that were considered to be mostly at risk were Liverpool, Bootle, Birkenhead and Wallasey. In some cases, the decision was taken to evacuate teachers and pupils of certain schools to a safer area for the duration of the emergency or until such time as it was felt that it was safe to return. It had been thought that due to the mass exodus of children from the city streets that they would be 'denuded of young life.' Eventually, across Britain, less than half of the children scheduled for evacuation in school parties actually left home.

A survey of all houses in Caernarfonshire had been undertaken as early as February 1939 to establish where children could be accommodated.[1] Three months earlier, Criccieth Urban District Council was approached by the local WVS leader with regard to setting up its own committee to receive evacuated children, but decided against participating even though the Ladies Evacuation Committee had already been functioning for some months. In anticipation of emergency accommodation being required

Evacuation leaflet issued in 1939. [Aled Jones]

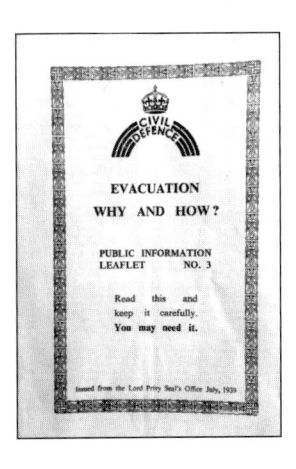

Cyngor Dosbarth Gwledig Gwyrfai.

At y Teuluoedd a'r Personau a gymerant i mewn Ffoaduriaid ar adeg o argyfwng.

CYFARWYDDIADAU A DARPARIADAU.

Dymuna Cyngor Gwyrfai ar ran y Gweinidog Iechyd a'r Cyngor ddatgan eu gwerthfawrogiad o'r cynorthwy parod a gaed gan breswylwyr y cylch, a chan y rhai fu yn cynorthwyo drwy ymweled â hwy.

Erbyn hyn cwblhawyd y trefniadau i symud mamau a phlant o ardaloedd peryglus ar adeg o argyfwng, drwy yr Awdurdodau Lleol, a chan ddatgan ein diolchgarwch am y cydweithrediad gaed, dymunwn roddi isod fanylion o'r trefniadau fel y byddwch yn deall yn hollol beth fydd ei angen a beth i'w drefnu.

PWY DDAW.

Trefnir i tua 2500 o gylch Lerpwl ddod i Wyrfai. Yn gyntaf, daw yr hanner fydd yn blant ysgol yng ngofal athrawon ac eraill, gydag un person i ofalu am bob deg o blant. Wedyn daw y gweddill yn blant bychain yng ngofal eu mamau ac eraill. Ni threfnir i rai gwael neu anafus ddod i gylch Gwyrfai.

SUT Y DEUANT.

Trefnir iddynt ddod gyda moduron i'r gwahanol ardaloedd, a bydd Swyddogion eyfrifol yn trefnu gyda chynorthwy lleol i'w dwyn i'r tai lle y byddant i aros.

The Gwyrfai Council have been advised that 1500 additional children are being evacuated to this area and are arriving here on Sunday.

We earnestly appeal for the co-operation of householders in providing the extra accommodation required.

Will householders who are willing to offer accommodation and those who are prepared to accommodate more than the number already allocated to them, please get in touch immediately with the Billeting Officers at the schools in their village or with the Council Offices, 22, Castle Square, Caernarvon,

Telephone Caernarvon 91.

Please Help

Public appeal by local councils for billets for evacuated children.
[Aled Jones]

initially in the schools and village halls of the county, blankets and beds were brought by lorries from Liverpool and some families, rather than be separated from their children, fled the anticipated attack on Merseyside and brought their own furniture to rented houses in Anglesey and Caernarfonshire.

A leaflet, issued and distributed by the Gwyrfai Rural District Council, was intended to make the public aware of the intended influx of evacuees. It stated that of the initial 2,500 evacuees from Liverpool to the area, approximately half would be schoolchildren, accompanied by their teachers, and the other half would be smaller children with their mothers. It gave information on travel arrangements, what they should bring with them and various other issues, such as billeting allowance, how to deal with illness, complaints, schooling and entertainment.

The first communication between Liverpool Education Authority and its equivalent in Anglesey was received on 13 July 1939 and it outlined the arrangements that would be put in hand in the event of a National Emergency. The original plan was for approximately 675 children to be evacuated from Alsop High School, Oulton High School and Blue Coat School, but the eventual number that arrived was 2,468. For the first week or two, several schools were closed to Anglesey children so that the Liverpool children and their teachers could have places to assemble. Anglesey teachers assisted their Liverpool colleagues in trying to resolve the inevitable problems that arose.

Liverpool children assembled at their individual schools on Sunday, 3 September 1939; some were taken to Edge Hill Station and others to Lime Street Station where they boarded trains for various destinations. Most of

Billeting Allowance Order Form for people accommodating evacuated children. [AC]

the children were filled with foreboding, separated as they were from their parents for no apparent reason, as far as they were concerned. Many were in tears, some with thoughts of a great adventure, others with the knowledge that at least for a little while there would not be the usual confrontation with one or both parents for some misdemeanour or another.

DEFENCE REGULATIONS
IMPORTANT ANNOUNCEMENT
BILLETING

The Government have announced that the dispersal of people in priority classes from certain large towns shall be put into effect immediately.

The area covered by the .... Council is a reception area* to which some of these people are being brought.

Occupiers of housing property in this area are required by law to provide accommodation for any persons assigned to them by the Billeting Officer. Every effort will be made to spread the burden of billeting fairly and equally between households.

It may be necessary to carry out billeting at night as well as day-time. Your co-operation in this emergency is requested.

An allowance will be paid to occupiers for the accommodation provided. To claim this you will need a billeting allowance order form. Watch the bottom of this notice for further information about how to obtain the form.

CLERK OF THE COUNCIL

*If only part of the area is scheduled as a reception area, the districts affected are shown below.

Local Council instructions with regard to evacuated children. [AC]

The arrival of approximately 2,000 children and teachers at Bangor coincided with the announcement by the Prime Minster, and relayed by tannoy system in Deiniol Road, that war had been declared with Germany. The children, accompanied by their teachers, walked from the railway station to the Central School where they were given a meal and medically examined. Suspected cases of scabies, diphtheria or scarlet fever were taken to the County or Borough Hospital for further examination and possible treatment.[2]

The first contingent of Liverpool evacuees destined for Caernarfon and the surrounding villages had arrived at 4.30 p.m. on 1 September. From Caernarfon railway station, they were marched to the County School where they were medically examined before being given tea and a bag of rations which were supposed to last for forty-eight hours. It was 10.30 p.m. before the exhausted children were eventually billeted for the night. Other children arriving in Caernarfon in the following few days were from the Prince Rupert School, Steers Street, Liverpool, accompanied by their headmaster, Harold Timbury, and Fred W. Jenkinson as first assistant. Children from the Clint Road, Heyworth Street and Earle Council Schools arrived during the next couple of days and were taken to Bontnewydd Orphanage, youth hostels at Glyn Padarn,

Evacuees possibly from Netherfield Road junior school, Everton on the first stage of their journey to an unknown destination in north Wales. [AC]

Evacuees leaving a suburb of London before boarding a train for Wales. [Doris Blackwell]

Snowdon Ranger, Bryn Dinas (in Nantgwynant), Royal Victoria Hotel (Llanberis), CS Holiday Home (Betws Garmon) and other locations.

In May 1939, the Blaenau Ffestiniog area was advised that it would be receiving 200 children and Llan Ffestiniog would receive 40, all from Liverpool. On arrival, they would be taken to the Council School where the Women's Institute were asked to supply crockery so that the 'refugees could be provided with a hot drink and food.' Sufficient malted milk powder, Ideal Milk, tea, sugar, biscuits and soap for the children to use, was bought at a total cost of £3 0s. 2d.[3]

A report prepared by the County Medical Officer of Health in Caernarfon at the end of September stated, 'approximately 8,204 evacuees [school children] and 3,746 women with children under 5 years of age were in the county. In addition, 1,000 other evacuees had arrived privately.'[4] The report also stated that seven cases of diphtheria and four of scarlet fever had been reported amongst the children. At the same time, the Public Assistance Office in Caernarfon reported that, 'During the last three weeks since the outbreak of war, the work of the department has increased, particularly in connection with applications received from evacuees from other areas for assistance under the Prevention of Distress Regulations issued by the Ministry of Health.'

The Evacuation Committee at Waenfawr met for the first time on 12 October at the Council School to discuss the welfare and care of the children allocated to their care from Heyworth Street and Clint Street schools in Liverpool. As many of the evacuees arrived in a very impoverished state, with little if any change of clothing, householders with whom they had been billeted took the trouble, at their own expense, of re-clothing them and supplying new footwear, only to find that many of the children returned home over the following weeks.[5] Such concern about the

Penisarwaen evacuees.
[Nora O'Brien]

welfare of the children was reflected throughout the region and a letter was sent to the Public Assistance Officer in Liverpool, stating that clothing and footwear were urgently required by the children, especially as winter was approaching.[6] When the items arrived, they were distributed at the school clinic in Shirehall Street, Caernarfon, to those children in greatest need.[7]

If the actual arrangements of transferring children from Liverpool to various towns were well organised, information about their life-style and home living conditions was sadly lacking. For many of the evacuees, a normal bath night (taken in a tin bath in front of the fire) was a new experience. Many children from poor areas of the large towns and cities, arrived infested with lice and had to be quickly treated before other children were infected with the same problem which caused concern in the host communities. 'There is certainly one thing that reception areas have a right to protest against and that is sending dirty and verminous children and people into their areas'.[8]

Even though every effort was made to help the children to settle into their new environment and to entertain them by showing educational films as well as the old favourites, such as Laurel and Hardy, by November 1939, 141 children had returned home to Liverpool from Port Dinorwic. Of the 400 original evacuees that arrived at Barmouth only forty-eight remained by November 1939. The remainder had returned home.

Initially, children from Liverpool were inclined to stay together because they were taught in their own classes by their own teachers and would only mix in a small way with local children. For many of the children, this was the first experience of seeing the countryside and being able to participate in nature walks, and those who were billeted on farms or smallholdings enjoyed sharing in the daily routine. The children destined for Beddgelert were taken to a school where they were allocated to local families. One girl, Eileen Hunt, who stayed with Hugh O. Williams, a headmaster, his wife and seventeen-year-old daughter, recalls hearing through an open window the sound of an evacuee crying on their first night in the village. To reassure her parents, the headmaster wrote them a letter,

> Glan Afon, Beddgelert, 15 September 1939 ... As you probably know we are a little village at the foot of Snowdon and one of the beauty spots of North Wales. Our climate all round the year is pleasant but a bit wet. About 70 children arrived here from the same school as your little girl and I happened to be in charge of finding billets for them. As two were to stay with me I, during the

sorting out at our local school, looked about for 'two nice little girls' those were my instructions from my wife ... I really must say here that you have a charming child nicely brought up. She is lovely in the house – very polite and has settled down well. Naturally she talks of Daddy and Mammy and at times is a little home sick especially after a visit from her mother but I have a daughter of 17 and a maid of similar age and they are both fond of children and together with my wife they soon have her happy again. My wife says she will be sorry when she has to part with her and we all shall be pleased to take care of her till this war is over and then hand over to you a happy child. She asked me quietly this morning if I could find a house for her mother somewhere near and I hope towards the end of the week to fulfil her wish and my promise to your wife and hope to find billet for her in a modern bungalow with kind people about a mile from here and then she will be able to see her girlie very often. There is certainly no need to pay me anything for what you are good enough to call kindness nor for anything we may give Eileen – She deserves it all as one who served in the last war and a lover of children can assure you that we shall take every care of your dear little girl.'[9]

For another couple in Port Dinorwic, Eileen Oldfield, a little girl of seven years-of-age who came to stay with them from Liverpool, was a timely replacement, for the only daughter whom they had recently lost through illness. The evenings were occupied in playing games of ludo, snakes and ladders, and draughts as well as reading stories. Within twelve months, Eileen was sufficiently accomplished in Welsh to be able to participate in both chapel services and the eisteddfod.

Where brothers and sisters had been evacuated together, they naturally clung to each other in a strange environment and would resent any attempt to separate them when it came to finding a place for them to stay. Three young evacuee sisters, Sarah, Dorothy and Hilda Woodward, after resisting all attempts to billet them in separate houses and surviving a seemingly endless journey, eventually found themselves in the quarry village of Llanberis. They knew that they had arrived in a strange land because they could not understand a word of what the people were saying nor, quite often, could they make themselves understood. They saw many strange words which they did not understand like *Bechgyn* (boys) and *Genethod* (girls) above the doors leading into the local school.

Because the billeting allowance was, more often than not, only payable until a child was fourteen years-of-age, most of those over that age returned to Liverpool. In the case of the three sisters, when the two older ones had departed, leaving the youngest on her own, she found herself becoming integrated naturally into village life, and the 'foreign' language was soon learnt without the necessity of enforced schooling. Consequently, this opened a new world to the young visitor who was able to converse in the Welsh language to the extent that she, like Eileen Oldfield, was able to compete at local eisteddfodau and participate in religious services.

Evacuees at Glan Menai, Port Dinorwic c1940 preparing the ground for potato planting. [W. W. Roberts]

The degree of welcome varied enormously from billet to billet and no doubt, this would reflect greatly on the happiness of the child and how soon he or she settled into the new environment. In some cases, the degree of integration resulted in some children who had grown up away from their natural parents, being reluctant to return home. Even when they did return home, it took some children a good twelve months to settle down.

Sadly, not all the children enjoyed their enforced stay in the country; indeed some were greatly relieved to return home. However, many were virtually adopted for the duration of their stay and benefitted from their experience. Some never did return home or, if they did, they would come back periodically to visit their 'uncles and aunts' with whom they found so much kindness and happiness. In the days of rationing and shortages, the kindly people who made the children welcome, invariably sacrificed a great deal to make them comfortable and happy for the duration of their stay.

The staple diet of fish and chips, which many of the evacuees were used to, caused many problems for their hosts when attempts were made to find acceptable alternative fare. The way of life of some of the children who came to north Wales made them adept at stealing and shop-lifting and therefore, they resented the inevitable chastisement and correction that followed. Even with such obvious potential problems, any householder who refused to comply with the requirements of a billeting order was liable to be taken to court and fined up to £25. Such a charge and fine was imposed in the case of Sophie Parry of Argoed, North Road, Caernarfon who failed to provide accommodation for a woman and two children. To sweeten the pill of having outsiders living in their homes, host families received a weekly billeting allowance and ration books. In 1942, the allowances for evacuated children were:

under five years-of-age	8s. 6d.
5-10 years-of-age	10s. 6d.

10-12 years-of-age	11s. 0d.
12-14 years-of-age	12s. 0d.
14-16 years-of-age	13s. 0d.
16 years-of-age	15s. 6d.
17 years-of-age and over	16s. 6d.

The allowance for a teacher was 5s. per week (for accommodation only), any food supplied was by arrangement between the teacher and the householder. A similar arrangement applied with regard to a mother with an under school-age child, with accommodation being charged at 5s. for the mother and 3s. for the child.

If the parents of evacuated children had the means, they were expected to make a contribution towards the billeting allowance. The only way of establishing who could and who could not make such a contribution was by means of the much-resented means test which resulted in at least a quarter of the parents not having to pay anything. The same system applied following the Ministry of Health's plan of co-operation between Education Authorities, the Public Assistance Committees and the Women's Voluntary Service in deciding which evacuated child could be given new clothes when the parents' circumstances precluded them from making a contribution towards the cost. In some cases, depending on income and the number of family members, free mid-day meals, halibut liver oil capsules and iron tablets were provided. If they had to be paid for, then the cost was 2d. per week for the capsules and 1d. for the tablets. Just before Christmas, 1939, the Liverpool authorities increased the evacuation allowance by 2s. per child to cover extras over the festive season. Liverpool was also asked to send sufficient school nurses and dentists, who were to remain in the county for the duration of the war, to attend to evacuated children.[10]

Organisations such as the WVS assisted with the influx of evacuees and did much by starting clothing depots so as to reclothe many of the children who came from deprived areas. Since clothing and footwear were strictly rationed, it was necessary to issue supplementary coupons to allow them to have a change of clothes. When boots required repairing, assuming that leather was available, it invariably meant that evacuated children had to either stay indoors until their shoes were returned or walk around barefooted.

Owing to the number of children evacuated to the village of Port Dinorwic, and the lack of space within the Council and National schools, it was decided that until alternative accommodation could be made available, schooling would have to be on a two-shift system. During the first week, the local children were taught until 12.45 p.m. and the Earle Road Senior Girls, of which there were 150, would then be taught by the headmistress, Miss A. Haslam, from 1.15 p.m. to 5 p.m. The following week, the visitors attended in the morning and the locals in the afternoon. By October 1939, the times of attendance had been changed to 9 a.m.–12 noon and 1–4 p.m. Eventually, the evacuees were relocated to the Memorial Hall in order that they could continue their lessons without interruption. Similar schemes were implemented in other schools throughout the country.

The provision of education for both local and evacuated children was as much a problem on Anglesey as it was on the mainland. The initial reaction of the local education authority was to dismiss the idea of educating both sets of children in the same premises because of language problems, children only receiving part-time education and difficulties for teachers in preserving the identity of their schools, 'Education of the English children has to be in their own language if it is to be effective, but the teaching of Anglesey children must not be impaired since the important function of our schools at this time is to safeguard the language, culture and traditions of Wales.'[11] A report stated,

> This concerns children evacuated from Liverpool to Anglesey under the Government Evacuation Scheme. First communication received from the Liverpool Education Authority was on the 13 July 1939 regarding evacuation of Secondary School Children to Holyhead and Llangefni. In the event of a National Emergency 540 pupils would be sent to Holyhead and 300 boys from Oulton High School to Llangefni. On the 4 August 240 Blue Coat School pupils would go to Beaumaris. In addition 325 Elementary School children would go to Menai Bridge and 350 to the Aethwy Rural District. This advance warning enabled accommodation to be arranged in Anglesey for Alsop and Oulton High Schools and the Blue Coat School (who were making their own educational arrangements). Instead of 675 Elementary pupils, 2468 arrived and they were distributed: 1184 to the Valley Rural District, 299 to Twrcelyn, 760 to Aethwy, 198 to Menai Bridge and 27 to Amlwch. In a few days, 3405 school children, 300 teachers and helpers and 413 mothers with 667 young children arrived from Liverpool into Anglesey. Many Anglesey schools were used as clearing stations.
>
> For the first week or two several schools were closed to Anglesey children so that the Liverpool children might have a place to assemble.
>
> There were three options for the children's education:
> 1. Educate evacuated children with local children.
> 2. Accommodate evacuated children in schools on the 'double-shift' system
> 3. Provide suitable premises for use as schools by Liverpool children.
>
> Due to the two languages, the first option was eliminated. Problems that could arise with the second were: half-time education for both local and evacuated children (nevertheless this system had to be used for a while). It was therefore decided that alternative premises for evacuated children would be required. Complications arose due to the large scale movement of evacuated children back to Liverpool often without the knowledge of the teachers. Arrangements were made for the purchase of necessary furniture and equipment as well as the provision of toilets etc. in hired premises taken over

for schooling. It was agreed that the cost would be borne by the Exchequer. Of the 3405 children originally evacuated to Anglesey, 1500 were to leave the county.

On the assumption that the war was to last at least three years, consideration had also to be given to children who would require in time to sit examination for Secondary School.[12]

The log book for the Earle Webster Road School, evacuated to Llandegfan, gives an indication of events during 1944 including the eventual return of the children to Liverpool as air-raids lessened,

10.01.44 School reopened this morning. Number of children present 24 (number on roll 31). Miss Long and Mrs Buckingham both present.
11.01.44 Nurse Garner visited the school this afternoon and examined the children. 3 cwts. of coal received.
08.2.44 Mr Jones (dentist) visited the school this morning and examined the teeth of all children present. Nine children had teeth extracted. Senior boys taken out for their first gardening lesson at Cyttir Bach which has been taken over for school use.
18.02.44 Five children attended the dental clinic at Bangor.
26.06.44 Two children reported with scabies.
22.09.44 112lbs rose hips collected and sent to Liverpool. More sent later making a total of 320lbs for the month worth £2. 13. 4d
23.11.44 Children returning to Liverpool November 29.
30.11.44 School closed and furniture and equipment taken away.[13]

Many of the evacuee children who came *en masse* from Merseyside to seek shelter in towns and villages in north Wales at the beginning of the war had returned home over the years. For the 186 evacuees that remained, it was decided that they too would return home on 29 November 1944, and it was Mr W. A. Jones, headmaster of Heyworth Street School, Liverpool, acting as train marshal, who had the responsibility for ensuring their safe return. The train started its nostalgic journey at Porthmadog and was to stop at most of the stations along the north Wales coast as far as Chester to allow the youngsters to embark. Those who had been staying in Anglesey boarded at Bangor. It had been as much an unique experience for the children as it had been for their temporary guardians who had the responsibility for caring for them during their formative years.

Dulwich College Preparatory School

Plans, which had been formulated as early as 1938 during the Munich crisis for the evacuation of children from the Dulwich College Preparatory School in south London were put in hand on 1 September 1939. The initial group of 135 boys, with ages ranging from 5–13$\frac{1}{2}$, was evacuated to Coursehorn, near Cranbrook, Kent. But, with the subsequent threat of invasion and the possibility of being bombed, it was decided that accommodation had to be found elsewhere.

After several enquiries, a member of staff was informed that there was a possibility of finding a hotel in Betws-y-Coed. The Waterloo Hotel was the initial choice until it was discovered, on arrival, that it had been requisitioned by the Royal Army Medical Corps as a military hospital. Eventually, the Royal Oak Hotel and the Llugwy Tea Rooms were taken over, whilst on the other side of the road, coaching stables were converted for use as a gymnasium.

Until the parents received a circular from Betws-y-Coed a few days after the arrival of the school party, they had no idea where their children had been taken. Nevertheless, the situation was generally accepted by parents and only two boys were withdrawn. Although the Ministry of Health (who at that time had responsibility for such matters) was not prepared to pay either the £700 cost of transport or some of the cost of alterations to the hotel, the parents generously contributed £800 which covered most of the expenses. For the five years that the school was in Betws-y-Coed, the average working time for the headmaster, his wife and the staff was in excess of twelve hours a day. Even during holidays, some of the boys remained at school which entailed some of the staff being on duty. But, as John Leakey states in his book *School Errant*, '… it does not show a true picture of the unending and devoted labour which the staff gave so freely during the five years, nor of the heavy responsibility for so many children's lives in which they took their full share.'

The boys became fully integrated within the community and participated in various schemes such as collecting salvage, helping with the National Savings campaign and making camouflage nets for the army in the Royal Oak stables. The work that they carried out in conjunction with the Forestry Commission resulted in a nearby plantation being named after

Dulwich College pupils at the nearby Royal Oak Hotel stables. [Dulwich College]

Pupils of Dulwich College receiving physical training at the Royal Oak Hotel, Betws-y-Coed. [Dulwich College]

Refreshment time for Dulwich College pupils at the Royal Oak Hotel, Betws-y-Coed. [Dulwich College]

the school. Whilst in the forest collecting wood for the hotel fires, the boys took the opportunity to collect sphagnum moss which grew there in profusion and which was used in its dried form to supplement cotton-wool for wound dressings. Male fern, foxgloves and nettles, which were used for medicaments and dye, were also collected for Bangor University and also rose hips in the autumn.

Whenever the weather was suitable, and in an attempt at evoking a suitable atmosphere, the children would accompany the teacher into the churchyard next door to the Royal Oak hotel where, seated amongst the gravestones, they would listen to a reading of Gray's *Elegy*. Similarly, when it came to the appropriate history lesson, the children would quite often be taken to visit Caernarfon or Conwy castles.

During their time in Betws-y-Coed, the school, which rented two fields from a local farmer, would play cricket, rugby and soccer against other schools in Colwyn Bay, Bangor, Ruthin and Trearddur Bay, sometimes travelling by train and at other times, using two (small) cars out of which would pour fifteen boys and two adults, to the astonishment of onlookers (in the pre safety-belt era!). Cricket matches were also arranged against the Catholic Approved School billeted at the British Legion camp at Capel Curig. These children, who were described as being well-fed and clothed, were comfortably housed in wooden huts and had the benefit of an 'excellent football field.' In his book, John Leakey made the observation that, 'It struck me as an extremely serious fault in the social system that it allowed a situation to arise where boys had to commit a misdemeanour to obtain what appeared to be a first-class boarding school education, where as the ordinary elementary school children were so pitifully neglected.' He added that, 'in spite of the Heath Robinson existence, or more probably because of it, we had achieved a standard of work, games and atmosphere, which was far in advance of anything the school had known before. We all of us felt that when peace came we must bring the spirit of Betws-y-Coed back to Dulwich.'

Subsequent to the school returning to London in 1945 and in acknowledgement of the years spent in Betws-y-Coed, it was decided to start an appeal in 1979 as a tribute to John Leakey's leadership and service to the school during the war years. As a result, a Visitor Centre was established in the restored Royal Oak Hotel stables which had served as classrooms for the school during the war. The centre, which was opened in 1985, with the approval of the Snowdonia National Park Authority, provides audio-visual aids and video programmes about the park for schools and visitors.

Other schools

There were at least three other schools evacuated to the Betws-y-Coed area, namely Edenthorpe School, which was resident at the Coed Derw Hotel in 1940, with Miss Bullock as headmistress; Kent House School at Plas Maenan and Aubyns Private School for Boys in Voelas Hall. Once Dulwich College Preparatory School had been established at the Royal Oak Hotel, Mrs Barnett, the wife of a master, started a school class for a few girls of around nine years-of-age in a small café nearby.

Directly after the evacuation of British and Allied forces from Dunkirk, the Lake House School in Bexhill, Surrey was requisitioned by the army and it became necessary for the pupils and staff to be evacuated in June 1940. They arrived at the Royal Victoria Hotel in Llanberis which they were to share with the army. The headmaster, Mr Alan Hugh Williams, together with three assistant masters and forty pupils, stayed there until September 1940 when they moved to the requisitioned Penygwryd Hotel, (Arthur Lockwood, the licensee, had to move out of the hotel and into the nearby house for the duration of their stay) four miles from Capel Curig. By 1943, the number of pupils had declined and the decision was taken to leave north Wales for a small village near Kirby Lonsdale.

Plas Machynlleth where the Dunluce School, stayed during the Second World War.
[Betty Roberts]

Dunluce School pupils off for a walk with the Machynlleth Fox Hounds accompanied by the Huntsman, Harry Roberts and Col. Beaumont.
[Betty Roberts

Dunluce School, Machynlleth.
[Betty Roberts]

Dunluce School pony club, Machynlleth.
[Betty Roberts]

Certificate of Appreciation from the Queen. [Margaret Jones]

Due to its location on the south coast and the property being requisitioned by the army, the pupils and teachers of the Sisters of the Sacred Hearts of Jesus and Mary School were evacuated from Hayling Island to Bryn Bras Castle, Llanrug, in June 1940 where they remained until May 1945 when their school building was released by the Ministry of Defence.

In Merionethshire, the Chelsea College of Further Education came *en bloc* to Pantyfedwen in Borth and Chatelard School was evacuated from Switzerland to the Trefeddian Hotel, Aberdyfi. Dunluce Private School, founded in 1880 and described in their brochure as, 'the pioneer of the Finishing School in England ... Now, under duress of war conditions it has moved (from Queen's Gate, Kensington, London) to Plas Machynlleth ... The old Ideals come with us, but the practical side must be strongly stressed to meet the needs of the moment. The modern debutante must now be not only charming and cultured, but useful, resourceful and practical.'

Conway Cadet Training Ship

Until May 1941, HMS *Conway* had been moored on the Mersey but, due to a close encounter with a magnetic mine, it was decided that she should be moved to a safer place in the Menai Strait. Her new mooring near to Bangor pier resulted in the *Conway's* captain, Commander T. M. Goddard, whilst writing to Captain Rees Thomas the Harbour Master at Caernarfon on another matter, making the observation, 'We have settled down in this delightful spot and I can see that I for one will never want to return to the Mersey. A perfect spot one dreams of at sea.'

The *Conway* remained there until 1949 when she was taken to new moorings near Plas Newydd, the home of the Marquess of Anglesey. Although the distance involved was short, it entailed negotiating the Swellies, a narrow passage which, due to the ship's twenty-two feet draft and fifty-four feet beam, only allowed fifteen feet on either side of the ship. Since she had the benefit of a spring tide travelling in the same direction, the role of the two tugs, *Dongarth* and *Minegarth* on that occasion, was to ensure that she kept in the correct channel. Nevertheless it was the skill of the Menai Strait pilots that brought her safely to Plas Newydd where she remained until 1953.

In that year, it was decided that the ship would be towed to Birkenhead where work to the hull would be carried out. The same two tugs that had brought her from the Mersey were allocated the task of guiding her through the Strait and on to Birkenhead. As she approached the Menai suspension bridge, the task proved too much even for two powerful tugs and slowly but surely, the *Conway* drifted slowly towards the mainland shore where she was to end her days. The school, however, remained at Plas Newydd until finally closing in 1974.

Conway Cadet Training Ship on the River Mersey prior to its departure for a safer venue on the Menai Strait 1941. [AC]

Tugs with Conway in tow entering the Menai Strait. [hmsconway.org]

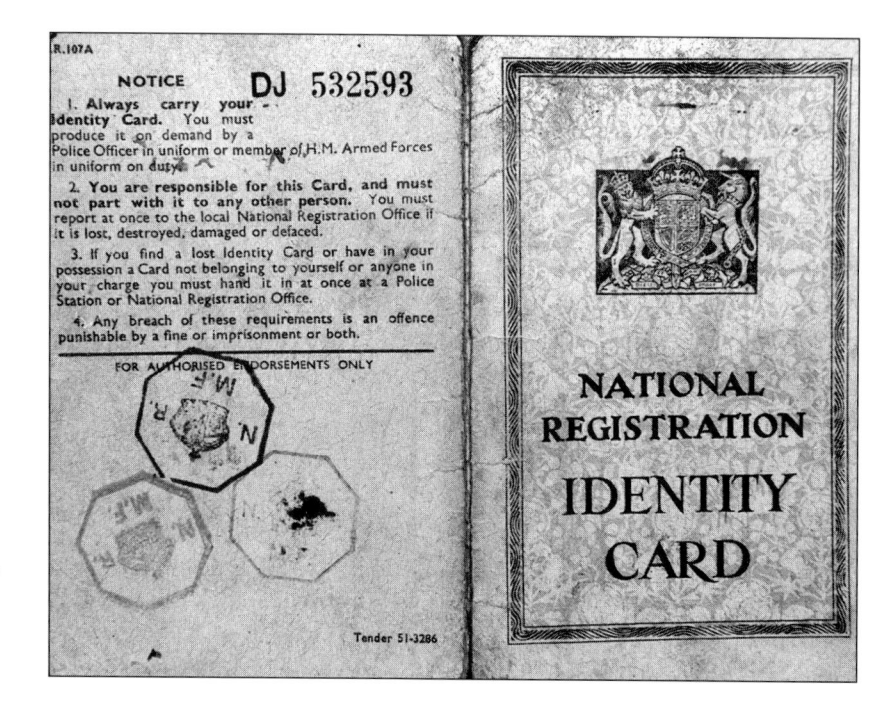

National Identity Card stamped by the Ministry of Food indicating that the holder had registered. [Ivor Wyn Jones]

Notes

1. *C&DH*, 10 February 1939.
2. *C&DH*, 15 March 1939.
3. BUA, Bangor Papers 5260.
4. GAS, XC2-2-32.
5. *C&DH*, 29 September 1939.
6. GAS, XM-3630.
7. GAS, ES/1.
8. *C&DH*, 8 September 1939.
9. Mrs Eileen Knight (née Hunt).
10. *C&DH*, 1 December 1939.
11. BUA, Bangor Papers 4594.
12. *The Education of Evacuated Children*, written by E. O. Humphreys, Education Officer, Llangefni, 27 November 1939.
13. Llangefni WA15-14.

Chapter 5
Home Guard and Police

Home Guard

When the Local Defence Volunteers (LDV), later renamed the Home Guard, was established on 14 May 1940, Sir Anthony Eden, Secretary of State for War, appealed for volunteers aged between seventeen and sixty-five to help the regular forces at a time when there was a strong possibility of an invasion following the German successes in France and the Low Countries.

The LDV (interpreted unkindly by some as 'Look, Duck and Vanish') were trained by those who had seen service in the First World War or by regular army personnel, and by the time they had been moulded into something like a defensive unit, the original LDV armband had been abandoned for a full uniform and they were issued with American rifles of First World War vintage, instead of the occasional shotgun. Both the Caernarfon LDV and Air-Raid Wardens were to share the north-east tower of Caernarfon Castle as their headquarters for the first few months of the war.

A letter sent on 31 January 1941 by a representative of the 3rd Battalion, 'A' Company, Llangristiolus, to the Officer Commanding the Anglesey Home Guard, indicates the concern that existed due to the lack of equipment:

> The enrolment of the Home Guard at Llangristiolus commenced in July 1940 and in a very short time over seventy men had volunteered. It was realised at the time that equipment could not possibly be obtained at once, and the men were assured that in the course of a few weeks each member would be fully equipped. Up to the present, seven months having elapsed, we are in possession of thirty (.33) rifles and eighteen bayonets.
>
> The scarcity of Arms and greatcoats is causing me great embarrassment as the men feel that they have a grievance … the members are aware by now that other units of the Home Guard in this County are much better equipped in every way than the Llangristiolus Platoon of 'A' Company.
>
> Another matter that is causing me concern is what would be the position of say forty members of one unit of the Home Guards (sic) in uniform without a weapon of defence during an invasion. (To my small mind they would be better off as civilians.)[1]

The initial role of the Local Defence Volunteers was that of a defence force and the instructions that were issued stated:

> 'MOBILE ARMED PARTY   this party needs constant training in rifle-shooting

Welsh language version of the instruction given by the Ministry of Information in the event of an invasion. [AC]

and the handling of arms so as to form it into a workmanlike and efficient unit capable of rapid and precise movement ... '

'ROAD BLOCKING Duties of LDV – 23 June 1940 – A census should be taken of all the available road blocking material in the neighbourhood of the proposed block – this means questioning at the farms around in order to find what carts, ploughs, harrows etc. are available ... '[2]

One of the first duties allocated to the LDV in Caernarfon in 1940 was that of 'guarding' the railway station, petroleum depot, post office and Bethel Road electricity sub-station.[3] Members of the LDV were allowed to use the rifle range at Glynllifon but, as the letter dated 9 July 1940 from Brigade Major HQ 23rd Army Tank Regiment, Glynllifon Park stated, all was not well, 'your LDVs turned up and shot on our range yesterday. They were very keen and showed considerable confidence in their rifles. Unfortunately a very high proportion of the ammunition was dud and they were only able to fire four out of their ten shots ... '[4]

Within three months, the initial 250,000 British volunteers had grown to a million, by which stage, the title had been changed from LDV to Home Guard. Eventually, all men had to join who were not eligible for the forces or other specified services, and who were aged between seventeen and sixty-five. Men who enrolled in the Home Guard were placed in one of two lists:

– those ordered to muster immediately when ordered to do so;
– those not available due to the importance of their civil duties were excused, but even they had to report to the unit within forty-eight hours.

Members of the Home Guard were expected to be available for training for a total of forty-eight hours each month. Failure to comply with a direction under the Defence (Home Guard) Regulations, 1940, could result in a summary conviction and imprisonment for a term not exceeding three months, or a fine of £100, or both.[5] Absenteeism was also an offence within the regulations and in a leaflet issued in August 1943 by R. J. Wordsworth, Col. Commanding Snowdon Section, he stated, 'Checking absenteeism is most distasteful to Home Guard officers ... as in some cases the delinquent may be a friend, neighbour or sometimes a client of the Home Guard Officer concerned ... '

The Home Guard sector responsible for the 'nodal points' (i.e. intersection of roads) at Beddgelert, Penygwryd, Betws-y-Coed and Llanrwst received the following ominous instruction,

> [they] must be prepared to resist all forms of attack. Resistance at these places must be maintained to the last man and the last round. In order to make plans to stock these places with ammunition, food, water and medical stores, it is necessary to know how many men will carry out the defence at each place ... please consider each nodal point and say what strength of garrison you recommend should be brought into each place ... Major Dolman, Craig-y-Dderwen, Betws-y-Coed, 24 July 1942.[6]

English language version of the instruction given by the Ministry of Information in the event of an invasion. [AC]

In the event of an attack in the Beddgelert area, sixteen men had been allocated to man a road-block on the edge of the village. A further four blocks were planned to be positioned on the Beddgelert to Penygwryd road, manned by twenty men. Eighteen men were to be held in reserve.[7]

It was also the task of the Home Guard to inspect bridges to ensure that no preparation had been made for demolition by saboteurs. The Capel Curig contingent was commanded by Major Arthur Lockwood (he had been involved with the building of Cwm Dyli power station c.1906 and was subsequently the licensee of the Pen-y-gwryd Hotel).

Whenever large-scale exercises took place, communication between the different sections and headquarters was always a problem. As radios were virtually non-existent, a request was made by the officer commanding to the Caernarfon postmaster that his men be allowed to make free telephone calls because 'it is difficult to ensure that each man engaged in such exercise has a sufficient supply of coppers on him,'

When the request was refused, an urgent appeal was issued asking for those with motor cycles to perform the duties of despatch riders for the Home Guard one night a week. A similar plea was made by Commander J. Goff Owen of 'C' (Llanberis) Company, Caernarvonshire Home Guard in

> HOME GUARD,　　　　　　　　　　　　No. 2 Platoon.
> 3rd (Caernarvonshire Bn.,　　　　　　December 3, 1940.
> "A" Company.
>
> Section Leaders,
> Sub-Section Leaders,
> Volunteers.
>
> Your earnest attention is drawn to this memorandum.
>
> Weather permitting, Saturday afternoon and Sunday open-air training will continue, but the importance of attending Musketry, Lewis Gun, Signalling Classes, etc., during the winter evenings cannot be over-emphasised.
>
> Volunteers in the Home Guard have undertaken an honourable obligation, not only to do a job of work, but also to train and drill to do that work efficiently. Regular and punctual attendance in classes is therefore imperative. The few Volunteers who have drawn clothing and equipment, and who are absenting themselves consistently from classes and parades do not fulfil their promises, and they are jeopardising the ultimate efficiency of the unit.
>
> Efficiency follows discipline. An enthusiastic Home Guardsman welcomes discipline, and obeys orders unreservedly. He becomes a friend of his Superior Officer, Section Leader and Sub-Section Leader after the "dismiss."
>
> Non-attendance or lateness on parade lead to slackness. Familiarity with Officers and N.C.O.'s will end in slackness and inefficiency.
>
> Standing about, waiting for volunteers, who are late for class or parade, is waste of good time. This is not the time to be idle. Serious and important work is to be done, and it must be tackled wholeheartedly.
>
> Road defences, etc., will not be of much use unless the Volunteers manning them are properly trained and inculcated with "team spirit" to win.
>
> Training takes time, but Home Guardsmen must submit to intensive training, which means hard but interesting work.
>
> A public parade, well done, is good drill. Steadiness in the ranks is imperative, but the admiration of the crowd must wait until the work solemnly pledged to achieve is done.
>
> The slogan now is ACTUAL TRAINING.
>
> In an emergency, the Home Guard must not surrender an inch of ground. Home Guardsmen must train to remain at their allotted posts and fight. To prevent panic amongst the civil population, you must stand firm, but before you are able to "stand firm" you must be proficient in squad drill, arms drill, musketry, field craft exercises, etc. The volunteer who stands to attention properly on the barrack square will not lose his head (in more than one sense) in an emergency.

Home Guard.
[Margaret Sheldon]

the *The Motor Cycle* magazine, February 1941), 'One night a week Motor Cycle Despatch riders required for Home Guard – petrol coupons issued and running allowance paid … '

It was intended that despatch riders would be issued with full uniform, which included the white Royal Corps of Signals armlet, boots, steel helmet and equipment (crash helmets, normally worn by despatch riders, were not yet available, nor was waterproof clothing). An allowance of 2d per mile to cover the cost of petrol, licence, insurance and running repairs would be paid to the owners of machines carrying out Home Guard duties.

Above: Officers and NCOs, 1st Battalion Anglesey Home Guard. [Holyhead Maritime Museum]

Left: 1st Battalion Anglesey Home Guard, Holyhead 1944: Rear L–R — L/Cpl Lewis, Pte J. E. Williams, Pte. J Roberts, L/Cpl Emrys Williams, L/Cpl Heath Middle —Lt Hewitt, Lt Timby, Major B. A. Gale, Major Roberts Lt T. Lloyd, Sgt. Major Thomas Front — Pte R. Hughes, L/Cpl Street, Sgt W. A. Milligan, L/Cpl Williams Cpl T. G. Jones. [Holyhead Maritime Museum]

Petrol coupons were available and an allowance given for wear and tear. Apparently, the first appeal for motor cyclists was answered mainly by Great War veterans.

The National Pigeon Service was an alternative method of communication under consideration (presumably for non-urgent messages), with birds being provided by local representatives – R. A. Bridges, North Road, Caernarfon; R. Williams, Cartref, Ala Road, Pwllheli and Robert Evans, 3 Clifton Road, Llandudno. However, in the event of an invasion, the following instructions had to be followed:

Destruction of pigeons in invasion – in any area which is likely to fall into the hands of the enemy all homing pigeons other than those in use for Army, Royal

Railwaymen Home Guard. [Holyhead Maritime Museum]

Air Force or other official purposes will be destroyed to prevent their use by the enemy. It will also be necessary as far as practical to destroy or dismantle lofts used by such pigeons in order to prevent any pigeons which may be flying out at the time of destruction from returning to the loft later ...[8]

The inconvenience caused to the public by the government directive to remove road signs and obliterate place names at railway stations, post-offices and telephone boxes was considered insignificant when compared to the problems confronting possible invaders requiring directions. A directive dated 16 September 1940 from General Staff, Kinmel Sub Area, Llanerch Park, St Asaph, stated, 'It is likely that at the time of invasion Germans will be landed in British battle-dress, mainly by air, but possibly also by sea ... All HQ units will therefore ensure that methods of identification are at all times strictly enforced ...'[9]

Members of the Home Guard were also expected to assist the police, 'Object – to check the movement of enemy agents while not slowing up the movement of troops or essential services ... examination shall be carried out by police ... there will be a detachment of Home Guard or regular troops in concealed positions from which they can cover the block by fire.'[10]

The method of 'halting motorists' was described as, 'By day – the sentry should use the ordinary police signals. By night – the sentry should stop motor traffic by waving a red lamp. In either case there should be another man 20 yards behind the sentry stopping traffic who is ready to fire if the car refuses to stop.'

The actual checking of identification passes at road-blocks made the task very difficult due to the variety of people that were travelling about the countryside, including Allied forces of various nationalities, vagrants and people of no fixed abode passing through the county. To further exacerbate the situation and add to the confusion, a list showed that there were sixteen different types of identity cards in use by a variety of people.

The regimental depot of the Royal Welch Fusiliers at Wrexham, which had become an Infantry Training Centre at the start of the war, was also on standby in case of invasion and was expected to take certain action on receiving the code word 'Cromwell' which was an indication that the invasion was imminent or had started. This message was actually received over the telephone at the depot and scribbled on a piece of paper which was left in a tray awaiting action. When it was eventually found and acted upon, a small contingent of soldiers were sent to their allotted station at Rhiw on the Lleyn peninsula, whilst the officer in charge followed in his 1935 Hillman Minx car, together with his twelve-bore shotgun in case he had time to spare for shooting! After languishing there for three weeks (during which time a number of game birds were disposed of), the company commander, based at the Oakley Arms, Tan-y-bwlch, ordered them to return to headquarters to await further instructions.

Although church bells were to be used as a warning when an invasion was taking place, it had been decided that 'church towers could only be used for observation and communication, but not for military purposes, no offensive weapons or searchlight to be installed and incumbent to remain in charge of the church and tower.'[11]

In the summer of 1940, every household in Gwynedd was given a

Penygroes Home Guard (Officers). [Aled Jones]

Penygroes Home Guard (all ranks). [Aled Jones]

Ministry of Information leaflet printed in both English and Welsh,

If the Invader Comes – What to do – and how to do it – The Germans threaten to invade Great Britain. If they do they will be driven out by our Navy, our Army and our Air Force. Yet the ordinary men and women of the civilian population will also have their part to play. Hitler's invasion of Poland, Holland and Belgium was greatly helped by the fact that the civilian population was taken by surprise. They did not know what to do when the moment came. You must not be taken by surprise … '

… Remember that if parachutists come down near your home, they will not be feeling at all brave. They will not know where they are, they will have no food, they will not know where their companions are. They will want you to give them food, means of transport and maps. They will want you to tell them where they have landed, where their comrades are, and where our own soldiers are.

Problems arising with over-enthusiastic members of the Home Guard regarding every parachutist as the German invading army and shooting at everything in sight, necessitated the following instructions to be issued (having failed to hit a stationary target on a rifle range, it was hardly likely that they would manage to be more successful hitting one that was moving),

Facing page: Deployment of Anglesey Home Guard. [Aled Jones]

Cases have occurred recently of our own pilots descending by parachute being injured by our own forces. All ranks of the Army and all members of Home Guard must clearly understand the following instructions:

SECRET
ZONE I. ANGLESEY.

ZONE I

DISTRIBUTION LIST — ANGLESEY HOME GUARD

APPOINTMENT	NAME	OPERATIONAL HEADQUARTERS	TEL. NO.
ZONE H.Q.			
Zone Commander	Col. R. R. Davies	Min y Garth	Glyn Garth 58
Second in Command	Lt. Col. R. D. Briercliffe	do.	do.
Zone Medical Adviser	Lt. Col. J. L. Moir	do.	do.
Intelligence Officer	Maj. Q. Wynne Jones	do.	do.
Staff Officer "G"	Maj. H. Thornton Jones	do.	do.
Chief Guide	Lieut. T. H. Currie	do.	do.
A.A.	R. R. M. Jones, Esq.	Council Offices	Beaumaris 46
Zone H.Q. Stores		Chapel Street	Beaumaris 128
NO. 1 BATTALION			
C.O.	Lt. Col. the Hon. O. H. Stanley, D.S.O.	Drill Hall, Holyhead	Holyhead 316
Second in Command	Maj. B. A. Gale	do.	do.
Adjutant	Capt. H. T. Finchett Maddock, M.C.	do.	do.
"A" Coy.	Maj. Conant	do.	do.
"B" Coy.	Maj. H. J. Seeds	Valley Hotel	76
"C" Coy.	Maj. F. N. Carpenter	Coffee House, Llanfaethlu	231
"L.M.S." Coy.	Maj. Smith, M.C.	Marine Buildings Holyhead	304
NO. 2 BATTALION			
C.O.	Lt. Col. L. Williams, O.B.E.	Parciau, Marianglas	Tyn y Gongl 29
Second In Command	Maj. Pery-Knox-Gore	do.	do.
Adjutant	Capt. I. B. Williams	do.	do.
"A" Coy.	Maj. I. Perry-Knox-Gore, D.S.O. M.C.	Hafod Lon, Menai Bridge	Glyn Garth 54
"B" Coy.	Maj. F. L. Arnold, M.C.	Police Stn.	Beaumaris 2
"C" Coy.	Capt. J. Royle	H.Q. Stores, Benllech	Tyn y gongl 37
"D" Coy.	Capt. W. J. Jones	Salvation Army Hut	Amlwch
"E" Coy.	Capt. S. Macneil	King's Head Hotel	Llanerchymedd 2
No. 3 BATTALION			
C.O.	Lt. Col. the Marquess of Anglesey, G.C.V.O.	H.Q. Stores, Bulkeley Sq	Llangefni 131
Second In Command	Maj. Pritchard Rayner	do.	do.
Adjutant	Capt. S. C. H. Livingston	do.	do.
"A" Coy.	Maj. T. Forcer Evans	do.	do.
"B" Coy.	Maj. O. Jones	School House	Bodorgan 83
"C" Coy.	Maj. J. Humphreys	School house, Bryngwran	Gwalchmai 237
"D" Coy.	Maj. J. E. Edwards, M.C.	Women's Inst. Llanfairpwll	32
"E" Coy.	Maj. Selwyn Jones	Maes y Porth Dwyran	Brynsiencyn 6

APN/2419

Home Guard Band (Caernarfon). [AC]

1. If fewer than six parachutists are seen descending they will not be fired at.
2. When parachutists are airmen in distress, either British or German, their aircraft will probably be seen or heard to crash in the neighbourhood at the same time.
3. The Air Ministry has issued the following instructions to RAF personnel forced to land by parachute.
   a. When persons approach to apprehend them they should stand still holding both hands over their heads with fingers extended and announce their identity loudly. They should make no movement until their identity is established.
   b. If ordered to produce proof of identity they should say where this can be found on them but should not lower their hands in case this action arouses suspicion that they are reaching for a weapon.
   c. If injured they should lie flat and stay still.[12]

On another occasion, it was stated that German airforce personnel who had landed in this country, either by parachute or by crashed aircraft, had been able to remain at large sometimes for hours and 'sometimes they have voluntarily surrendered to totally indifferent bystanders.'[13]

The Llanberis company of the Home Guard organised a full training programme during the winter of 1941–2 which included rifles and machine guns, grenades and bayonets, map-reading, signalling, camouflage, tank hunting and destruction, fieldcraft, tactical exercises, guerrilla warfare, discipline and morale.[14] Even though they had been supplied with flame throwers, their use was restricted by the quantity of petrol available and 'it would be necessary for them to apply for coupons like everyone else!' This company, which was responsible for the NECACO aircraft factory in the

Dinorwic Quarry, was expected to maintain a continuous all-night patrol with approximately twelve men, whilst a reserve patrol of six men slept at the premises. In addition, road blocks with 'Blacker Bombard' positions were maintained along the Llanberis pass and adjacent to both Llyn Peris and Llyn Padarn.[15]

There were occasions when certain appointments proved unpopular with the men as was shown in a letter of 3 October 1940, addressed to a Dr Parry, and signed by thirty-one members of the Llanberis members of the 3rd Battalion, Caernarvonshire Home Guard, stating,

> We the undersigned ... beg to draw your attention to the discord which is displayed in our platoon following a recent appointment made by Mr E. Thomas our Company Commander. We would be glad if you could meet us so that we can discuss the matter with you. We have no objection whatsoever to Mr E. Thomas being present at this meeting and we would like to point out that this communication is prompted only by a very sincere need for harmony in our platoon.[16]

Whenever training took place at Belan Fort camp near Dinas Dinlle, rules were issued stating that the cookhouse and the aerodrome were out-of-bounds to all ranks except those employed therein. It was also necessary to warn all ranks 'of the danger of throwing stones, etc into the minefield (which was clearly marked) or interfering with them [the mines] in any way.' It seemed ominous for the following to be added, 'Training: It is also the Medical Officer's wish that there should be a few men in each section who have an elementary knowledge of First Aid. The quick removal of the killed and immediate attention to the wounded will do much to keep up the morale of the fighting men.'[17]

Whether such a recommendation was made because of the following

Officers, 3rd Battalion, Caernarvonshire Home Guard. [Bangor University Archives]

SNOWDON SECTOR.

Distribution List Revised July, 1943.

Appointment.	Name.	Address	Tel. No.	Pte. No.
Sector Commr.	Col. R. J. Wordsworth, D.S.O., T.D.	Barracks, Caernarvon	Caer. 539	Bangor 86
Staff Officer	Major E. H. Jarvis, D.S.O.	Craig Lledr, Bettwsycoed		Bettws. 9
Sector Adjt.	Capt. T. Holloway	Barracks, Caernarvon	Caer. 539	Caer. 361
Sector M.O.	Lieut.-Col. W. Hilton Parry, M.C.	Barracks, Caernarvon	Caer. 539	Caer. 207
Intell. Officer	Lt. E. A. K. Webber	Glan Conway, Bettwsycoed		Pentrevs. 207
Sigs. Officer	Lt. D. Williams	15, Newborough St., Caernarvon	Caer. 539	Bangor 192
Transpt. Offr.	Lt. L. A. Russell	Bronwylfa, Caernarvon	Caer. 517	Caer. 338
Training Offr.	Lt.-Col. V. L. S. Cowley, D.S.O., M.C.	Poste Restante, Criccieth		Criccieth 87
Training Offr.	Major E. G. Utley	Ty Newydd, Bangor		Bangor 278

CAERNARVONSHIRE TERRITORIAL ASSOCIATION

Appointment.	Name.	Address.	Tel No.	Pte No.
Acting Secry.	Capt. E. W. Hughes	Barracks, Caernarvon	Caer. 161	
Admin. Asst.	Capt. R. O. Jones	Barracks, Caernarvon	Caer. 161	

2nd BATTN., CAERNS. H.G., BANGOR

Appointment.	Name.	Address.	Tel. No.	Pte. No.
C.O.	Lt.-Col. H. G. Carter, M.C.	284, High Street, Bangor	Ban. 785	Ban. 553
2nd I/C	Major I. Griffiths	Drill Hall, Bethesda	Beth. 304	Beth. 234
Adjt.	Capt. J. L. Anderson	284, High Street, Bangor	Ban. 785	Ban. 700
Qr. Mr.	Capt. G. B. Wright	284, High Street, Bangor	Ban. 785	Ban. 156
Battn. M.O.	Major R. J. Helsby, M.C.	Wellfield, Bangor		Ban. 55
"A" Coy.	Major A. R. Breese	Eagles Cafe, Bangor	Ban. 785	Ex. 4
"B" Coy.	Major T. R. Magee	Britannia House, Bangor	Ban. 785	Ex. 5
"C" Coy.	Major D. R. Llewellyn	Drill Hall, Bethesda	Beth. 304	
"D" Coy.	Capt. G. W. Griffin	H.G. Hqrs., Portdinorwic	Port. 296	
"E" Coy.	Major H. L. Pierce	H.G. Hqrs., Deiniolen	Llanberis 238	

3rd. BATTN. CAERNS. H.G. BARRACKS, CAERNARVON

Appointment.	Name.	Address.	Tel. No.	Pte. No.
C.O.	Lt.-Col. T. G. Wynne-Parry	Barracks, Caernarvon	Caer. 523	Caer. 197
2nd I/C	Major D. R. Jackson, D.S.O.	Necaco, Llanberis	Caer. 523	Llan. 287
Adjt.				
Qr. Mr.	Capt. R. Hughes	Barracks, Caernarvon	Caer. 523	
Battn. M.O.	Major J. G. Dods	Bron Menai, Caernarvon	Caer. 523	Caer. 46
"A" Coy.	Major T. Jones	Drill Hall, Caernarvon	Caer. 105	
"B" Coy.	Major E. Thomas	Drill Hall, Penygroes	Pen 32	
"C" Coy.	Major E. Thomas	Church Hall, Llanrug	Caer. 173	
"D" Coy.	Capt. J. Somerville	Drill Hall, Llanberis	Llan. 287	

4th BATTN. CAERNS. H.G., HENDRE GADREDD, CRICCIETH.

Appointment.	Name.	Address.	Tel. No.	Pte. No.
C.O.	Lt.-Col. R. C. O.'Farrell, M.C.	Hendre Gadredd, Criccieth	Criccieth 87	Nevin 229
2nd I/C	Major R. C. G. Vivian	Hendre Gadredd, Criccieth	Criccieth 87	Llanbedrog 29
Adjt.	Capt. A. T. Taylor	Hendre Gadredd, Criccieth	Criccieth 87	
Qr. Mr.	Capt. R. Chambley, T.D.	Hendre Gadredd, Criccieth	Criccieth 87	Portmadoc 62
Battn. M.O.	Major K. V. Trubshaw	Nant Glyn, Criccieth	Criccieth 73	
"A" Coy.	Major R. Belton Jones	Drill Hall, Portmadoc	Port. 314	Portmadoc 70
"B" Coy.	Major J. C. Burnell	Drill Hall, Criccieth	Criccieth 124	Criccieth 155
"C" Coy.	Major G. R. Prys	Drill Hall, Pwllheli	Pwllheli 332	Pwllheli 110
"D" Coy.	Major H. Parry	Church Hall, Nevin	Nevin 237	
"E" Coy.	Major R. C. G. Vivian	Haulfryn Lodge, Abersoch	Aber. 116	Llanbedrog 29

1st. BATTN. MER. H.G., PLAS WEUNYDD, BLAENAU FESTINIOG.

Appointment.	Name.	Address.	Tel. No.	Pte. No.
C.O.	Lt.-Col. M. Williams-Ellis	Plas Weunydd, Blaenau Festiniog	Blaen. 67	Blaen. 67
2nd I/C				
Adjt.	Capt. R. W. Jones	Plas Weunydd, Blaenau Festiniog	Blaen. 67	
Qr. Mr.	Capt. W. T. Lee	United Services Club, Bl. Festiniog	Blaen. 114	Blaen. 85
Battn. M.O.	Major J. W. Morris	Bryn Marian, Blaenau Festiniog		Blaen. 61
"A" Coy.	Major L. F. Davies	Soar Chapel, Blaenau Festiniog	Blaen. 129	Blaen. 119
"B" Coy.	Major D. M. Jones	Church Hall, Festiniog	Festg. 11	Festg. 2
"C" Coy.	Capt. W. Jones	1, Bull Street, Maentwrog	P'rhyn'th 285	
"D" Coy.	Capt. T. Williams	Park Square, Blaenau Festiniog	Blaen. 140	

Facing page and above: Deployment of Caernarvonshire Home Guard (Snowdon Sector). [GAS, XM1301]

observation is not recorded, 'Standard of training in Anglesey is not high enough: some Home Guard members cannot hit a 4ft target at 200 yards.'[18]

Exercise 'Dwrog' was intended to check the Llandwrog airfield and Belan Fort defences, and a detachment from the Royal Welch Fusiliers, the 560th Coast Regiment Royal Artillery and the 3rd Caernarvonshire Battalion Home Guard took part. It was intended that 'A' Coy of the Home Guard was to proceed by boat at 07.30 hours, (provided the sea was not too rough) from Caernarfon to Belan Fort where the 403rd Coast Battery, RA was responsible for three light machine-guns and two naval guns. Everything went off according to plan until, after successfully negotiating the mines laid on the beach, they were confronted by a furious OC RAF Llandwrog yelling, 'Get off my bloody runways!' as he thought his flying schedules were going to be interrupted by these interlopers.

A document described as *Consolidated Instructions to Invasion Committees (England and Wales)* issued in 1942 stated, 'The general military plan for our troops is that there will be no withdrawal and that such enemy forces as penetrate will be counter-attacked and destroyed or driven into the sea … 6th Marquess of Anglesey, Lt-Col OC, N° 3 Battalion Home Guard Anglesey.'[19]

Women were also encouraged to form teams in support of the men, 'And all are invited to come and learn how to be of the greatest use in the case of invasion. The Women's Home Defence do not drill or wear uniform but they do learn Self-Defence, Anti-Gas Treatment, First-Aid, Field Cooking etc. Do not forget that the Germans have proved themselves to be ruthless

Clynnog Fawr Home Guard with Evan Pritchard (left) given the honour of holding the Lewis light machine-gun. [Evie Wyn Jones]

barbarians, sparing neither women nor children but using them in the most brutal fashion and killing them without mercy ... '[20]

As far as the Morfa Nefyn Repeater Station was concerned, it was the 22nd Cheshire (GPO) Battalion Home Guard that had the responsibility of guarding it. Major F. Baldwin commanded the eight-man section and his deputy was Capt Tennyson.[21]

The Saunders Roe factory at Beaumaris had its own Home Guard detachment but, because some of the members lived in Bangor, they were told that if the Menai Bridge was destroyed, they were to muster on Bangor pier where they would be picked up by launch and brought across the strait

Nant Peris Home Guard. Note the two Lewis guns on the ground (left and right) and the Boys Anti-tank Rifle (centre). [Griff Roberts and Dafydd Whiteside Thomas]

Home Guard and Police 73

Llandudno Local Defence Volunteers.

Above: First all-night patrol on the Great Orme before the allocation of uniforms or weapons. [H. L. Wilson]

Left: After some members had been issued with overalls and rifles. [H. L. Wilson]

Llandudno Home Guard. Three members armed with a rifle, an air-cooled Lewis gun and Sten gun, training in a busy Mostyn Street, watched by an amused schoolboy. [H. L. Wilson]

A Company, Llandudno Home Guard leading a parade past the War Memorial on the promenade. RSM Tom Owen at the front.
[H. L. Wilson]

Despatch Riders, Llandudno Home Guard on Gloddaeth Avenue. [H. L. Wilson]

Machine-gun Section, Llandudno Home Guard with two Vickers .303 machine guns.
[H. L. Wilson]

Penisarwaen Home Guard.
[Norah O'Brien]

to Beaumaris. They had plenty of armaments to defend the factory, including fifty-seven rifles, five light machine-guns, one light Browning automatic rifle, one heavy Browning machine-gun, fourteen Sten guns and a variety of hand-grenades. Even the matter of the men's welfare was very much in mind when they appointed Private Gravenell to be responsible for the catering 'in the event of an emergency.'

Similar arrangements applied at the Daimler factory in Bangor which also had its own Home Guard section, but the responsibility of looking after the Port Penrhyn stores was naturally delegated to the three storekeepers. They had the advantage of being able sit in the comfort of their office and gaze through the window in the direction of Beaumaris and beyond, thus ensuring that nothing untoward was happening within their line of vision. Provided the weather was fine and the forecast reasonable, two out of the three would take a walk along the quay while the third member took turns in preparing refreshments and manning the telephone. At night, when nothing could be seen through the window, they took on the role of fire-watching which gave them an opportunity of improving their card-playing. They were never provided with a uniform, not even an arm-band, to signify their role, possibly because they were not entirely sure whether they were members of the Home Guard, the Royal Observer Corps or represented the Air-Raid Wardens. Their only form of protection was a form of truncheon, but no instructions had been given as to its use if the occasion arose. There had been a rumour that a twelve-bore gun was kept

Llanfairfechan Home Guard. [John Lloyd Roberts]

in a locked cupboard, but they never found the key to establish whether it was true or not.

To maintain morale, a competition was arranged within the 3rd Battalion Caernarvonshire Home Guard on 6 November 1942 to 'foster a competitive spirit within the sector.' It was intended that points would be awarded and prizes given to the winners based on, 'Battle Drill; Battle Craft including turnout, smartness of movement, words of command. NB. Turn out will be as for a Fighting Soldier NOT as for Ceremonial Parade'.[22]

On 15 August 1942, the Pentraeth Home Guard organised an Open Athletics Sports Day at Bryniau Field with competitions for children, open platoon events and Home Guard events only. Admission was 6d., and the proceeds were in aid of British Red Cross and Prisoners-of-War Fund. Another public relations event was arranged for the Liverpool Blue Coat Hospital School at Beaumaris.

The Estate Office at Glyn Hall, Talsarnau, which was involved in organising a similar event for the Merioneth Home Guard in July 1942, received a letter from the Ministry of Food, Rural Food Control Committee (Bank Buildings, Penrhyndeudraeth) stating,

Manod Home Guard. [Royal Welch Fusiliers Museum]

Machynlleth Home Guard.
[Y Tabernacl, Machynlleth]

I enclose herewith the special permits as promised. You will observe that I have made out the meat permit for N⁰· 8 Platoon in favour of Rowlands, Maentwrog, as the doing is a sort of rehearsal [sic]. Everything will be all right regarding the supplies from Mr Roberts, Meirion Stores. He will also supply dried milk. I have also arranged with the Canteen Bakers regarding the Bread. They will have 45, 4lb. Loaves ready for Friday and they will bake another lot of 30, 2lb. loaves on Saturday in case you will require them. Everything will be all right at Messrs J. Ivor Jones, Harlech, as well, – Groceries, Milk and Bread. I forgot about Sausage when you were here. They would help your bacon and they are off ration. Asst. Food Executive Officer. PS The price of carrots will be reduced to $3^{1}/_{2}$d. per lb. as from the 13th July.[23]

The register of hours of attendance for the 6 Platoon, C Coy, 1st Merioneth Battalion, Home Guard listed a total of fifty-five men in November 1943.[24] By April 1944, 6 Platoon had been issued with seven Remington, six Winchester and thirty-seven other makes of rifle.[25]

When the junior officers of the 1st Battalion, Anglesey Home Guard celebrated their Second Annual Dinner at The Bull Hotel, Llangefni on 24 February 1943, the Austerity Menu stated, 'There'll be some soup, I've been promised a bit of pork and/or beef, we can get vegetables alright, we'll put on a good sweet.'[26]

These menus were in marked contrast to the fare which the Felinheli (Port Dinorwic) Home Guard contingent experienced. They met at Menai View, a house on Brynffynnon Road, with the cookhouse conveniently situated on the other side of the road in the National School where the meal, such as it was, was eaten while sitting at a child's desk. It was here where the culinary prowess of two retired sea captains was put to the test, for they were the official cooks for the local detachment of about thirty men. Normally, their expertise only stretched to boiling a kettle for a cup of tea, but they did manage occasionally to produce a dish of *lobscaws*

Aberangell Home Guard 1943. [Y Tabernacl, Machynlleth]

(stew), which, after a hard day's work, if not a gastronomic experience, was at least palatable and warming. When it came to identifying what they were about to consume, it was carried out in a simplistic way – if it was salty it was a stew; if it tasted sweet it was a pudding![27]

The Port Dinorwic Home Guard had to be on parade by 6 p.m. and remain at their post until 6 a.m. when breakfast (that was purported to be porridge) was produced by the maritime experimenters. Since it would be expecting too much of the men to drill under such adverse conditions, this was usually undertaken in the evening or at the weekends in the vicinity of their headquarters. Most exercises could only be conducted over a weekend, which unfortunately coincided with the time when the local children, who were at a loose end and looking for trouble, had the disconcerting ability of finding the heavily camouflaged Home Guard members wherever they sought refuge. A report made in August 1941 described exercise 'Arfon' as a farce because a machine-gun was surrounded by a crowd of children, 'and the position of other hidden posts being given away to the enemy by the attitude of onlookers.' Inevitably, there was a tendency for the Home Guard to be treated in a rather fatuous way and consequently, people generally could not or would not treat them seriously.

From time-to-time, the local Home Guard was tested against the army to establish its capabilities. Although the amateurs were no match for the regulars, the exercise did provide the local force with some practical experience rather than relying on monotonous drill. Similar exercises were also carried out against other Home Guard units in neighbouring counties. When this was an exercise between the Caernarvonshire and the Anglesey battalions, a decision had to be taken as to the best method of getting across the Menai Strait to enable an 'invasion' to take place. It could be done either by using the Menai Suspension Bridge, or by boat. Rather than invade unobtrusively by boat which could be wet, uncomfortable and even dangerous, the unadventurous majority decided that the Strait would be crossed the 'dry way' via the bridge.

Generally, accommodation was always a problem since every available building had been requisitioned for some purpose or another. The Rhostryfan Home Guard, after carrying out necessary repairs, used an old Welsh Highland Railway waiting-room as accommodation. The Rhyd Ddu section also used the local waiting-room as well as the booking-office of the same railway. Carmel, Cesarea and Nebo Council Schools were used two or three nights a week, where an 'efficient blackout' had been fitted, although the only means of lighting was from paraffin lamps.

As far as the Home Guard in Caernarfon was concerned, it was naturally expected that the town Drill Hall would be available to them for training purposes. However, since the building had been taken over by the Ministry of Labour, and the staff were proving intransigent, consideration had been given to taking over the building by force, but before that became necessary the 'trespassers' left to take up residence in Siloh Chapel schoolroom instead.

The 3rd Battalion Caernarvonshire Home Guard had the distinction of having formed a brass band in 1942 with E. W. Hughes as bandmaster and president, Owen E. Owen as his deputy, E. H. Williams as secretary and Cpl R. Parry as librarian. The twenty-two bandsmen practised on Wednesday evenings at 7 p.m. in the Caernarfon Drill Hall. Their first public performance was on Remembrance Sunday, 8 November 1942, at Llanrug and in the afternoon, at Caernarfon. On the 28 March 1943, they gave a concert at the Majestic Cinema, Caernarfon in the presence of their Commanding Officer, Lt-Col T. G. Wynne Parry.[28]

Even at the time when an invasion could have occurred, the Caernarfon Home Guard still found time for a periodic game of football at the Oval. During the 1941/42 season, the team consisted of H. H. Roberts, E. Roberts, B. Pierce, F. Henderson, R. Hughes, C. Rutherford, A. Jones, L. Carter, B. Lovell, W. E. Evans and J. Simmons.

Cemaes Home Guard.
[Y Tabernacl, Machynlleth]

Above left: Certificate of Service in the Home Guard. [Y Tabernacl, Machynlleth]

Above right: Membership certificate for the 3rd Battalion Caernarvonshire Home Guard. [Derek Jones]

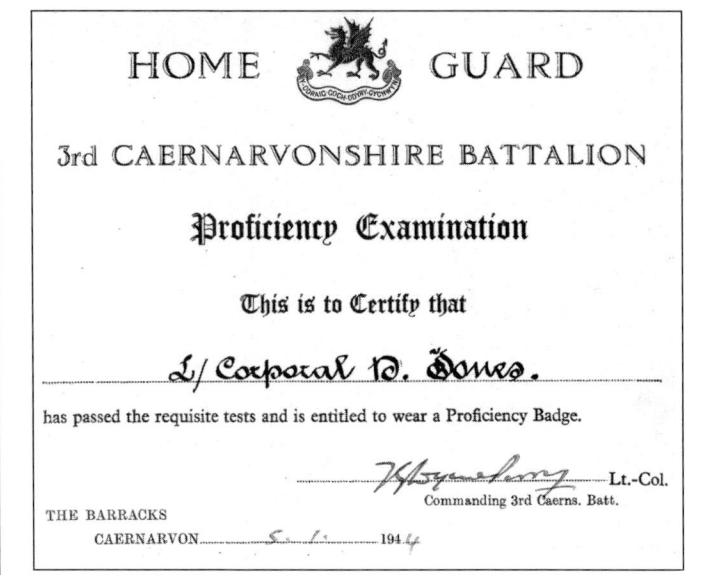

A letter, dated 22 April 1943, sent by the officer commanding the Caernarvonshire Home Guard (Col R. J. Wordsworth), Zone 2, based at Penrhyn Estate Office in Bangor, to the Clerk of the County Council, Caernarfon stated that, 'The Prime Minister had expressed a desire that special Demonstrations of the Home Guard shall take place on Sunday afternoon 16 May (1943) to Commemorate the third anniversary of their formation … Such demonstration to be carried out for the benefit of the public to give them some idea of the strength and efficiency of the force.'[29]

Fortunately, no invasion came and as Germany turned her attention eastwards to Russia, the importance of the Home Guard declined and it was eventually 'stood down' on 1 November 1944, but was held in reserve until finally disbanded on 31 December 1945.

Police Force

It was the duty of hoteliers and boarding-house keepers to make a record of everyone staying at their establishment. Failure to do so could result in police prosecutions. When eleven Dutchmen and one Belgian were found to be staying at the Railway Hotel in Bangor, it was stated in court by solicitors acting on behalf of the hoteliers, that they were diamond-cutters working in Bangor.[30]

In the Police Aliens Day Book, covering the early period of the war, a variety of people of various nationalities were recorded as passing through the town of Caernarfon, including circus performers at the Pavilion, an American carrying out missionary work in Caernarfon, as well as Russians, Argentinians, Egyptians, Iraqis and Turks, together with 128 Germans. Others recorded as having been 'Removed to Internment Camp at Huyton' were:

Giovanni Antoniazzi, 260 High Street, Bangor – confectioner & tobacconist.
Joseph Valla, 341 High Street, Bangor – chip potato saloon proprietor.
Ernest Hochsinger, Haulfryn, Park Crescent, Llanfairfechan.
Ernest Halbertstadt, Balmoral Hotel, Llanfairfechan.
Alfred Schild, 8 Penrhos Drive, Bangor – student.
Arnold Goldberger, 39 Strand Street, Bangor – artist.
Antonio Miserotti, 23 Pool Hill, Caernarfon.[31]

Those few individuals who owned a camera in the 1940s and intending to use it even for an innocuous holiday snap, needed to take care especially if it was near a sensitive area such as an airfield. Entries in the Police Day Journal for 1939 and 1940 indicate that a number of individuals were arrested for 'surreptitious taking of photo,' 'man using camera at Llanberis' and 'persons taking photos at Vaynol.' A man was even arrested for 'sketching at Dinas Dinlle', presumably because of its nearness to the airfield.[32]

As part of their duty, the police were expected to arrest enemy parachutists 'as soon as they landed' and that they were,

> To be questioned for name and find out if he is a member of the armed forces of the enemy. No detailed interrogation is to be carried out by you. Prisoner to be held in rigorous custody if possible by an armed guard ... if you have any reason to think that the prisoner is a parachutist or saboteur or a member of the enemy armed forces in disguise, you will remove everything from him

Police and Special Constables, Port Dinorwic. [Olive Bocking]

Police, Observer Corps and NFS at Penygroes.
[Aled Jones]

including his clothing ... question him as to his identity, destination ... and make arrangements with MI5 to dispatch an interrogating officer or to give instructions as to the disposal of the prisoner ...[33]

An allowance of 9d. (later increased to 1s.) was made for each meal (breakfast, dinner and tea) supplied to prisoners in police custody in Caernarfonshire.[34]

To assist the police in such duties, 'Bloodhounds may be made available for the tracking of missing parachutists, etc ... The hound will have to come some distance but will travel in a fast car; part of the training of these particular hounds has been a journey by motor car in order that the hounds may associate travelling in a car with serious work.'[35] When it came to identifying enemy agents the following points were made, 'A clear and new Identity Card; clothing of a foreign cut; new tabs on old clothing; address written in continental fashion; possession of a large sum of money; foreign accent; lack of knowledge of the neighbourhood; possession of large scale maps; check ration card against Identity Card for consistency; check on passport (any issued in Luxembourg should be regarded with the gravest suspicion and reported at once to HQ).'[36]

If any part of the country had been invaded, the police were told to obey instructions given to them by the 'competent military authority.' Their role was to control the civil population and take precautions against espionage and sabotage and to prevent petrol or other materials falling into enemy hands. Because of the fear of bacteriological sabotage, any leaflets, parachutes, etc dropped on this country were, 'To be sent immediately ... to the Emergency Public Health Authority Laboratory at Conway for examination.'[37]

The question of communication between police stations and their officers working away from base was always a problem, especially so during a time of emergency. Even as late as 1941, many police stations in north Wales lacked telephone facilities. In an attempt to improve matters, the Home Office was asked by the Chief Constable for a police wireless system to be installed in Caernarfonshire. It was eventually decided that the Home Office was, 'To arrange for three fixed station receivers and transmitters ... at Headquarters (Caernarfon), Conway and Pwllheli and four medium frequency receivers and four transmitters for the patrol cars. The cost of this will be approximately £500.'[38]

At the time when the Menai Suspension Bridge was being reconstructed in the late 1930s, a great deal of correspondence was being generated between the police, Home Office, County Councils and Ministry of Transport as to whether it was necessary for it to be guarded and if so, by whom. The extra cost was also a contentious issue, especially if it had to form part of the normal budget of the two police forces of Anglesey and Caernarfonshire. The consulting engineers, Sir Alexander Gibb & Partners, were concerned that with the work at a certain stage, 'an act of sabotage would have dire results and might indeed lead to the stoppage of road communications over the Menai Strait for a long period' (this opinion was expressed to the Chief Constable at Holyhead). It was also said that 'it was quite a simple matter to sever the temporary cables that hold up the bridge.' In addition to the police stationed on the bridge, road blocks set up 200 yards from the bridge entrance on the mainland side, would be manned by special constables. Their duties included stopping all cars and pedestrians in order that their identity cards and driving licences could be examined.[39]

Other places in Caernarfonshire which were described as being most at risk at the beginning of the war were the Britannia Tubular Bridge, the Conwy Tubular Bridge, RAF Penrhos aerodrome, the North Wales Power

Police and Special Constables, Penygroes.
[Robert Hughes]

Station at the Dolgarrog Aluminium Works, the petrol storage tanks at Caernarfon, the BBC Studios at Bangor, the North Wales Power Station Cwm Dili as well as railway stations and water works.[40]

On 13 August 1945, G. W. Roberts, Deputy Chief Constable, sent the following message, 'The time has come when the part-time special constables can be released from the war-time restrictions on their right to resign … Although you are now entitled to resign should you desire you will realise … that the special constabulary must continue to play its historic part as an integral and essential element of the peace time Police Service.'[41]

Aerial photograph of Caernarfon taken from Short Sunderland of N$^{o.}$ 461 (RAAF) Squadron, August 1944. [Roy Sloan Collection]

Notes

1. GAS, WDT/15152.
2. GAS, XM/1301/6, 11.
3. GAS, Z-DDW-27.
4. GAS, 1301/19-20.
5. GAS, XC2-2-43.
6. GAS, XM1301/6.
7. GAS, XM/1301/6.
8. GAS, XJ1234/42.
9. GAS, XM. 1301/11.
10. GAS. XM 1301/6.
11. GAS, XM 1301/9.
12. Directive issued by General Staff, North Wales Area, Shrewsbury.
13. GAS, XM 1301/2.
14. GAS, XM/1301/13.
15. GAS, XM-1301-6.
16. GAS XM1301/13.
17. GAS, XM 1301/15.
18. GAS, XM 1301/16.
19. PPP 469.
20. PPP 474.
21. GAS, XM9062.
22. GAS, XC2/2/43.
23. GAS, ZDDW/43.
24. GAS, Z-DDW-43.
25. GAS, Z-DDW-47.
26. PPP 470.
27. NLW, 23037 D.
28. GAS, 1301/28.
29. GAS, XC2/2/43.
30. *North Wales Chronicle*.
31. GAS, XJ 1375, 1387 & 1469.
32. GAS, XJ375.
33. GAS, XM 1301/2.
34. GAS, XJ1234/11.
35. GAS, XM 1301/2.
36. GAS, XM 1301/2.
37. GAS, XM 1301/5.
38. GAS, XM 1388/163, 162.
39. GAS, XC2-39-24.
40. GAS, XJ1234/11.
41. GAS, XM1388-162/163.

Chapter 6
The Nation's Treasure

Long before war had broken out, there had been considerable fears that priceless treasures housed in major British cities might be lost forever in the event of aerial bombardment and discussions were held as early as 1933 for the removal of works of art from London galleries and museums in the event of war. The Rt Hon. Ormsby-Gore MP (later Lord Harlech), First Commissioner of the Office of Works, had called together the directors of all the libraries, museums and art galleries in the capital and, on the advice of the Air Ministry, had decided that Wales would be the safest place for the irreplaceable National Heritage and a list was compiled of country houses and other repositories where such material could be removed for safety.

With increasing tension in Europe and the possibility of war, ten institutions, including the National Gallery and the British Museum, applied for space in the National Library of Wales at Aberystwyth. To test the feasibility of plans made by the National Gallery, a number of pictures were sent from London at the time of the Munich Crisis, but were returned unpacked when the crisis passed. The plan had been to move the National Gallery pictures from London to Bangor and on 30 September 1938, Kenneth Clark (later Lord Clark) wrote to E. H. Jones, Registrar of the University College of North Wales (UCNW). 'Now that the chances of our having to use the Hall at Bangor University as a storage for our pictures have considerably diminished I must write to thank you and the University Authorities for your generous offer to let us use this Hall.'[1] This matter was considered so confidential by the college authorities that no reference was ever made to the subject in the Council Minutes.

A short time later F. I. G. Rawlins, Scientific Adviser to the Trustees of the National Gallery wrote, 'Should our plans for the dispersal of pictures in Wales ever have to be put into operation it would seem that Bangor would be an ideal place.'[2] Further confirmation of the availability of the UCNW was sent on 19 February the following year to the First Commissioner, 'The UCNW has placed at the disposal of the National Gallery in the event of war, for the purpose of picture storage, the Pritchard-Jones Hall.'[3]

Rather than having to face the formidable task of virtually emptying the gallery, consideration was given to selecting certain paintings. However, the invidious task of deciding which pictures merited being saved and which did not, resulted in the authorities opting for the easier solution of transferring the greater part of the gallery to a safe depository. In August, even though the declaration of war was still more than a week away, the

National Gallery paintings in temporary storage on the lower floor of the Eagle Tower, Caernarfon Castle. [The National Gallery]

National Gallery paintings at Plas y Bryn, Bontnewydd. [The National Gallery]

Paintings stored at the Prichard Jones Hall UCNW, Bangor prior to being transferred to Manod Quarry. [The National Gallery]

decision was taken to start evacuating the pictures from the National Gallery and the first container-load left Trafalgar Square on 23 August. Rail transport was provided by LMS to Bangor and GWR to Aberystwyth, and each journey was meticulously planned so that, in the event of an air attack the travelling time was reduced as far as possible. The timetable also ensured that the consignment would arrive at its destination in daylight to facilitate unloading. To make the task of handling easier, the weight of individual paintings was reduced by removing the larger picture glasses and frames which were retained at the gallery. Once the final destination of the pictures was known, glasses and frames were reunited with the appropriate picture. Around 6,000 pictures were moved out of London and the whole operation was completed by the 2 September, the day before the declaration of war.

About a thousand of the smaller pictures and eighty-two boxes of valuable books were stored in the underground tunnel which had been constructed near the National Library of Wales at Aberystwyth, in anticipation of such an eventuality, and were retained there for the duration of the war. Most of the material at Aberystwyth remained packed and inaccessible, but the opportunity was given for research workers to study Welsh manuscripts, part of the British Museum collection, whilst at the library. Although the library was closed to visitors and the general public for about six years, the Readers' Room remained open throughout the war to those who had been provided with special permits. Other pictures that were deposited at Aberystwyth came from the Royal Collection at Hampton Court and from a Dutch museum.

Even though the paintings destined for Bangor had arrived safely, problems then arose with their transportation from the railway station to their eventual repository, especially where the larger pictures were concerned. It was necessary to take into consideration the size of doors,

Paintings being loaded on to an LMS lorry for transporting from the Prichard Jones Hall UCNW Bangor to Manod Quarry. [The National Gallery]

Paintings leaving the Pritchard Jones Hall at UCNW, Bangor for Manod Quarry. [The National Gallery]

passages or even windows in order to gain access to buildings. Apart from the main task of housing the pictures, the question of suitable atmospheric conditions had also to be considered. Due to its size, and the fact that it was heated by coke-fired boilers, the task of maintaining anything approaching a constant heat level in the Pritchard Jones Hall at Bangor was virtually impossible. The situation was further exacerbated with the variation in temperature between the severe winter of 1939–40 and the unusually hot summer of 1940. Difficulties were also experienced when trying to access the Pritchard Jones Hall with certain paintings, whereas those destined for storage at Penrhyn Castle presented no problem. The smaller pictures were stored in the castle's dining-room, whilst the larger items were easily put into the garages with their large doors (required in the days of horse-drawn carriages). Variations in temperature and humidity, however, presented many problems, but were largely overcome by the installation of small office electric fans which circulated the air. Due to the size of the garages, temperature variations between the ceiling and floor could be as much as 5°F and relative humidity could be about ten per cent higher at the bottom than at the top. Such differences were particularly critical as far as the larger pictures were concerned and some were as big as thirteen feet in height.

On the assumption that, subsequent to the fall of France, there would be an increase in the number of German planes flying over Bangor on their way to bomb Manchester, Liverpool and other north-west targets, there was always the danger of bombs being dropped deliberately or otherwise on the city. A letter (dated 26 November 1940) addressed to the Ministry of Works at the Palace Hotel in Rhyl, refers to the mounting of a machine-

Painting of 'Charles I on Horseback' being transferred from Penrhyn Castle to Manod Quarry.
[The National Gallery]

The painting 'Charles I on Horseback' passing beneath a railway bridge on its way to Manod Quarry.
[The National Gallery]

National Gallery painting 'Charles I on Horseback' being transferred to Manod Quarry.
[The National Gallery]

gun on the college tower for the defence of the building. Whether this related to an anti-invasion measure or for the purpose of guarding the paintings, is not stated. It was therefore decided that the risk could be reduced by transferring some of the paintings to the lowest floor of the Eagle Tower at Caernarvon Castle which had been adapted for the purpose, and also to Plas-y-Bryn, a private house in Bontnewydd. However, Samuel Courtauld, Chairman of the Gallery Trustees, was still concerned for the safety of the pictures and considered an underground shelter to be the only option. Although Aberystwyth was not considered as vulnerable as Bangor as far as aerial attack was concerned, it was decided nevertheless to transfer 'a considerable number of pictures' from the National Library of Wales to Crosswood, about nine miles away, the home of Lord Lisburne who had allocated a room as a depository.

During the summer of 1940, due to the difficulty in supervising different locations and the ever-present danger from bombing, it was decided to find a more secure location. A number of sites were inspected, including various railway tunnels and caves, but none was considered suitable because of difficult access and the possibility of flooding. The National Gallery eventually decided that Manod Quarry at 1,750 feet above sea level, in the mountains near the town of Ffestiniog, could be adapted to their needs.

In order that the larger paintings could be put into the cavern, the first priority was to increase the size of the quarry entrance from six feet by six feet, to thirteen feet six inches by ten feet. This, and the levelling of part of the cavern floor, involved removing some 5,000 tons of slate rock. Within the cavern, with its 200–300 feet thick slate roof that provided adequate protection from a possible air attack, six brick structures were built to house the paintings. Each building had its own conditioning system. The warm air which was generated and controlled by thermostats, was drawn into each building by fans, thus ensuring four changes of air per hour which prevented the growth of mould. The atmosphere within

National Gallery painting 'Charles I on Horseback' approaching Manod Quarry. [The National Gallery]

Right & below: Narrow gauge railway used for transporting paintings at Manod Quarry.
[The National Gallery]

Above & below: National Gallery paintings being examined at Manod Quarry (note narrow gauge rails below the picture being handled). [The National Gallery]

Above: Restortion work at Manod. [The National Gallery]

the units was maintained at 65°F and forty-two per cent humidity and, as an additional precaution, an axial-flow fan was installed adjacent to the tunnel entrance to extract any possible dust from the air.

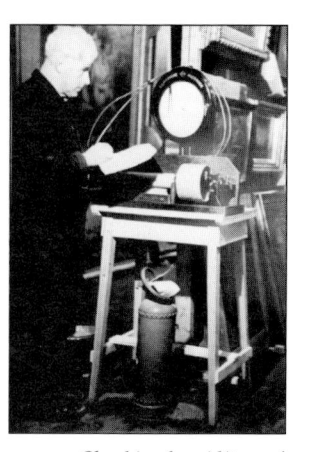

Transformers stepped down the high potential 11,000 volts from the transmission lines to 400 volts for heating and 230 volts, or in some cases, 100 volts, for lighting. Since certain paint materials, such as oil and tempera, react badly to the lack of light, a certain level of illumination had to be maintained in the quarry at all times. The wisdom of installing a 150hp Crossley diesel engine with a 90kW alternator as a precaution against the possible failure of mains electricity power supply was proven on many occasions when wintry conditions caused an interruption in the supply from North Wales Power Company.

On 12 August 1941, eleven months after the quarry had first been seen by officials of the National Gallery, the first pictures began to arrive at Manod, conveyed in LMS container lorries from Bangor and Caernarfon, and in similar vehicles of the GWR from Aberystwyth.

Checking humidity and temperature at Manod. [The National Gallery]

The movement of the lorries, which were arriving at the rate of four a day, had to be carefully programmed to prevent a clash with returning empty ones on the narrow four-mile road leading to the quarry. The journeys were made more difficult during the dark hours of the snowy winter of 1940–1 as visibility from vehicle headlights was greatly reduced by wartime restrictions. Although 600 to 700 pictures were arriving each week, the only problem was with Van Dyke's *Charles I on Horseback* and Piombo's *Raising of Lazarus*, when it became necessary for the road beneath a bridge near Ffestiniog to be lowered by two and a half feet to enable the lorry carrying the pictures to pass underneath.

Having negotiated a far from ideal narrow mountain road to the quarry, the enlarged opening into the cavern allowed the pictures to be unloaded from the lorries unobtrusively and safely, and be transferred by means of narrow-gauge wagons, two enclosed and one open (a bogie seventeen feet long specially built at Derby), to their allocated space within the cavern and its associated building. These same wagons were also used for carrying equipment, timber and general stores.

The new location enabled all the pictures to be properly supervised and stored in a controlled atmosphere which was to prove as good, if not superior to, that of the National Gallery in London. The collection held at the National Library had all been removed to the quarry by September 1941.

The National Gallery staff stationed at Manod Quarry consisted of the Head Attendant, E. B. Harrison, who had responsibility for fourteen men. Such a number was required because Manod had to be guarded day and night. Extra men were also required to move the pictures when necessary. The remoteness of Manod was an advantage, as it was away from prying eyes, but problems did arise in winter-time when staff and administrators had to be transported to the nearest village three miles away.

Although the artificially created atmosphere was conducive to the storage of the pictures, it caused problems with the cavern roof. The possibility of a roof fall necessitated the making of regular checks. Paradoxically, the inevitable slate dust had no damaging effect on the pictures but had the pictures remained in London, many would have been irretrievably lost when the National Gallery was badly damaged by bombs in 1940. Mr Holder, a picture restorer for the National Gallery, and Mr Ruhemann, worked in a daylight studio which was purpose-built near the main entrance, to ensure that no harm came to the pictures. They also took the opportunity of cleaning those that required it.

Plans for the return of the pictures to London began in October 1944, when the end of the war was considered to be in sight. By the Saturday following VE day, about fifty of the masterpieces were back in the National Gallery. By the first week of December 1945, all the evacuated items had been returned to Trafalgar Square, some six and a half years after the first pictures left London to seek sanctuary in Wales. Manod Quarry had served its purpose well, so much so that it was retained by the Government for many years after the war because of the possibility of further conflict, particularly during the Cuban Missile Crisis.

Rest time for maintenance staff at Manod.
[National Gallery]

Notes

1. BUA, Records Box 32 File 3 (uncatalogued).
2. BUA, Records Box 32 File 3 (uncatalogued).
3. BUA, Records Box 32 File 3 (uncatalogued).

Chapter 7
Agriculture and PoWs

The shipping losses caused by U-boat action during the First World War and the resulting food shortages, caused severe problems throughout Britain. But, rather than develop an efficient agricultural industry during the inter-war years, Britain was still importing sixty-percent of her food requirements when hostilities broke out in 1939.

A farmer writing in 1931 (*Farmer's Glory* magazine) reflects the feeling of frustration that the industry felt at that time:

> Probably one of the hardest things for farmers to realise today is that they are considered unimportant people by the majority of the community. When the townsman is hungry the food producer is a very important person, but today the consuming public are being fed by foreign countries very cheaply ... The zest has gone out of farming ... It is not pleasant for a man to discover that he is engaged in an occupation for which his country has neither use nor interest.

Almost half of the land supposedly allocated to crops was derelict, as were many buildings and roads. Much of Welsh farmland had been given over to sheep and cattle breeding. In an attempt to encourage farmers to improve their neglected land, the Agriculture Act of 1937 allowed a fifty percent grant towards the cost of lime, considered to be the major cause of land dereliction. Although there was an inadequate supply of phosphates available at the beginning of the war to meet the increasing acreage of land being cultivated, basic slag was plentiful and there was a plentiful supply of other fertilisers. Even when fertilizers were available, much of the land had been left fallow during the 1930s as many farmers could not afford to plough it, let alone purchase fertilisers.

However, with the threat of war and the realisation that once again the country would be dependent on home-produced food, grants were introduced to enable fallow land to be tilled. At the same time the quality of stock and breeding was improved and, in particular, efforts were made to eliminate bovine tuberculosis. Although the selling price of agricultural products was controlled by the government during the war, returns were slightly better when compared to the prices of the 1930s and, since costs were reasonably stable, it meant farmers were able to generate a reasonable income. However, the long hours of work and low wages did nothing to attract new labour, nor to retain skilled agricultural workers at a time, prior to eventual mechanisation, when so much depended on them.

Even though names had not been published, nor permission sought, individuals considered suitable to serve as county chairmen of War

*Harvesting c.1940.
[Ivor Wyn Jones]*

*American Caterpillar tractor pressing air out of silage. The machine on the left is a silage blower.
[Ivor Wyn Jones]*

Preparing for bailing with a sweep attached to a Standard Fordson tractor at Plas Llansadwrn. [Cledwyn Jones]

Agricultural Executive Committees (WAEC, or 'War Ag' as it was generally known) throughout Britain had already been selected by the Minister of Agriculture. The Munich Crisis caused the minister to instruct the chairmen, executive officers and secretaries and certain other members of each committee to be prepared to act upon receipt of further instructions. These instructions, sent by telegram, were sent on 3 September 1939, demanding that the committees take immediate action and, at the same time, informing them that they were empowered by the Ministry of Agriculture to enforce wartime measures. The face of British agriculture was to be changed from its neglected appearance to that of a thriving industry simply because the country was at war and the people had to be fed. The Anglesey War Agriculture Executive Committee, based at the Shire Hall in Llangefni, was chaired by Sir Wynne Cemlyn Jones. It sent out letters early in September 1939 indicating what was required of the farmers, 'landowners are asked to put all their lands in their occupation and/or lands annually let by them for grazing in a state to produce the maximum of food ... The Minister of Agriculture in his broadcast on 4 September 1939 mentioned as a round figure that 10% of the grassland in this country should be put under the plough and cultivated for 1940 crops.'[1]

A survey of twenty-nine agricultural holdings in Llanfairisgaer (Central) carried out by the Caernarvon War Agricultural Executive Committee as far back as 1919, included the following details: farm occupant, landlord, acreage of holding/farm, pasture or cultivable, waste or plantation, nature of soil and whether land was steep, undulating or fairly level. Information was also required with regard to the number of workers employed and whether they were men, boys or women. The type of stock, number of horses, dairy cows or other cattle, sheep and pigs was also required.[2] Compared to these details, the National Farm Survey called for by the Ministry of Agriculture in 1940, and undertaken mostly by the members of the Executive Committees or retired farmers, required a great deal more information. The awesome task of detailing every holding with more than five acres of land and coming within the county's jurisdiction, was carried out with the aid of the six-inch scale Ordnance Survey maps. Details had to be recorded on: the condition of each farm, the state of the land, composition of the soil, the acreage of crops and grass, and the areas of dereliction. Other required data related to the state of buildings, cottages, cart-roads, fences, ditches and water. They also had to note whether electricity was available and whether the farms were infested with rats, rabbits or other pests. Furthermore, an opinion had to be given as to whether or not the farmer was a good one or not and, if the survey found the land to be in a poor state, suggestions had to be made to improve it. Such information was used for both immediate needs and future planning. A later questionnaire required every farm to categorise its land as heavy, medium, light or peaty and each category as a percentage of the whole. It asked whether the farm was conveniently laid out and what percentage of

Caernarvonshire War Agricultural Executive Committee, 1945. [Heulwen Williams]

land was good, fair or bad. Questions were also asked with regard to the position of the farm relative to a main road and the railway. From the answers given, a great deal could be deduced to the state of the farm generally and, in particular, how much work was required and the relevant cost of improvements.

Each Executive Committee was made up of seven unpaid local people who were connected with agriculture, plus two to represent the Women's Land Army (WLA) and agricultural workers. Sub-committees were formed to deal with specific duties such as: cultivation, labour, farmers' requirements, machinery, drainage, finance, animal feed and ploughing. In addition, groups of men numbering from four to seven, were formed into district or parish committees who were directly responsible to fellow farmers. The members of each Executive Committee usually met once a month and those on the District Committees met bi-monthly. Such regular meetings allowed any problems to be dealt with quickly and efficiently. Although these members were acting on a voluntary basis, they devoted a tremendous amount of time and effort to the organisation, and its success was due to their personal farming experience, knowledge of local conditions and empathy with the farmers in their district whom they were ready to guide and assist. The farmers themselves readily accepted such assistance as it was an opportunity for them to improve their land and make it more productive.

Those who could not plough land as directed by the Executive Committee, because they had neither the implements to undertake the task nor the money to pay for the work to be undertaken on their behalf, usually had the land ploughed by workers employed by the WAEC. If farmers refused on principle to carry out the WAEC's instructions or, if the land being cultivated by the tenant or land owner was not of the standard required due to poor farming methods, then the land could be arbitrarily taken over. If this was the recommended course, then the farmer was entitled to an explanation as to why the land was being requisitioned. To compile such a report, the Executive Officer, one member of the Agriculture Committee and the owner-occupier or tenant would walk the farm. The report was then considered by other members of the committee and the owner-occupier/tenant advised of the final decision. Since the national interest was paramount, the decision had to be made objectively rather that subjectively.

The first task at the outbreak of war in 1939 was to bring in the harvest as quickly as possible so as to clear the fields for action. Such was the sense of urgency, that the War Office agreed to a request made by the Ministry of Agriculture for soldiers to assist on the farms at this critical time. This was followed by land, previously used for grazing, being successfully ploughed in time for winter frosts and the sowing of seeds the following spring.

The severity of the 1939–40 winter brought many problems and the

War Agricultural Executive Committee members, Dolgarrog, with anti-tamk blocks in the foreground. [H. Vaughan Jones]

cessation of nearly all work on the land at a time when much needed to be done. The situation was further exacerbated when, for a period, most forms of transport came to a halt, especially in the Snowdonia hills, due to the volume of snow. When spring came, it brought with it additional problems with melting snow creating floods and mud that clung to everything, including farming implements and footwear.

The Minister of Agriculture, having decided that an additional two million acres of land had to be ploughed nationwide, would advise the chairman of each County Committee of the quota of additional acreage required. Such a quota would in turn be shared between each District Committee and sub-divided even further between each Parish Representative. This last allocation would then be divided between each farmer in his section according to the size of the farm.

To help the committees, the government provided them with a staff of experts, under the guidance of an executive officer, to supply information about modern farming methods and techniques. Apart from the voluntary, unpaid committee members, who gave up much of their spare time to the job, the Ministry of Agriculture had the benefit of the best technicians in the country, specialising in a particular branch of husbandry. Also, each Executive Committee had a back-up of about twelve paid office staff, being a mix of youngsters, retired people and technicians.

Caernarvonshire War Agricultural Executive Committee Implements Section, 1945. Hugh Owen (Chairman) 9th from left, front row. [Mr & Mrs Tecwyn Evans]

Caernarvonshire War Agricultural Executive Committee, 1942. Front row (L–R): Miss Elsie Griffith; R. Alun Roberts; G. Hughes Roberts; D. G. Jones; G. Gregory Williams; Hugh Owen. Middle row: J. H. Jones; William Williams; T. J. Owen; E. Morgan Humphreys; Evan R. Jones; W. A. Jones. Back row: Gwilym T. Jones; W. R. Williams; R. O. Williams; Frank Griffith. (Mr & Mrs Tecwyn Evans]

All this additional work, made that much harder because of the exodus of agricultural workers into the armed forces or to other industries paying better wages, necessitated the recruitment of alternative labour. In an attempt to retain or even attract agricultural workers, council houses were specifically built for them with the WAEC deciding on their allocation.

In March 1940, the Ministry authorised the WAEC to organise and employ mobile gangs of workers on drainage and ditching schemes. However, apart from difficulties in recruiting men there was also the problem of finding sufficient qualified individuals to supervise them in their allocated tasks and to train newcomers. Apart from the lack of foremen, the nature of the work on widely-scattered pieces of land, often the worst in the area, and fields which no farmer was prepared to tackle, resulted in a low level of achievement at a high level of cost which led to considerable criticism of the committees by the farming community.

The Scientific Food Committee, appointed by the Lord Privy Seal in July 1940 and chaired by the President of the Royal Society, had the task of considering and advising on problems relating to national food requirements and, more especially, difficulties arising from reduced imports from abroad of food and animal feed which this country had relied upon in the 1930s. The committee had to establish the minimum food requirements of the people on the assumption that the quantity being imported would get progressively less and less due to enemy action. It had to calculate an individual's basic needs in terms of vitamins, calories, minerals and proteins and also in terms of a worker's additional requirements. Apart from some fats and wheat, which had to be imported, the committee was of the opinion that all other foods could be produced at home in sufficient quantities to meet the needs of the whole population provided that milk production could be increased by twenty percent and potato output by one hundred percent, together with appropriate increases in other foods. This was the time when the National Growmore fertiliser, based on a ratio of 7:7:7 phosphates, potash and nitrogen, was developed by Government scientists to assist in increasing food production.

From a situation where little interest was taken in agriculture, suddenly, because the country was at war, the farmer had at his disposal, the free advice and assistance of experts on every conceivable subject. District Committees arranged evening 'Fireside Chats' which took place at designated farms with a few neighbouring farmers being invited for an informal talk on agricultural matters given by a WAEC speaker. These talks were not a recent innovation, as it had always been the custom for farmers to congregate at different farms and, whilst the men discussed 'official' matters, the wives would be in the kitchen preparing a meal and having their own fireside chat.

At the start of each year, a district officer, such as the late Griffith Williams of Tyddyn Perthi, Port Dinorwic, would have 'walked the farm' with the aid of an Ordnance Survey map, and discussed with the resident farmer which fields were to be cultivated. The resulting knowledge of each farm under his control and the close working relationship with the farmer, enabled disputes to be kept to a minimum. Common sense usually prevailed but, if any disagreement arose as to the area to be cultivated or indeed on any other matter, then it was discussed in the monthly district committee.[3]

Such was the demand for additional land that public parks and golf courses, both public and private, were ploughed up for food production. Welsh hillsides, normally bracken-covered, were transformed with the aid of caterpillar tractors, the only vehicle capable of tackling such terrain, and prepared where and when possible, to grow potatoes. Even land between fruit trees was ploughed for potato planting.

When potatoes were planted, a careful note was made by the cultivation officer of the acreage involved and the quantity of seed supplied by the Potato Marketing Board particularly since it was virtually impossible to

Caernarvonshire War Agrcultural Committee Implements Department, 1943.
[Mr & Mrs Tecwyn Evans]

Young Farmers Club at Vaynol. [Beryl Owen Jones]

check the quantity actually planted (seed potatoes were invariably coloured with a dye to make them less attractive for human consumption and as a means of tracing them). However, at the time of harvesting of the crop, it was possible to quantify the amount produced against the seed supplied. A suitable proportion of the harvested crop would be retained as seed for the following year.

Paradoxically, although there was a desperate need for extra land for cultivation and crop growing, an estimated 600,000 of acres were taken over by the Ministry of Defence for training by the armed forces, coastal defences and some 444 airfields in Britain. The anti-landing devices placed in large fields to prevent invading planes from landing, would be as much, if not more, of a handicap to the tractors working in the fields as they would have been to a potential enemy.

Early in the war, Lord Anglesey became personally involved with Plas Newydd Home Farm of 223 acres and Plas Newydd Park of forty-four acres, as well as the other tenanted farms belonging to the estate. In September 1941, he advised the WAEC that he had decided to plough up the Plas Newydd cricket ground in order that winter oats could be sown but this could only be done when a tractor and plough had been released from the corn harvest. Similarly, he decided to plough the golf course, which covered some thirty-four acres, and asked the WAEC to carry out the task. Early the following year, he had to inform them that he was unable to plough as much of the golf course as he wished as the military authorities had requisitioned about eight or nine acres.[4]

To save on capital outlay and ensure that farm machinery was fully utilised at a time when there was a shortage, it was the policy of the WAEC (through its machinery department) to hire tractors or implements to the farmer at a cost of £5 per week. Requests for assistance were handled by a central control and would result in the appropriate machine (when available) and driver being allocated for the task. A similar hire arrangement existed with contractors who used their own drivers. The hiring arrangement would, in principle if not in practice, ensure that the machinery was fully utilised at a time when there was an increasing workload.

The working horse, a familiar sight on farms in the 1930s, was still being traded on a regular basis as the following report shows, 'Menai Bridge Horse Fair – John Pritchard & Co. conducted … their two day sale … on Tuesday when 270 seasoned horses, three year old, light horses, Welsh cobs and ponies (were sold). A further 400 were sold on Wednesday.'[5] The introduction of the tractor ensured that a great deal more work could be accomplished when compared to what a horse could manage. The tractor was capable of hauling a variety of implements and would continue working for hours on end, each and every day (unless there was a shortage of fuel as did occur on occasions), whatever the weather. It could also expedite the work of the harvester by providing power through a belt-

Caernarvonshire War Agricultural Committee, Machine Section, 1943. [AC]

drive. When a job required to be completed, provided a driver was available, work would quite often continue into the night through the use of screened headlights and a lamp placed in the hedge to act as a guide for the tractor driver. The normal British summertime was extended by an extra hour, so creating double summertime. Even so, there was a tendency for some farmers in the remoter parts of the country to leave the clock undisturbed, irrespective of summer of double-summer time.

Early tractor wheels were made of steel with the rear ones having the benefit of lugs along the edge to give additional traction, whilst the front wheels had a rim running along the centre to give better steerage. There was at least one farm on the outskirts of Caernarfon which had the benefit of a Titan tractor, a legacy of the pre-war period. Compared to present-day heated and air-conditioned vehicles, the only concession allowed for the Titan, Ferguson or Fordson tractor driver was a folded sack placed on the cold wet metal seat in an attempt to alleviate some of the discomfort. These vintage machines were started by means of petrol prior to switching over to Tractor Vaporising Oil (TVO). Compared to the early tractors, limited as they were to the type of implements that they could tow, the Ferguson TE20 (known as the Little Grey Fergie or *Ffergi Bach)* developed in 1945, had the benefit of a 'three point link system' which allowed the driver, through the hydraulic system on the tractor, to make adjustments, such as the depth of a furrow when ploughing, without dismounting from the vehicle. Sixty years on, these reliable and popular tractors which revolutionised farming, were and still are in use, long after production ceased. In Wales, the tractor with caterpillar tracks was considered to be a very versatile vehicle because it could tackle the most difficult hillside terrain where neither tractor nor plough had ever ventured before. These powerful machines, turning over four or five furrows at a time, could do the work of many horses and men.

As the result of pressure being applied to increase food production, implements hired through the WAEC were subjected to heavy usage and wear and tear. A periodic maintenance inspection of implements disclosed that they were often returned damaged, or even unusable, due to lack of care. It was also found that they were hired for longer periods than was necessary and to some farmers who could well afford to buy their own.[6] As agriculture became fully organised, associated rural trades such as blacksmiths, carpenters and wheelwrights were called upon to maintain and repair farm implements, whilst village garage mechanics became responsible for ensuring that the few tractors that were available, especially in the early years of the war, were properly maintained.

When the WAEC considered the method of farming or rate of production to be unacceptably poor, they would arbitrarily take over the farm in question. This happened with the tenanted farm of Plas Llwynon in Anglesey which they found to be in a 'disgraceful condition, both arable and pasture ... [being] semi-derelict.'[7] As a result, the tenant was dispossessed by the WAEC and the farm was taken over by the owner, Lord Anglesey, in 1942. This also happened with the Vaynol Estate's Trefarthin Farm on Anglesey as late as 1944. In a futile attempt at having the decision changed, a letter was sent by the farm manager to Miss Megan Lloyd George, the local MP, asking her to see the Minister as it was felt that 'a great injustice would be done if the WAEC was allowed to take over the farm.'

The various government campaigns did everything possible to make the public as well as the farmers aware that every small piece of ground was to be used for growing food. Amongst the many posters that the Ministry of Agriculture issued from time to time were those stating 'Grow More Food', 'Lend a Hand on the Land', 'Dig for Victory' and, as a reminder of the role and risks being taken by seamen in bringing food into the country, 'The

Caernarvonshire War Agriculture Committee Standard Fordson tractor, with binder cutting corn. [Cledwyn Jones]

Baling at Plas Llansadwrn farm, Anglesey. [Cledwyn Jones]

Life-Line is Firm, Thanks to the Merchant Navy.' The BBC programme *Kitchen Front*, which was broadcast at 8.15 a.m. every day, provided information about the latest cooking methods and recipes with a concoction of strange ingredients, at least by present-day standards, but which, nevertheless, were palatable and provided nutritional meals. As the result of the 'Dig for Victory' campaign, the number of persons participating in growing their own vegetables in gardens and allotments grew from a figure of around 700,000 to double that figure by 1943, with possibly half of them being women. In addition, the popular radio gardening programme with 'Mr Middleton' was listened to by millions, and undoubtedly persuaded the majority to turn from flowers to the more pressing need for vegetables in whatever form. It was not only the man in the street that was expected to sacrifice his floral garden, stately homes converted rose gardens, and even tennis courts, into productive vegetable patches.

As more land became available for cultivation and output increased, so did the need for extra labour to deal with the harvests. Anyone who was willing, including children, evacuees, shop girls and office workers, was enlisted in the gathering of the crops. Indeed, many preferred to spend their holidays working on the land and so help the war effort. Such a vast army of temporary workers were provided with accommodation where they could eat and sleep – at camps, hostels, village halls and schools. Of the 12,000 youngsters who were to assist with the 1941 harvest and accommodated in the 300 camps created for them throughout Britain, a contingent from the Liverpool Boys Institute came to work at the Schoolboy Harvest Camp at Plas Newydd in Anglesey. Children were not allowed to work for more than thirty hours a week and for this they were paid 8d. an hour.[8] Even when hostilities ceased, the food situation still remained critical for a number of years and school children continued to assist during harvest time. When possible, work was allocated as near as possible to the homes of the children but for those having to travel, 7s. 6d. was contributed towards a return railway ticket. Harvest-time labour was organised in conjunction with the WAEC.[9]

In order that the work could be completed quickly and efficiently, particularly during favourable weather, threshing time was usually a joint effort between a number of adjoining farms. The gathering of farm labourers would ensure that the harvester, which usually worked with power provided by a belt drive from a tractor, would complete the task and move on to the next farm with as little delay as possible, and leave the grain safely stored. Threshing time, because of the quantity of food that was required to be prepared for the workers involved in the work, was equally as busy for the wives, daughters and maids as it was for the men.

The Federation of Young Farmers' Clubs, formed in 1942, arranged for Ministry of Information films to be shown and talks to be given by a WAEC technical officer such as Ivor Wyn Jones, who would advise them about the latest farming technology and methods.[10] The rally held at Plas Newydd, Llanfairpwll on Anglesey on 10 June 1944 allowed the latest farm machinery, including a 'robot transplanter' to be demonstrated, as well as organising various competitions between clubs to demonstrate skills at machine and hand shearing of sheep, milking, rope-making, weight judging, potato peeling, thatch making and welding.[11] Similar rallies were held at the Oval football ground in Caernarfon.

In the 1940s, a pick-up baler cost about £299 and a tractor about the same price. Even when second-hand farming implements were offered for sale, permission had to be obtained from the WAEC before the transaction could be completed. By February 1944, the WAEC had 884 machines in use on Anglesey farms, including seventy-seven tractors, but by 1953 this number had risen to 1,273. At the same time, there were 1,651 tractors in use in Caernarfonshire.

Although British manufacturers began to produce tractors in greater numbers during the war, they had to compete for raw material with the munitions industry. To make up for this shortfall, tractors and other farming machinery were imported from Australia and Canada as the result of the Mutual Aid arrangement and, similarly, from America under Lend-Lease (passed by US Congress in 1941, it authorised the President to supply war materials to other countries 'whose defence he deemed vital to the United States'). The first Sunshine binder came from Kilkenny in Australia in 1940 and, in the same year, Massey Harris and International implements arrived from Canada and the USA. They would arrive mostly assembled and ready for use, the exception being the binder with its fans and blades packed separately. For those destined for Anglesey and Caernarfonshire, they were usually delivered by rail to Llangefni or Caernarfon but, if there were transport problems due to a shortage of railway wagons as was often

Harvesting with an International tractor (JC790), driven by Bob Thomas, cutting corn at Glynllifon College, Caernarfon, 1939. Hugh Owen, Chairman of the Caernarvonshire War Agricultural Committee on the right. [Mr & Mrs Tecwyn Evans]

the case during and directly after the war, they were collected by lorry from a distribution centre in Cambridge. This underpinning of the war-time economy was suddenly ended by President Truman with the surrender of the Japanese in 1945.

At the time that the Lend-Lease Act of 1941 was being discussed in Washington by the British Food Mission, additional supplies for the British civilian population and armed forces were also requested. Even when all the necessary arrangements had been made and agreed, there was no guarantee that the ships carrying the food and other vital supplies would ever reach British ports due to the high number of U-boats operating in the Atlantic. With improving methods of detection, and the intercepting and decoding of German wireless transmissions, more and more U-boats were being sunk and, correspondingly, more and more ships carrying vital supplies were reaching their intended destinations. 'No weapon ever invented is more deadly than hunger; it can spike guns, destroy courage, and break the will of the most resolute peoples. The finest armies in the world, courageous enough in the face of bombs or bullets, can be reduced by it to helplessness and surrender.'[12]

At the same time as the land was being improved, so too was the quality of stock, although the eradication of tuberculosis from cattle was not accomplished until after the war. The milk officer employed by the WAEC carried out a periodic check on the quantity and quality of milk and if insufficient was being produced or it was not up to the required standard, then the farmer or milk retailer was liable to lose his licence and the right to sell milk.

It was the custom in Anglesey for farm workers to present themselves for employment for a period of six months at a biannual fair (*ffair cyflogi*) held at Llangefni in May and October. Increasing agricultural wages by eight shillings, to a minimum wage of forty-eight shillings, added £14.9 million to farming costs. Further increases occurred in December 1943 when the minimum wage went up to sixty-five shillings and then seventy shillings in March 1945. As a further inducement to attract agricultural workers, meals and accommodation were provided at the farms for single men. Unfortunately, wage increases could not always be absorbed because of insufficient income and this resulted in a tendency for farmers to rely more and more on employing casual rather than regular labour and by contracting the WAEC to carry out work on their behalf.

Evan Hughes of Tŷ Mawr in Pontllyfni, milked by hand until around 1943, when a Pelton wheel, powered by the flow of water at the nearby Afon Llifon, generated sufficient electricity for lighting in the house, the use of some small appliances and a milking machine. The milk, which he produced to retail amongst his customers at around 3*d*. a pint, was delivered daily from house to house, within a radius of five miles from the farm, by means of a horse-drawn milk float. Any surplus milk was sold to the Milk Marketing Board (MMB) and taken by rail from Chwilog to Liverpool. The milk was taken in ten gallon churns by tractor from the farm to the nearest road, where it was placed on a purpose-built (usually slate) shelf on top of a hedge or wall, accessible to the MMB lorry driver for collection twice a day. Some of the smaller farms also churned their own butter which could be for home use, for selling or for exchanging at a local shop for other provisions. A wooden stamp, which gave an impression of an animal or flower, applied to the half-pound of butter, would be the means of identifying the source.

In preference to purchasing meats from a local butcher, it was possible for a farmer to apply for a Ministry of Food permit for a pig or lamb to be taken to a local slaughter house, such as Isaac Parry's abattoir near the Victoria Dock in Caernarfon. In the days before the advent of deep freezing, the meat was preserved by covering in saltpetre prior to being wrapped in muslin, or by soaking in a slate tank filled with brine, where it would remain for three or four weeks. The farmer's ration book would be adjusted in accordance with the weight of the animal slaughtered. Preserved hams or joints of meat hanging from the farmhouse ceiling were quite a familiar sight and in this state, they could be kept for about six months. The alternative to such preservation methods was for the animal to be slaughtered and the meat made available at the butcher's shop the next day.

Each year of the war saw an improvement in the state of British farms, with waste land being converted into productive acres. Between 1939 and 1944, 6.5 million 'new' acres were ploughed in the UK and, because of a six-fold use in the application of lime and fertilisers, there was a tremendous improvement in the land and subsequent yield. In the case of animals, there was an increase of 300,000 milking cows and beef cattle increased by 400,000 whereas sheep numbers decreased by 6,300,000, pigs by 2,500,000 and poultry by 19,200,000 in the same period. The mechanisation expansion programme continued after the war to the extent that in the decade between 1942 and 1952, the number of tractors in use on British farms generally rose from 101,500 to 324,960. During the same period, there was a large increase in the number of hay-balers and combine-harvesters being used.

Whereas the plans of many peacetime industries were disrupted or even abandoned as the result of the war, agriculture was given the opportunity, albeit in an arbitrary manner, of improving land and productivity. But it was the agricultural community itself that transformed the face of the countryside and brought about a remarkable increase in food production. This entailed War Agriculture Executive Committee officials spending long hours visiting farms, field by field, by day and by night, in all seasons of the year as well as attending numerous committees and, inevitably, form filling. Farming was transformed from neglect and inactivity to a thriving industry. As the result of ditches and water courses having been cleaned and widened, and the general laying-on of water supplies to fields and buildings, the state of farms in Britain improved drastically during the war. Agricultural wages had improved and the disparity of farm workers with those employed in other industries had, to a certain extent, been reduced. A vast increase in mechanisation had taken place, both to assist in increasing production and to ease the difficulties which had arisen from the loss of men to the armed forces and other industries.

Women's Land Army

The Women's Land Army (WLA) was formed with the object of providing a mobile force of full-time workers available for regular employment on the land for the duration of the war. Although the main campaign to persuade women to join the WLA came later, the realisation that there would be a need for women to assist in agricultural work came before war had been declared. By the beginning of 1939, nearly 4,000 applications for enrolment in the WLA had reached the Ministry of Agriculture, and continued to be received from women in every walk of life, with an age range of thirteen to eighty-two! Most of them came from women in their twenties and thirties, many of whom had already had some experience of work on the land.

When Ernest Bevin, Minister of Labour and National Service, urged women aged over twenty years to register voluntarily for war work, the WLA being one option, only 300,000 did so nationally. As a result, conscription was introduced and this applied to men (who had not

Women's Land Army armband and lapel badge. [Megan Edwards]

*Women's Land Army at
Caernarfon Castle, 1943.
[Megan Edwards]*

been called up to the forces), single women and also mothers with children over fourteen years-of-age. It was estimated that nine out of ten women were eventually engaged in one form of war work or another.

Inexperienced WLA volunteers, and later, those who were conscripted, were provided with four weeks' training at the government's expense, before being placed in employment where directed. Such training included instruction in milking, tractor driving and the care of stock and poultry. During training, the farmer was paid a billeting allowance of 15s. a week and the volunteer a personal allowance of 10s. a week. The welfare of those who were directed to work at a specific place became the responsibility of an appointed county committee and its local representative.

Although there had been initial reluctance on the part of farmers to employ women on the land, the increasing workload imposed by the WAEC, ensured that any prejudice was soon dispelled resulting in 19,000 being employed by the autumn of 1941. A report in a local paper stated that, by September 1939, only a few had joined the WLA in Caernarfonshire and an appeal was launched for more to enrol.[13] Its members were recruited from shops, offices, hair salons and even the theatre, all coming to fill the gaps created when the men went off to war, but the work was more physically demanding than they were used to in civilian life.

Each girl was guaranteed employment for twelve months, with one week's paid holiday and, unless there was urgent seasonal work to be carried out, free time on Saturday and Sunday afternoons. Wages were not deducted for sickness, injury or wet weather stoppage. Those under eighteen years-of-age were paid a wage of 18s. per week together with their keep and those over eighteen received £1 2s. 6d. per week (by 1944 this

Women's Land Army rat catchers, (L-R): Betty Williams, Emily Evans, Megan Williams. [Betty Williams]

Marion Birchall at Plas Tirion Farm, Llanrug. [Glenys Edmondson]

had been increased to £2 8s. per week) plus keep. This wage was sometimes enhanced when 9½d. overtime was paid on weekdays.

They were provided with a uniform that consisted of a pair of brown corduroy breeches, a beige shirt, a green jumper, a khaki overcoat, a brown hat, a thick pair of stockings, wellington boots, a pair of heavy brown shoes and two pairs of boots. Houses such as Plas Glyn-y-Weddw at Llanbedrog and Abergwynant Hall, Penmaenpool were used as hostels for those members who were not living at their place of work or at home.[14] One such worker was Marion Birchall, who was born in Spain and worked at the British Consulate in Barcelona until she and her mother left the safety of a neutral country in November 1942, to fly to Portugal. From there they were able to obtain a passage in a cold and draughty Empire seaplane (*Golden Hind*) which flew them from Lisbon to Northern Ireland, without the benefit of food or drink during the flight, to land on a lake near Belfast from where they continued their journey to Poole in Dorset. Mary came up to Caernarfon to join her brother, who was serving in the RAF at Llandwrog airfield, and by January 1943, she had joined the WLA. For many of the recruits, training took the form of practical work on the farm but Marion and others had the benefit of a month spent at Madryn Farm at Aber, 'we had to learn how to milk by hand. Some of us would be milking in the morning and the others in the afternoon. We only milked one cow per day! We also learned about dairy, poultry, garden and farm work.' From Madryn, she was posted to a farm in Dolwyddelan where she worked for six weeks before being transferred to Plas Tirion Farm in Llanrug in October 1943, where she worked and lived until January 1946 when she left the WLA.

At Plas Tirion I was taught to drive by Malcolm and Jessie Mackinnon. I learnt in three weeks and then I was on my own. During the war one didn't have to pass a driving test ... I was taught to drive so that I could deliver milk in the Ford van to Llanrug, Cwm-y-Glo, and Llanberis. [I was] called at 6 a.m. to milk. Then I would go in for breakfast and change into clean overalls and start on the milk round. No bottles, the milk had to be measured so I carried a quart, pint and half pint measure.[15]

Members of the WLA employed by the Vaynol Estate near Bangor at a rate of £2 8s. per week were:

Forestry Department – Gwyneth Jones, Elizabeth Butcher, Megan Edwards, Megan Davies, Gwyneth Chambers, Elsie Owen, Gwyneth M. Edwards, Ida Bradshaw, Annie Davies and Megan Jones.

Farm Department – Elizabeth Beasley, Annie L. Goodman and Vera Goodman; gardens – D. M. Roberts, Betty M. Kitto, Eunice Child, Joyce C. Taylor and Doris I. Parker and dairymaid, Ceinwen P. Hughes, who was paid £3 3s. per week.

For the girls who were used to a warm and comfortable office or shop, the transformation to working with the WLA, often in cold and wet conditions, proved too much of an extreme. But many became very capable and took on the challenge of every type of job including the destruction of pigeons, sparrows, rabbits, squirrels and rats, considered to be pests because of the vast quantity of human food that they consumed.

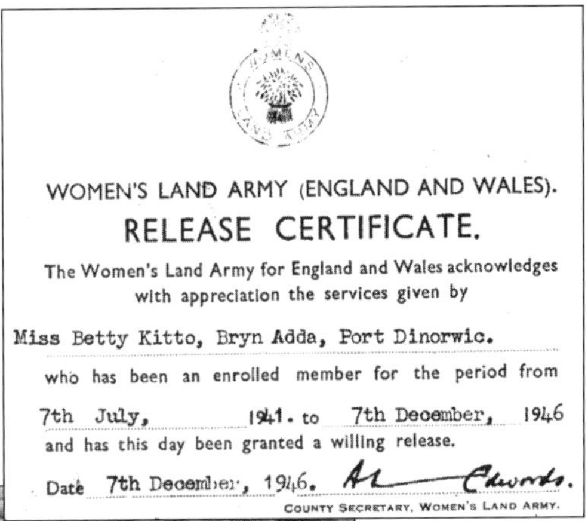

Members of the Women's Land Army at work on Anglesey. [Holyhead Maritime Museum]

Women's Timber Corps

The Women's Timber Corps, formed in 1942, undertook the task of tree-felling with the aid of axes, weighing up to seven pounds, and cross-saws. Many of the trees planted on a hill a few miles from Llanberis to commemorate the Jubilee of Queen

Women's Land Army Release Certificate. [Charlotte Evans]

Caernarvonshire Women's Land Army being inspected by the King and Queen at Caernarfon Castle, 1946. [Charlotte Evans]

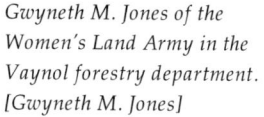

Gwyneth M. Jones of the Women's Land Army in the Vaynol forestry department. [Gwyneth M. Jones]

Gwyneth Walters, Mary Jones, Megan Edwards, Ida Huston of the Women's Land Army, Vaynol forestry department. [Megan Edwards]

Victoria, were cut down to be used as telegraph poles and pit props depending on their dimensions.[16] After felling, the trees were dragged by horses, with the aid of chains, to a suitable clearing. It was here that Mrs Megan Edwards from Llansadwrn and other members of the team went to work, cutting or trimming the trees as the case may be. She recalls that the area where they worked was also used for bomb storage and entry could only be gained by the production of a special pass to the police. Similar work was carried out at the plantation on the other side of the road to the Royal Victoria Hotel in Llanberis.

Mrs Ida Houston, another member of this indomitable team, recalls her time in the woods, 'In the winter, when it was snowing, we used to have a bonfire and burn all the odd twigs and bits of wood. This was fun and we used to roast potatoes on the embers. A little finch used to come by. He had only one leg and we called him *Hoppity*. Naturally we gave him crumbs.'[17]

When bad weather brought work to a halt, Mrs Mary Jones (from Speke in Liverpool) stated that cover was sought in an RAF underground air-raid shelter until such time as the foresters built a wooden hut for them where they were able to enjoy a cup of tea and obtain warmth from a wood-burning stove. On such occasions, the peace and solitude of the forest were often disturbed by raucous singing emanating from within.

From the weekly wage of £2 8s. paid to members of the WLA and WTC, there would be little pocket money available after paying £1 2s. 6d. for accommodation. At that time, every penny mattered and for that reason, if they went to a cinema, it would be to Llanberis or Caernarfon at a cost of 6*d*., the same as the forces, whereas civilian (or non-uniform) rates applied in the Plaza and City cinemas in Bangor. Also at Caernarfon, they had a similar concession at the YMCA paying 2*d*. for a cup of tea and cake. The same concession, with regard to the cost of admission, applied at the weekly dance held at the Royal Victoria Hotel in Llanberis and the twice-weekly dance at the village hall.

Rationing
Even though by the winter of 1916, food shortages had caused severe malnutrition, especially amongst the poor, David Lloyd George's First World War government did not introduce food rationing until 1918. With the knowledge that war was imminent and that the country was even more dependent on imported food, the Food (Defence) Plans Department of the Board of Trade had formulated plans for rationing in 1936, so that by the outbreak of war, the machinery of food control and distribution was largely in place although actual rationing was not to start until 8 January 1940. By the time the Battle of the Atlantic had reached its zenith in 1940, 2.6 million tons of merchant shipping had been sunk by German U-boats and desperately needed supplies of food were being lost at an alarming rate.

The staff of the Ministry of Food in London was evacuated to Colwyn Bay where the country's food rationing system was operated by some 5,000 clerks, accommodated in commandeered hotels. The head office was established at the Pwll-y-Crochan Hotel where they were to remain for the duration of the war. Lord Woolton, Minister of Food, who was also accommodated at the hotel, had a team of advisers headed by Jack Drummond, Chief Scientific Adviser, who were able to produce what was described as a balanced diet under wartime conditions for the population generally. As far as imported food was concerned, priority was given to skimmed dried milk, cheese and tinned meat and fish. Other items, such as bananas, took up too much space and priority was given to oranges.

The Divisional Food Offices, in addition to their supervisory function, were responsible for providing accommodation for emergency food stocks which became known as 'buffer depots' for supporting normal distribution services. A number of buildings were requisitioned for temporary storage, including the Pavilion at Caernarfon, until new buildings were erected.[18] Major W. Lloyd Griffith, as Divisional Food Officer responsible for the whole of north Wales was based in Caernarfon. A regional office of the Ministry of Food in Bangor Street, under the charge of Mr Quinn (previously employed by J. Bibby & Sons, Liverpool), dealt with the allocation and distribution of oils and fats to wholesale users, such as bakeries, cafés and ice-cream makers. A third office, at Pool Side,

Ration Book still in use 1952–3.
[Ivor Wyn Jones]

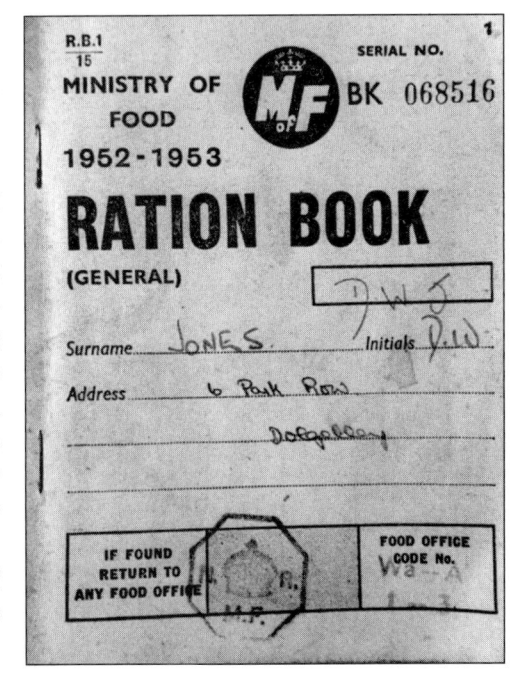

Ministery of Food staff at the Caernarfon Pavilion. [Doris Rogers]

dealt with the distribution of ration books.

Food rationing began with a weekly allowance per person of:

4 ozs bacon or ham
2 ozs tea
4 ozs butter
4 ozs margarine
4 ozs cooking fat
2 ozs cheese
12 ozs sugar.

Within six months, the weekly allowance was reduced to 1 oz cheese, 2 ozs cooking fat and 2 ozs butter which was later further reduced to 1 oz. Meat was rationed from 11 March 1940, with a weekly allowance of 1*s*. 10*d*. rather than by weight, which enabled people to choose the type and quality they preferred. Within the next twelve months, further commodities were rationed including jam, marmalade and honey.

Other foodstuffs such as poultry, game, fish and bread were restricted by availability. Every opportunity was taken to purchase eggs so that they could be preserved in water glass, a chemical that sealed the shell. Many substitutes came on the market such as powdered milk and dried powdered egg, but they were not very popular, nor was the coffee substitute made from ground dried acorns. Because icing was banned, tiered wedding cakes were often made of cardboard and hired from bakers.

The national wholemeal loaf was of a bran-like texture and was an unpopular substitute for white bread. In an attempt to supplement the allocation of food controlled by rationing, many decided to use their back garden to keep pigs and hens, and to use the household food waste for feeding them.

Although many items of food were rationed, it did not follow that they were always available, some went 'under the counter' and were sold at the discretion of the shopkeeper. This discriminatory distribution caused considerable animosity, especially amongst housewives who had queued patiently and then discovered that the items required were not available. Shopkeepers generally would try and look after people who had been regular customers before the war.

The Ministry of Food would not allow people to shop wherever they wanted and any change had to be registered. The quantity of food distributed to individual shops was dependent on the number of customers registered at each premises. When people stayed at hotels or bed and breakfast establishments, special forms provided by the local Ministry of Food office would authorise the place to provide meals. Ration books were marked according to the meals eaten, so that there was no possibility of anyone getting more than their permitted ration.

As a result of the very successful 'Dig for Victory' publicity campaign launched by the Ministry of Agriculture, production of vegetables and milk output increased, which ensured that essential calcium and vitamins were available to improve the health of the young and old. The Chief Scientific Adviser to the Ministry of Food emphasised the importance of sufficient carbohydrates, especially for the working population. As the result of his investigation into the level of food that was required to maintain health generally, it was stated that the health of people in Britain had not only been maintained during the war, it had even improved, especially as far as children were concerned.

Members of the Women's Institute arranged for collected fruit to be preserved or made into jam. The organisation also had the task of co-

Ministry of Food officials at a Baby Clinic in Caernarfon.
[AC]

Wartime recipes.
[Y Tabernacl, Machynlleth]

ordinating, collecting and distributing fruit and vegetables produced in thousands of allotments and gardens, and also the collection of rose hips by children, which in syrup form, supplied beneficial vitamins. To maintain a certain standard quality of product and hygiene amongst the many voluntary organisations involved, the Ministry of Food and Agriculture appointed twenty 'Inspectors of Jam Makers.'[19]

In the summer of 1943, wartime cookery classes were organised by the Caernarvonshire Education Committee for anyone who cared to enrol.[20] The Ministry of Food published recipes in daily newspapers to help housewives produce palatable meals for their families at a time when there was little choice of ingredients available. Many of these recipes were based on the potato which housewives were urged to use when baking in preference to imported flour.

> Potato Carrot Pancake:
>
> Well-seasoned mashed potato combined with cooked carrot makes a wholesome and savoury-tasting pancake. Whip the mashed potato to a loose creamy consistency. Season well with pepper and salt and add some diced carrot. Pan-fried slowly in very little fat it develops a deliciously crisp crust, but it can be baked to a gold brown colour in the oven if preferred.[21]

Clothes, materials and shoes were rationed from 1 June 1941 and availability was controlled by the ubiquitous clothing ration book. At first, each person was allowed to use sixty-six coupons per year – enough for one complete outfit of clothes – but in 1942, the number of coupons was reduced to forty-eight. Standardisation of clothing produced utility garments which, although well-made from good materials by well-known firms, were nevertheless devoid of style or character. A limit to the amount of cloth per garment regulated the number of pleats, pockets, buttons, skirt length, etc. Such clothing was identified by the symbol CC41 (Civilian Clothing 1941).

With the introduction of petrol rationing on 16 September 1939, only one grade was available thereafter and this was sold and distributed as 'pool' motor spirit at 1s. 6d. per gallon. The normal petrol coupons were obtained from post or taxation offices but applications for supplementary coupons had to be submitted to the Divisional Petroleum Office.[22] The lack of transport and shortage of fuel often caused farmers to move sheep and cattle on the hoof to market or to and from summer or winter pasture. It was not uncommon for animals to be walked a distance of more than twenty miles. This was the case with sheep from Dyffryn Mymbyr near Capel Curig which were moved as far as Colwyn Bay where they would graze on the golf course during the winter months. A private vehicle, of which there were few on the road, was liable to be stopped by the police, and the driver had to justify the journey. For this reason, farmers had a tendency to carry suitable merchandise, such as a sack of potatoes, in the boot of the car. It came as no surprise to learn that such farming merchandise travelled many miles but never seemed to leave the car or to arrive at a destination.

In an attempt to overcome the problem of petrol shortage, the Crosville Bus Company converted ten per cent of their fleet to run on coal or producer gas which reduced the speed of the vehicles to between fifteen and eighteen miles per hour. Most owners simply took their cars off the road and placed them in store for the duration of hostilities and consequently very few cars were sold during the war years. A new Morris 10 could be bought at the Red Garage in Caernarfon for £175 (road tax £7 10s.) and £160 would buy a second-hand 2·5 litre Jaguar at Braid Brothers in Colwyn Bay. But few could afford them, even at such low prices.

Domestic power supplies

The rationing of electricity, coal and gas supplies was introduced in September 1939. However, because of administrative problems, it was abandoned after a fortnight and no further attempts were made to control either sales or usage. Thereafter, as with some foodstuff, it was a question of availability and affordability.

Prisoners of War

In anticipation of the influx of Prisoners of War (PoWs) arriving from Europe, particularly after 1943, the Ministry of Works Planning Department in Rhyl, stated in a letter to the Caernarvonshire County Council in January 1943, that sites would be required at Ty'n-y-groes, Bontnewydd, Sarn and Fourcrosses where camps were to be established for the Ministry of Agriculture and Fisheries.[23] Similar sites were planned in Anglesey and Merionethshire.

After the experience of staying in camps in Oswestry and Sheffield, many PoWs gladly accepted the offer of agricultural work in preference to being incarcerated within barbed-wire fencing, especially when it was realised that the British had no intention of releasing them in the near future, even after hostilities had ceased.

The first prisoners to arrive in Caernarfonshire were Italians and they were housed in camps in Bontnewydd on the outskirts of Caernarfon, Vaynol near Bangor, Sarn, Ty'n-y-groes and Four Crosses near Pwllheli. They were controlled from the headquarters at Pabo Hall in Llandudno Junction. In retrospect, conditions in the camp were generally regarded as being quite good, with plenty of reading material available and studying encouraged. When the Italians were replaced by German prisoners, the same facilities were provided, together with German newspapers printed in London and newsletters printed in Ruthin. As part of their recreation, the prisoners at Bontnewydd were allowed to play football against RAF personnel from Llandwrog.

The German prisoners allocated to Vaynol, near Bangor were brought by train in August 1945 from Oswestry to Menai Bridge from where they were marched some two miles, to accommodation which consisted of tents previously occupied by Italian PoWs. Eventually, three Nissen huts were erected, each capable of housing twenty prisoners. The camp, which was

German Prisoners of War at Vaynol camp, 1947.
[Ludger Lonnemann]

Prisoner of War Camp 119F at Four Crosses. This camp was originally opened to accommodate Italian POWs. They were replaced by German POWs towards the end of the war. It remained as a POW Hostel until the late 1940s (when German POWs were eventually released). The buildings were later used as temporary housing for the local civilian population until council houses were built in nearby Four Crosses (Y Ffôr) in the 1950s. The camp accommodation has survived and is now incorporated into the Welsh Lady jam factory.

Four Crosses POW Camp had three accommodation blocks (housing a total of about fifty prisoners) as well as a kitchen block and a toilet and bath block.

Top: Accommodation block.

Middle: Accommodation block (left), with kitchen block attached.

*Bottom: Toilet and bath block.
[W. Alister Williams Collection, via Dio Jones]*

located near to the Capel Graig Lodge, was guarded by five British soldiers who were regarded as superfluous as none of the prisoners had any desire to escape.

From 1943, many PoWs, both Italian and German, were allocated agricultural duties and for such assistance, the farmer had to pay the War Agriculture Executive Committee (WAEC) between £2 10s. and £3 per week.[24] However, the prisoners were only paid 1d. per hour – 8d. for an eight-hour day, starting at 8 a.m. and finishing at 5 p.m. (with one hour off at lunch time).

The work carried out by these prisoners was very much appreciated by farmers, especially at a time when they were desperately short of labour and crops needed to be harvested. The German prisoner, considered to be the more diligent worker compared to other continental nationalities, worked well alongside regular farm workers and members of the Women's Land Army. They were popular because they were willing and capable of tackling most jobs on the farm, even though many of them had not experienced similar work in civilian life.

During the period when the army was responsible for the prisoners, the men were taken by lorry to the allocated farm and, in an attempt at preventing familiarity between prisoners and farmers, the venue was changed each week. The following instruction was issued by the military authority,

After a period working on a farm as a PoW Richard Stuhlfelder settled to live and work in Port Dinorwic. [Richard Stuhlfelder]

> PoW labour (described as Italian co-operators) not to leave employer's land during the working day. Do not go to any villages or towns or any shops, houses, hotels or restaurant. Do not receive money or gifts. Do not send letters except through the hutment hostel to which they are attached. Food will be provided with normal rations including a haversack lunch by the Military Authorities. It will not be necessary for the employer to provide co-operators with food but only with hot liquid refreshments (eg cocoa, coffee or soup) during the day.[25]

Amongst the prisoners who came to Vaynol was Lonnie Lomeman who had been conscripted into the *Wehrmacht* (the German Army). After serving as a paratrooper in the 2nd Parachute Division in Poland and Russia, he was posted to France where he was captured near Brest by the US Army in September 1944. Lomeman eventually returned to Germany, but his friendship with the civilians who worked on the Vaynol farm ensured that he maintained contact with them for a number of years after the war.

Richard Stuhlfelder was another prisoner who stayed at Vaynol, on the site later used by the forestry department. He was conscripted in 1942, at the age of seventeen, into the German airborne forces. It was however, as an infantryman that he fought in Normandy in 1944. He was wounded in both knees at St Malo and taken by German hospital ship to Jersey, and

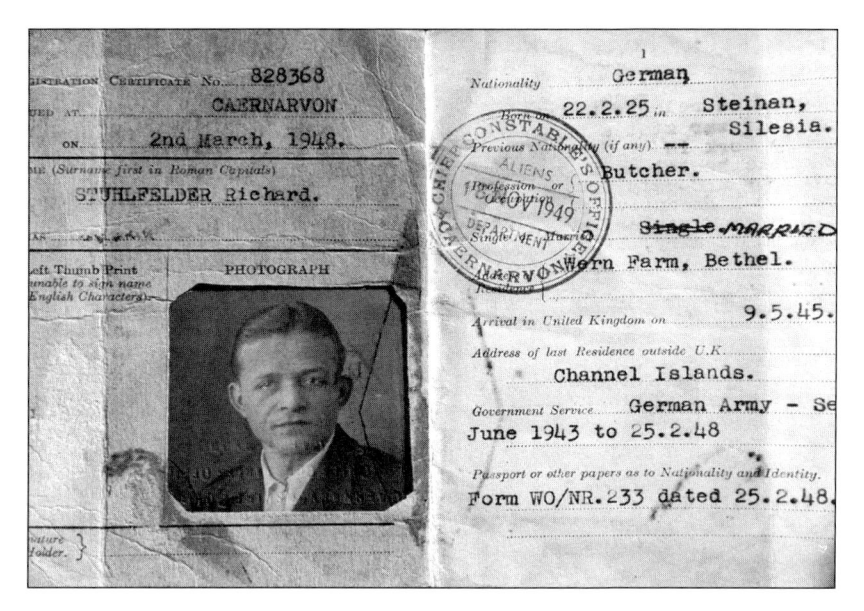

Aliens pass issued to German Prisoner of War whilst working on farms after the war. [Richard Stuhlfelder]

then to Guernsey. Both the Germans and the inhabitants of the Channel Islands were by then very short of food. The only food that was plentiful was cockles. In time, Red Cross ships were allowed to bring in food to relieve some of the shortages. At the end of the war, a warehouse full of tinned food was found but, for some reason, had been withheld from both the soldiers and the inhabitants. Having been trained as a butcher before conscription, Stuhlfelder was put in charge of catering for 110 prisoners and three guards at Vaynol (skills which were to eventually find him employment at Roberts & Sons in Port Dinorwic where he stayed for thirty-six years). Food, such as bread, butter, corned beef and boiled ham, was delivered to the camp from the Pavilion at Caernarfon (where emergency food supply had been kept during the war) by army or civilian lorries. In addition to catering, he was also involved with agricultural work, first at Wern farm in Bethel and, subsequent to marrying, at Carreg Goch farm in Port Dinorwic.

Heinz Nowack, a native of East Prussia, was recruited into a German artillery regiment, and was captured near Arras in France, aged twenty, in 1944. He and other prisoners eventually arrived at a camp in Sheffield where they were given the choice of remaining in the camp for an unspecified period, or doing agricultural work. He, together with many other prisoners, accepted the latter option and were taken by train to Pwllheli, and then by road to the camp at Bontnewydd. Here, they found conditions very regimented, or at least they were for the first few months. A Dutchman recruited into the *Wehrmacht* was responsible for the camp catering, such as it was. Lunch was supposed to consist of a

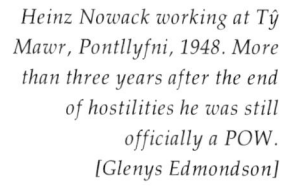

Heinz Nowack working at Tŷ Mawr, Pontllyfni, 1948. More than three years after the end of hostilities he was still officially a POW. [Glenys Edmondson]

IDENTIFICATION PASS

German Prisoner of War No. 366 841 Rank L. Cpl.

Name LONNEMANN, Ludger

Quartered at Vaynol-Park

has permission to be absent from his quarters, daily when not on duty, until **LIGHTING UP TIME**, or **2200** hours, whichever is the earliest.

He has strict orders to produce this pass on demand, by (a)—members of the Camp Staff; (b)—Military Police; (c)—Civil Police; (d)—German P.O.W. Police.

1st JAN, 1947.   MAJOR.
Commandant, 119 German P.W. Working Camp.

German Prisoner of War Identification Pass. [Ludger Lonnemann]

piece of bread but, because the prisoners were so hungry, this would invariably be eaten with their breakfast. The initial antipathy that existed between the prisoners and the local people soon changed to an air of acceptance. Some petty rules instigated by the military authority, such as the non-fraternisation policy, were difficult, if not impossible, to maintain, especially when prisoners had a daily working relationship with farmers. In fact, more often than not, the prisoners were soon invited to join the farmer and his family for a mid-day meal. Another petty restriction when the PoWs were the responsibility of the army was that of restricting their movements to within half a mile of the camp. However, when the prisoners were eventually billeted at a farm rather than in a camp, the distance was increased to one mile. Although this was sufficient to allow a visit to Pen-y-groes, they were still not supposed to visit cafés, pubs or the cinema. They soon overcame this restriction by wearing borrowed raincoats which hid their uniforms and were able to gain admission to various places previously denied to them. Although the local policeman at Pen-y-groes was well aware of the situation, he pretended not to notice them.

When the prisoners were the responsibility of the military, Nowack and his fellow prisoners were transported around the locality to various farms by army lorry. However, at the end of the war, the WAEC took responsibility from the army for the distribution of labour and allocation of work, a different attitude prevailed to the extent that it was not unusual for farmers to telephone the camp and indicate which prisoner they would prefer to work for them. By this stage, the prisoners had been allocated bicycles as a means of transport.

Women's Land Army girls together with local farm workers and German POWs at Vaynol, 1945. [AC]

After his peripatetic agricultural experiences, Nowack worked at Morfa Goch, Dinas Dinlle for about six months, before moving to Tŷ Mawr in Pontllyfni at the beginning of 1948. Many of the men who had arrived in this country as prisoners of war, when eventually given the option of returning to their own country, chose to stay here. Nowack remained at Tŷ Mawr and when Evan Hughes moved from there to Yokehouse near Pwllheli in 1961, Heinz went with him and eventually completed forty-five years with the family by the time he retired. He was presented with a Long Service Medal at the Royal Welsh Show in 1986, in recognition of his dedication and contribution to the success of the farm.

Notes
1. BUA, PNP 487.
2. GAS XC20-5-27/29.
3. GAS XC20/5/27.
4. BUA, PNP 572.
5. *C&DH*, 27 October 1939.
6. BUA, PNP 5723.
7. BUA, PNP viii 5723.
8. BUA, PNP 5723.
9. GAS, XC2-4086.
10. BUA, PNP 5723.
11. BUA, PNP 5719.
12. *Land at War 1939-44*, HMSO, 1945.
13. *C&DH*, 15 September 39.
14. GAS, X/Gorddinog/19.
15. Interview with the author, 1984.
16. NLW Ms 23073D.
17. Interview with the author, 1984.
18. GAS, 1301/24.
19. NLW 23073D.
20. GAS, XD 39/240.
21. Ministry of Food - Food Facts published in the national press.
22. Supplementary coupons were issued to essential users of motor vehicles, e.g. farmers and doctors.
23. GAS, XC2-6-248.
24. BUA, PNP 5724.
25. BUA, Bangor Papers 11821 and PNP VIII/3660.

Chapter 8
Industry

NECACO

Rollanson Aircraft Services, formed by Bill Rollanson and Freddie Kent in 1935, had its workshops conveniently located on Croydon airfield, enabling it to service aeroplanes for British Continental Airways, Imperial Airways, Vickers and Hawker Aircraft. It also had contracts with the Air Ministry to repair and recondition service aircraft such as the Fairey Battle and Hawker Hurricane, and manufactured components for the Wellington bomber on behalf of Vickers. Within four years, Hunting & Son had become the majority shareholder in Rollanson, and its chairman, Percy Hunting, had joined the board of directors.[1]

A bombing attack by German aircraft at 7.10 p.m. on Thursday, 15 August 1940, resulted in Rollanson's Aircraft Services' Croydon factory being extensively damaged and six workers losing their lives. Aircraft, both inside the factory and outside on the runway, were damaged or destroyed. Further damage was inflicted when the raiders returned two days later. Since there was always a possibility of further air raids, it was decided that a safer location would have to be found.

On 27 August, Percy Hunting, accompanied by a couple of officials from the factory, travelled by train to Caernarfon where they were met by the Mayor, Philip Davies, the Town Clerk and his wife, The Rt Hon. David

The Dinorwic Quarry showing the cutting and splitting sheds that were taken over by NECACO in August 1940.
[Iris Morley Jones]

Official visit to the NECACO factory. L–R: W. A. Summers; David Lloyd George, MP; Percy Hunting; Mrs Frances Lloyd George; Sir Goronwy Owen, MP. October 1944. [Ann Richmond]

Blow: Lloyd George and his wife are conducted around the factory by W. A. Summers. [Ann Richmond]

Lloyd George, MP and Maj Goronwy Owen, MP. The next day, after breakfast at the Royal Hotel, Hunting, accompanied by Lloyd George and Goronwy Owen, had a look at a couple of quarries before lunching with Sir Michael Duff Assheton Smith, Mr Vivian (Vaynol Agent, described by Hunting as 'an old man of eighty-nine but full of vigour') and O. T. Williams (General Manager of the Dinorwic Quarry). Later, Hunting had further discussions with Mr Lloyd George and his family over tea in Criccieth. On 30 August, the decision was made to go ahead with the Llanberis project (it is understood that Lloyd George had already persuaded Lord Beaverbrook, Minister of Aircraft Production, that the Dinorwic Quarry site would be an ideal location for Hunting Aviation).

According to a letter, dated 16 September 1940, sent by O. T. Williams to the quarry solicitors, it seemed that he was anything but pleased with losing the quarry sheds and the consequential loss of production, 'the government have demanded the taking over on behalf of Rollanson Aircraft Services Ltd. certain sheds and other small buildings from the Dinorwic Quarry ... at a rental of £1,200 plus £20 for the use of the tunnel.'[2] When Percy Hunting returned on the 30 September, he made the following observation in his diary, '... they have made wonderful strides since we were away. The whole shop is cleared which in the time must have been some job.' However, he may well have anticipated problems as a result of the

NECACO officials with W. A. Summers, Works Manager (3rd from left front row). [Ann Richmond]

requisitioning of the quarry sheds according to a letter of 28 April 1941, that he sent to the General Manager of Dinorwic Quarry, '[NECACO] ... carrying on a very big aircraft production industry under Government orders ... also appreciate that slates are now of considerable national importance and that the two industries must try and work smoothly together.' On 6 May, he made the comment, 'I am afraid that in this part of Wales they have had such a peaceful time that they have not realised the importance of this aircraft manufacture.'[3]

The use of 'the tunnel' (originally planned as an Air-Raid Shelter according to some of the letters passing between the Dinorwic Quarry manager and solicitors), was a contentious issue with NECACO. They were accused of trespassing onto the part allocated for use by the quarry even though the manager had been told by the quarry solicitors that NECACO was acting within the rights bestowed upon them by war-time requisition laws. Nevertheless, 'he [the General Manager] was of the opinion that they were abusing such powers especially when he considered that they would lose £35–45,000 in output' and letters continued to be exchanged on the subject.

The fact that Dinorwic Quarry had been instructed to pay half the cost of camouflaging the sheds, with the other half being paid by the government, with no contribution from NECACO, did nothing to ease the situation between the parties. In what appeared to be a further attempt at non-cooperation and procrastination, the quarry owners introduced various inappropriate clauses and phrases into the draft lease. It was even stated that 'the tunnel' had been pledged to the National Gallery for use in storing pictures. A number of letters passed between the solicitors acting for the two parties before the matter was resolved and the final document agreed and signed.[4]

The North East Coast Aircraft Company (NECACO) had been formed before the war in Newcastle-upon-Tyne, as a subsidiary of Hunting, for the manufacture of aircraft but the idea was abandoned because of the possible danger from air attacks in the north-east. When the decision was taken to relocate Rollanson's Aircraft Services to Llanberis, the opportunity was taken to use the deliberately misleading acronym of NECACO (rather than 'The New Factory' as it was known locally). The factory continued to be known as NECACO until the decision was taken to change it to Hunting Aviation in August 1944, by which time it had become obvious that the company's association with Llanberis would soon end.

Arthur Summers, who had joined the company in 1940 to take charge of the relocation, had the responsibility in the first place of preparing one shed (which was 561 feet long, previously used to house some one hundred and fifty machines for splitting and cutting slate) to house equipment that was brought by road from Croydon. Another shed (184 feet long) was also acquired and used by NECACO. Engineers such as Bill Lavender and Fred Lane planned the layout of the machines within the larger shed. Lane later took charge of the training of personnel in a building originally owned by the Caernarfon Electric Company on the Bangor side of Victoria Dock in Caernarfon. Summers, together with a small band of employees from Croydon, completed the task of relocating the machinery by the end of September, thus enabling the production of some components and aircraft parts to start by November and full production by spring 1941.

When Percy Hunting looked after matters in north Wales, he lived at Llywenarth, Pen-y-groes, the home of Col Jones-Roberts, with the resident housekeeper taking care of the place, but when it was necessary to discuss

NECACO work's pass issued to Haydn Hughes.
[Haydn Hughes]

NECACO staff. [Dewi Ellis]

matters with representatives from Rollanson Aircraft Services, meetings were occasionally held in Worcester which was considered to be half-way between the two factories.

If unemployment had been a problem in north Wales in the 1930s, it was certainly not during the Second World War. On the contrary – with the exodus of men and women to the armed forces and other destinations, the task of finding sufficient people to work in munitions and similar occupations, was a daunting one. The role of the Unemployment Office was changed from finding work for people to that of finding people for work. Even men who were unsuitable for military service because of ill-health or age, could still be considered for work in munitions. Women who were within a certain age category and in reasonable health, were usually given the option of either enrolling in the armed forces or being directed into work of national importance, such as munitions.

When NECACO started in Llanberis, the company had the difficult task of training some 3,000 people, many of whom had never even seen the inside of a factory, let alone operated machinery. Limited training in operating machines was given at a building called the Victory Works on Victoria Dock in Caernarfon, but most apprentices became proficient within a short space of time by practical experience in Llanberis.

Women, who had previously been involved with housework and caring

NECACO staff. [AC]

for husbands and children, were suddenly transformed into experts in the assembly of intricate and vital aircraft components. Interviews for secretarial staff were conducted at the Royal Hotel (now the Celtic Royal) in Caernarfon and the initial office for their use was set up there until such time as facilities were available in Llanberis. Tea or coffee was brought to them on a silver salver by Sir Michael Duff's valet who had been directed there for war-time work. In time, Summers (the General Manager), Cowan (the Assistant Manager) and Young (the Works Manager) moved into an office consisting of two huts near the main shed in Llanberis but, because it was so basic, use was made of toilet facilities at the Padarn Villa Hotel. Eventually they joined the accountants, Sanderson, Bowran and Tongue, in the main shed which by then included all the clerical staff.

The first jigs to be installed at Llanberis were those for producing wings for the Boulton & Paul Defiant night fighter. When it was fully operational, the factory produced parts for the Handley-Page Halifax, Avro Lancaster, Short Stirling and Vickers Wellington bombers. It also undertook occasional work for Saunders-Roe at Beaumaris.

In addition to the main factory at Llanberis, there were three sites in Caernarfon involved with the manufacture or assembly of various parts: the Central Garage (where components were made for the de Havilland Mosquito and Bristol Beaufort aircraft); a building built on the site of the old Peblig brickworks (taken over by 3 October 1941 as 'an outstation') for the outer casing for the newly-developed jet engines for the Gloster Meteor; and the Victory Works, on the side of the Victoria Dock, for training and producing small parts used in the main factory at Llanberis. Rivet annealing was also carried out at the Victory Works when the plant

The NECACO Peblig factory. [AC]

NECACO canteen at Peblig. [Griff Roberts]

at Llanberis either broke down or could not cope with demand.

The tooling machines had initially been installed in the main shed, but they were later moved to the safety of the nearby tunnel which ran from the site occupied by NECACO, through slate rock to Gilfach Ddu. Zinc sheets lined the roof to prevent water, which seeped out of the rock above, falling onto the capstans, lathes, planers and grinders and their respective operators. They also had to work in an atmosphere that was dank and damp and with the pervading smell of oil. The various machines were located on one side of the tunnel which barely left room for a small low-loader Lister pick-up with its engine mounted on the single front wheel, to travel inside. A hydraulic press for rubber parts was installed at Gilfach Ddu and the quarry pattern shop was also used for certain items. A Rushton engine, brought from Preston, enabled a generator to provide emergency power, if or when the national electricity supply had failed for any reason.

Since there was always the possibility of an air attack, teams of personnel from each of the factories paid periodic visits to Llandwrog airfield where they were instructed in the art of fire-fighting and extinguishing incendiary bombs with stirrup pumps, by Sgt W. A. Wilson the RAF fire instructor. As part of the training, he would also let them have the experience of walking through a fire, clad in asbestos suits.

Personnel at NECACO worked two shifts of twelve hours each – 7.30 a.m. to 7.30 p.m., and 7.30 p.m. to 7.30 a.m. Day shifts were limited to two weeks, followed by night shifts for two weeks. The latter shifts were much quieter because there were fewer people working. Unless there was pressure for certain parts, work usually finished at 4 p.m. on Saturday and resumed when the Sunday morning shift came in. When the workload began to ease, because of greater expertise and organisation, production staff were allowed to finish at 5 p.m. on Wednesdays and mid-day on Saturdays.

Crosville buses, both single and double-decker, some starting from Beaumaris at 6.10 a.m., would tour the countryside picking up men and women until the bus, full of budding songsters, arrived in Llanberis at 7.15 a.m. in time for the start of the shift. Similar arrangements applied for the workers at the Peblig works, the Central Garage and the Victory Works in Caernarfon.

During the daytime shift, a fifteen-minute tea break was allowed in the morning and afternoon, together with a one hour break for lunch, which in the summer-time, was often taken by the side of Llyn Peris. Similar concessions were allowed on the night shift. During the winter months, when employees worked from 7.30 a.m. until 7.30 p.m., and consequently saw little, if any, daylight, they were given the opportunity of sun-ray lamp (ultra-violet) treatment at the medical centre. Provisions for the canteen were replenished periodically by sending a works' lorry to the Pavilion at Caernarfon where butter, tea and sugar were stored for general and emergency use.

Wages varied, with the basic pay supplemented by piece-work or

The front fuselage sections of Avro Lancaster bombers being assembled at the NECACO factory, Llanberis. [Hunting plc]

NECACO staff. [AC]

bonuses, depending on the output. Girls at the factory were paid 1s. an hour, but if special training had been received, then the rate was increased to 1s. 3d. per hour with 11d. bonus, as compared to the men who were paid 2s. 6d. per hour. The clerical staff were also subjected to long hours of hard work, resulting in a strong desire for nothing more than sleep after a hasty meal at home at the end of a shift. If anyone complained of the long hours, they were suitably reminded that members of the forces fighting on their behalf, never complained. At the end of a shift, irrespective of how tired they were, enough strength was mustered to run the distance between shed and bus so as to grab a seat rather than having to stand. The period at home was short, but long enough for a meal and sleep that would enable them to recuperate sufficiently before the next onslaught.

The employees received regular instructions that they were not to talk about their work to anyone. The ubiquitous 'Careless Talk Costs Lives' posters that were prominently displayed in various buildings, were a further reminder of their responsibility. The chairman issued what was described as an important notice on 1 December 1940, 'All works Personnel are hereby notified that Machine Guns have been posted throughout the area covering the works on both sides of the lake. These posts are manned day and night. Armed patrols are working in the vicinity also day and night in addition to the guards at the usual fixed points ... necessary for all personnel to stop at once if challenged ... '5

Most of the local factories had their own Home Guard contingent from their own employees. NECACO's detachment, with Maj Jackson in charge and housed at The Lodge, was responsible for security at Llanberis as well as Peblig, Central Garage, Victory Works and the store section at Schofield's yard near Pont Saint, Caernarfon. However, the officer

NECACO Staff Drama Group. [Iris Hughes]

commanding N⁰· 3 Platoon was rather critical of an exercise called *Padarn* which took place in February 1942,

> He [Jackson] relied too much on 'token strength.' On paper he has 60 men to call upon from Llanberis but in actual fact less that 20 turned out. Can these others be relied upon in actual emergency? Speaking from my own experience in the Home Guard I much doubt it and I think it would be better for such men to receive the 'order of the boot' forthwith; obviously the number of men at Major Jackson's disposal were very inadequate for the job in hand. A point in favour of conscription.[6]

An entry for 25 July 1941 in Percy Hunting's diary stated, '[they are of the opinion] that we are paying the Home Guard which of course is nonsense. We are not, we are paying factory watchers who are members of the Home Guard. I'll bet our friend O. T. Williams is making trouble that we have pinched his quarrymen.'[7]

Problems with the workforce were not unknown from time-to-time, but more often than not, these were quickly settled. However, one strike at Llanberis was caused by one of the girls taking more time than she should 'powdering her nose.' A confrontation with a foreman and the involvement of an union official caused a strike at the factory which lasted a couple of days.

Until purpose-built lorries were available, vehicles were commandeered from local firms in order that raw materials could be brought to the factories and the finished product conveyed to its eventual destination. By the time production at Llanberis had reached its zenith, fourteen 'Queen Mary' lorries were being used to carry aircraft sections made at Llanberis and Caernarfon. These vehicles always carried two drivers to deal with any problems encountered on the journey, and to ensure that no driver exceeded the permitted maximum eleven hours' duty. A delivery to Weybridge, south-west of London, entailed leaving Llanberis at 4 p.m. and arriving some time after 10 a.m. the following morning. Parts were also delivered from Llanberis to the Fairey Aviation factory at Alston, Cumbria. The lorries, rather than returning empty from the south, would bring material from various locations, including Gloucester, for use at Llanberis. During the appropriate season, whatever else was being transported to Llanberis, there would always be room for a load of fruit purchased at Evesham at 1s. a basket which the drivers sold to the eagerly-awaiting factory workers at Llanberis, for 1s. 6d., a profit of 6d. per basket!

The recreation centre or NECACO works club, Pool Lane, Caernarfon, was officially opened on 11 August 1943, in the company of Percy Hunting and the Mayor of Caernarfon. The twelve-hour shift at the factory left most of the workers feeling very tired with little incentive to enjoy the facilities provided. Nevertheless, the dances, especially on Saturday nights, were enjoyed by most employees.

Music for the dances was provided by the works' band with J. L. Jones on drums (he was responsible for designing the Horn with Wings logo of the company), together with Geoff Roberts on piano, Bill Collins on violin and Haydn Hughes as the popular vocalist. In another room, J. L. Jones' wife ran a lending library, and snooker tables were available on the ground floor. A drama group was formed with Iris Hughes, Lionel Hughes, Arthur Hutchinson, Kathleen Mason, Olive Roe and Betty Williams, to name but a few of the local talent, who performed in plays such as Agatha Christie's *Alibi* to packed houses at the Guildhall in Caernarfon.

Concerts held in Gronant when local personalities were given an opportunity to display their talents, were always very popular. Indeed, the standard at such concerts was considered by many to be far higher than the entertainment provided by ENSA (Entertainment National Service Association) concert parties when they occasionally performed at the works canteen. The popular NECACO male voice and mixed voice choirs, with Aled Owen as choir-master, practised at the Gronant club and entertained many in the district as well as competing at the Eisteddfod in Llandudno. David Lloyd, a well-known tenor at that time, used to sing to an appreciative audience at the Peblig canteen. The BBC radio programme *Workers' Playtime*, which was broadcast from various factories around the country, visited NECACO in Llanberis, but brought their own piano because of the poor condition of the canteen piano. Before the days of the transistor radio, the inspection team had procured a gramophone on which an endless number of records were played, with a scratchy sound emanating from a large horn speaker. Although cumbersome to carry, it would be taken out when the weather was suitable so that those dining on sandwiches by Llyn Peris could enjoy Glen Miller's *String of Pearls* and *Moonlight Serenade*. For further relaxation, if time allowed, members of staff ran a tennis club at the Padarn Villa Hotel, with matches against members of the BBC Variety Club in Bangor and RAF personnel from N[o.] 31 MU [Maintenance Unit] Llanberis.

Many officials and visitors called from time-to-time at NECACO but, because of the dearth of suitable accommodation (most of the local hotels had been taken over by the armed forces) in this relatively remote area, Hunting Aviation formed a company called Red Dragon Hotels Ltd which bought the Padarn Lake Hotel (later to be re-named Padarn Valley Hotel), the Swallow Falls Hotel at Betws-y-Coed and the Café Royal at Colwyn Bay. Although the company was reasonably successful, Hunting Group decided that this was one line of business that it would not pursue in the future. The Duke of Kent, who visited the NECACO factory on 8 May 1942, stayed with Sir Michael Duff at Vaynol, as did Princess Marina when she visited Llanberis on another occasion.

The bombing that Rollanson experienced in Croydon had occurred in many other parts of the country, including in and around Coventry, with many aircraft factories being damaged. As a result of these raids, the Ministry of Aircraft Production built a factory in 'safer' areas, including one in Bangor for Darwen British Electric Motor Company (it later became the Dennis Ferranti factory). It also took over the Bangor Crosville garage on behalf of Daimler Motor Company. Radcliffe Engineering Company Ltd was also involved in the manufacture of 'war materials' in a specially-built factory in Llandudno Junction by May 1940.[8]

Undoubtedly, NECACO was a very successful operation with everyone from machinist to clerical staff making a valuable contribution. Although the work was often tiring and demanding, the consensus of opinion expressed by those who worked at the factory, was that they had enjoyed

Duke of Kent at NECACO, 8 May 1942, together with Percy Hunting, Sir Goronwy Owen MP and W. A. Summers (Works Manager).
[Ann Richmond]

Capel Norton, Machynlleth, where aircraft components were assembled during the Second World War.
[Y Tabernacl, Machynlleth]

the experience, in particular, the camaraderie.

With the Second World War at an end, the numbers employed at the factory had fallen to approximately 500 by September 1945, and the sheds that housed both employees and machinery for over four busy and productive years, would soon be empty and silent.

Saunders-Roe

During the early part of the Second World War, at a time when Britain was in desperate need of aircraft, the Ministry of Aircraft Production arranged for American aircraft intended for use by the Royal Air Force (RAF) to be appropriately modified in the United States, to take British equipment that would meet the country's operational requirements. However, by the time the aircraft arrived in Britain, it was found that the required modifications had become out-of-date, and additional changes had to be carried out before they were operationally acceptable to the RAF. Due to delays, the volume of changes and the fact that modifications involved design work, Saunders Roe was awarded a contract by the Ministry of Aircraft Production. As a result, it became the central firm responsible for work on the Consolidated Catalina flying boat and eventually, the Vought-Sikorsky Kingfisher, Consolidated Coronado, Curtis Seamew and Martin Mariner aircraft in accordance with RAF requirements.

The firm of Saunders-Roe was started by S. E. Saunders in 1830 to construct boats on the banks of the River Thames in London. It remained there until 1906 when it was relocated to Cowes on the Isle of Wight. Between 1914 and 1939, Saunders specialised in high-speed craft such as *Bluebird*, *Maple Leaf IV* and *Miss England* which, in turn, were destined to hold the World Speed Record. After a period of building motor cruisers and lifeboats for the Royal National Lifeboat Institution, it began constructing wooden hulls for flying boats during the First World War. The name of the firm was changed to Saunders-Roe in 1928 when Sir Alliott Verdon-Roe (of Avro aircraft) provided financial backing. Just prior to the Second World War, the decision was taken to form two separate companies – one to build boats and the other (in association with Short Brothers) to build flying-boats, .

In September 1940, as the result of enemy action at Cowes, the design department was transferred to the comparative safety of a property known as Fryers, a large house situated at Llanfaes near Beaumaris on the east side of Anglesey, with Harry Broadsmith as joint managing director. The office staff were housed in the main house, and various sheds and hangars, some of which had been brought from Cowes, were erected in the surrounding fifty acres of land. The transfer to Beaumaris was completed by the end of

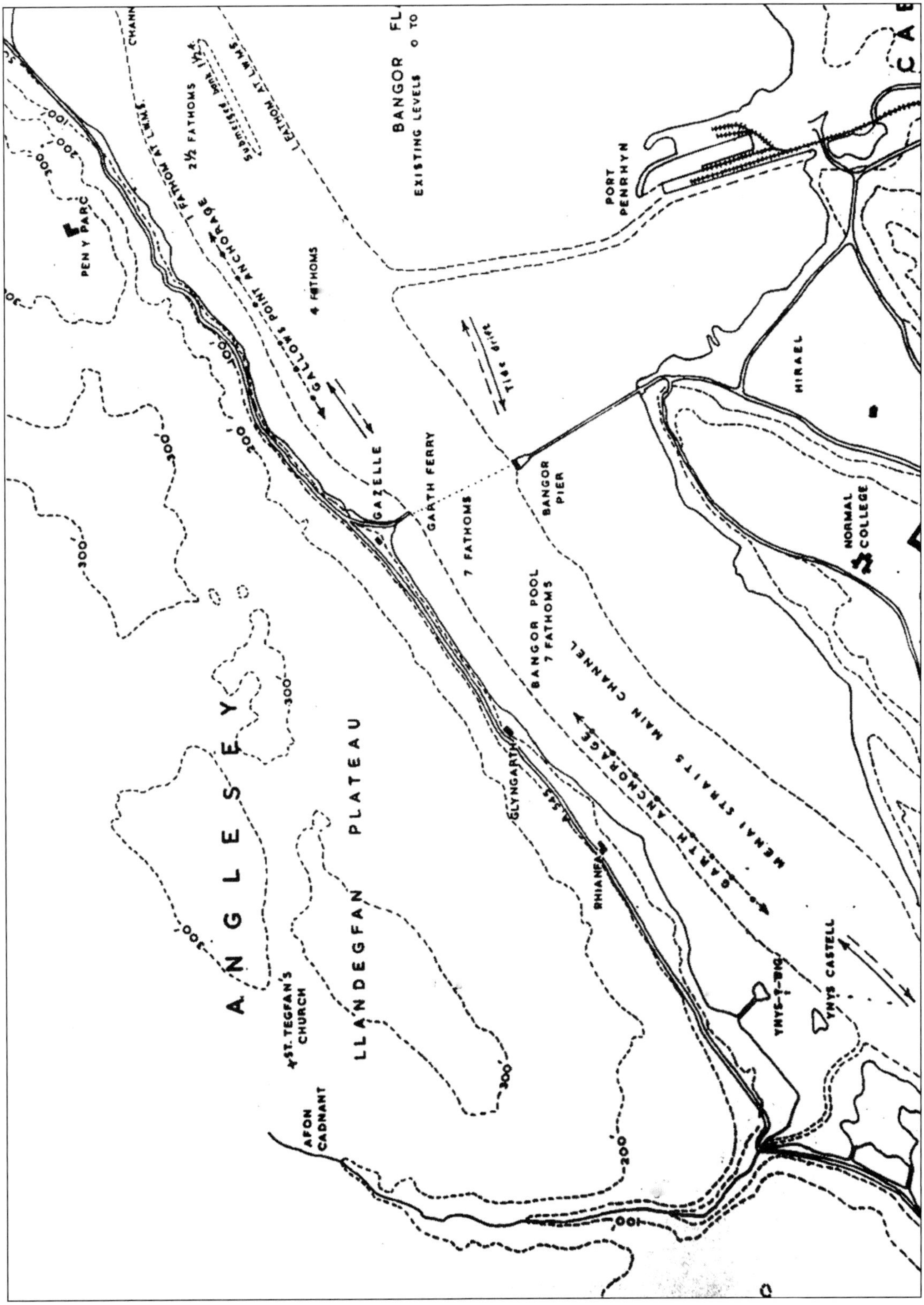
ANGLESEY
PLATEAU
LLANDEGFAN
ST. TEGFAN'S CHURCH
AFON CADNANT
PEN Y PARC
GALLOWS POINT ANCHORAGE
4 FATHOMS
1 FATHOM AT L.W.M.S.
2½ FATHOMS
BANGOR FL
EXISTING LEVELS
PORT PENRHYN
HIRAEL
Tide drift
GAZELLE
GARTH FERRY
BANGOR PIER
7 FATHOMS
BANGOR POOL
7 FATHOMS
NORMAL COLLEGE
MENAI STRAITS MAIN CHANNEL
GARTH ANCHORAGE
GLYNGARTH
RHIANFA
YNYS-Y-BIG
YNYS CASTELL
300
200
100

October 1940. In the early days, because of the lack of equipment at Beaumaris, most of the detailed work that involved a large amount of heavy jigging was subcontracted to NECACO at Llanberis.

In January 1941, at the time when the RAF was desperately short of flying boats, a personal arrangement was made between President Roosevelt and the Prime Minister, Winston Churchill, to divert seven United States Navy PBY-5 aircraft to Britain, the first aircraft arriving at Greenock on the Clyde in February 1941. However, it became apparent that a considerable number of changes in equipment would have to be made before the aircraft could be used operationally by the RAF. Despite the damage caused to aircraft and buildings when Greenock was attacked by enemy bombers on 4 May, Scottish aviation workers were able to produce the aircraft more or less on time, without the benefit of overhead cover.

The Consolidated aircraft due to arrive in Beaumaris were initially named 'Plymouth' but within a few days, this was changed to 'Catalina', a name which was subsequently applied to all of its variations throughout the world and by all air forces. The first Catalina (AH564) to arrive in Beaumaris in June 1941 was used specifically for fitting and testing equipment that was new or adapted, including new devices from the Royal Aircraft Establishment Centre at Farnborough. Its replacement in February 1944, a Catalina IV, was also used for testing equipment.

To enable RAF Coastal Command to carry out anti-submarine patrols that usually lasted fourteen to sixteen hours, or even up to twenty-six hours, Catalinas were fitted with long-range fuel tanks. As a result of the additional weight created by the tanks, it became necessary for the hull to be strengthened. As an additional aid in its fight against the U-boats, a

Harry Broadsmith Manager at Saunders Roe.
[Roy Sloan Collection]

Previous page: Flying-boat moorings on the Menai Strait.

Aerial photo of Saunders Roe.
[William Williams]

Catalina on a compass base at Beaumaris. Aircraft were placed on this circle to check the calibration of their compass. This aircraft has been fitted with a Leigh Light under its starboard wing. Built by Consolidated, this maritime patrol aircraft carried a crew of eight or nine. [Hilary Date]

Leigh searchlight was fitted on the underside of the aircraft to provide a powerful beam for detecting surface submarines during night-time operations. The bomb-carrying capability of the Catalina was increased from 500 *lbs* to 1,000 *lbs* (later versions carried 1,500 *lbs* of bombs), which allowed depth charges to be slung underneath the plane in special racks. Long-distance flights required reliable navigational equipment and the British DR Compass was installed. The Sperry automatic pilot, fitted by the Americans, was removed from the aircraft as it was unsatisfactory and a cabin heater had to be stripped out because it interfered with several important British requirements.

Space was always at a premium in Beaumaris and even though the 'red hangar', had been brought from Cowes, it was found necessary to make use of buildings within the town of Beaumaris, including Chesterton's garage in Chapel Street, where the wooden hulls for the Supermarine Walrus aircraft were constructed prior to being transported to the Isle of Wight for final assembly. The pavilion at the end of the pier was brought into use to store loose equipment removed from aircraft on arrival whilst conversion work was carried out on the planes. Even the stables at a house called Bryn Hyfryd were utilised as the Embodiment Loan Store. The Red Hill and Baron Hill stables on the outskirts of Beaumaris were also used for storing equipment such as wing trestles. By November 1943, all the stores were brought back under one roof in the west hangar. With the increasing amount of work, it was necessary to divide the Beaumaris staff between the three sections dealing with the Short Shetland, R.14/40 (code for the Supermarine Walrus) and the Consolidated Catalina.

The number of people working at Beaumaris varied – between August 1941 and December 1941, the staff had increased from 35 to 167, and then to 200 by April 1942. By July 1942, the number employed on the American aircraft had dropped to 100, reflecting the fall in the number of Catalina arrivals from America. By September 1942, the number had again increased to 200 because with more Catalinas were arriving in Beaumaris.

Catalinas at their moorings on the Menai Strait.
[R. E. Roberts]

Landing party preparing to bring Catalina 1b FP115 ashore at Beaumaris. Note the row of radar antennae on the hull towards the front. Beaumaris Lifeboat Station can be seen in the distance and two other Catalinas moored out in the Strait.
[Hilary Date]

Three Catalinas moored out in the Strait with the mountains of Snowdonia as a background. [Hilary Date]

A Catalina being moved off the compass base at Fryers.
[Hilary Date]

A foreman and some of the female staff at Saunders Roe, Beaumaris alongside a Catalina. [John Stops]

Production planning was extremely difficult, if not impossible, due to the numbers and types of aircraft arriving at Beaumaris. Nevertheless, such aircraft still required extensive modifications due to changes to planned specifications. Rather than change the specification during production in America, it was decided to deal with modifications at Beaumaris. Many of the problems arose because of confusion between the terms 'alteration' and 'modification' and their application to aircraft. It was eventually agreed with the Modification Centre at Roosevelt Field in America, which was responsible for dealing with aircraft destined to be flown to this country, that any changes to aircraft in America would be described as 'modifications' and any changes in this country would be 'alterations.' In addition, the prefix 'A' was allocated to Catalina aircraft, 'B' to Kingfisher, 'C' to Coronado, 'D' to Seamew and 'E' to Mariner.

Considerable difficulties were experienced with defective instruments having been installed in incoming aircraft and, since spares were not available and repairs were dependant on specialist knowledge, a representative from Carlux of Chester would call to inspect such instruments and, when possible, repair them on the spot. RAF personnel were also involved in rectifying faulty electrical equipment due, it was stated, to lack of care in its installation in America.

Once a flying boat had landed on the Strait, it had to be guided to its allotted mooring by one of two official launches, *Saro I* or *Saro II*, crewed by individuals well-versed in the tidal conditions of the Strait. Once the aircraft was secured, the crew would then be taken ashore. A third vessel, *Perula*, owned by Winifred Brown, was also involved in a variety of tasks for Saunders Roe.

Winifred Brown was asked in the 1920s whether she had thought of taking up flying as 'she was good at handling cars!' After a few lessons in a Tiger Moth G-EBLV, with communication between pilot and pupil restricted to 'shouting down a gas tube purchased from Woolworth', she obtained her licence on 13 April 1927. Within three years, she entered and

A tractor being hitched up to a Coronado at Beaumaris.
[John Morris]

won the Royal Aero Club King's Cup at an average speed of 102.7 mph, the first and only woman to do so.

After ten years of flying, she sold her aircraft and re-invested the proceeds in a 45-foot ketch, *Perula* (originally named *Alec Randles*) built as a fishing boat in 1932 by A. M. Dickie & Sons, Bangor and powered by a 4-cylinder 40 hp RN diesel engine. Subsequent to re-conditioning the seized-up engine at a cost £161 10s., and a further £584 15s. to make the vessel seaworthy, it was launched from the Bangor boatyard in June 1936, with a new main mast and Bermudian yawl-rigged.

It was whilst returning from a trip to Norway aboard the vessel that Winifred Brown and her husband heard the news that Britain had declared war on Germany. Ever watchful for planes and U-boats on their journey home, they arrived safely at their base at Ynys-y-Big, Menai Bridge on 5 September 1939. Even though their vessel (listed as FD61 for the duration of the war) was a converted trawler, their first attempt at earning a living by catching fish ended with a loss rather than a profit. Early in 1941, Brown was advised that *Perula* was being requisitioned by the Admiralty but, before the requisition order could be served, Harry Broadsmith, Joint Managing Director at Saunders Roe, decided that due to the increasing workload at Beaumaris, the services of the vessel would be required on the Menai Strait.

Winifred Brown and Ronald Adams on board the Perula.
[Hilary Date]

With the increase in the number of aircraft arrivals, Les Ash, Second-in-Command and Chief Test Pilot at Saunders Roe, decided that the number of moorings spaced between Beaumaris and Menai Bridge had to be increased to thirty to accommodate the additional aircraft expected, and

Martin Mariner (PBM-3B) Mk1 JX103 on the front lawn at Fryers, Beaumaris, October 1943. It flew with 524 Squadron. [W. Williams & Hilary Date]

Vought-Sikorsky Model OS2U-3 (Kingfisher) at Beaumaris. [W Williams]

An experimental Spitfire floatplane at Beaumaris. [Hilary Date]

Saunders Roe works staff, Beaumaris. [John Morris]

Leslie Ash, chief test pilot at Beaumaris.
[Roy Sloan Collection]

that Brown would be responsible for their location. The difficult and heavy task of laying these was undertaken by the well-experienced crew of the *Lydia Eva*. However, future maintenance work on the buoys would be undertaken by *Perula* and, to enable inspections to be carried out on a monthly basis, a derrick capable of lifting a ton, was fitted to the deck.

Whenever a seaplane landed on the Menai Strait, directions were given by Flying Control, either by radio or Aldis Lamp, as to mooring arrangements and *Saro I* or *Saro II* would be instructed to assist the plane to its moorings and then take the crew ashore. If space ashore was limited and the plane had to remain at its moorings, a pilot would run the engines every seven days or so whilst the aircraft taxied along the Strait. As soon as a space became available ashore, the plane would be towed by its stern, so as to give more control to the direction of travel, to a point where the aircraft could be handed over to a beaching party waiting on the concrete apron (built in April 1941). Later models were fully amphibious but, for the earlier versions, a set of wheels would be temporarily fitted to enable it to be hauled onto dry land. Once ashore, after it had been washed with fresh water, all (attractive) portable equipment, such as clocks, emergency rations, thermos flasks, etc inside the plane were listed, checked and stored. A period of twenty-one or so days was usually sufficient to allow checks, alterations or conversions to be carried out to the plane whilst inside a hangar. Once reloaded with the appropriate loose equipment, it would then have its magnetic compass checked on the Compass Base.

When all the necessary alterations and adaptations had been completed, and prior to being handed over to the RAF, Leslie Ash, Saunders Roe's Chief Test Pilot would take the aircraft for a test flight (S/Ldr Ash was a First World War fighter pilot and it was in an Auster IV floatplane VF517 that he piloted his last aircraft having 10,000 flying hours to his credit and having flown over 100 aircraft).

A. M. Dickie & Sons Ltd

The Dickie family took over the boatyard at Hirael, Bangor in 1925 and in the following forty years, some 328 boats, ranging from the smallest dinghy to large luxury yachts, were built there. During the Second World War, the yard's production role changed from boats for the leisure industry to vessels for the Admiralty including eleven Motor Launches (MLs), six Motor Gun Boats (one of these, MGB 314 commanded by Lt Dunstan Curtis, took part in the St Nazaire raid in 1942, see Chapter 8), ten Motor Torpedo Boats, one landing craft and four forty-five-foot motor fishing vessels. The craft used by the coastal forces were designed for mass production for the Admiralty by the Fairmile Marine Company. Pre-fabricated hull parts, consisting of wooden diagonal planking on plywood frames, were assembled at a number of boat yards in the United Kingdom, including Dickie's. The living space on board for the crew was uncomfortable and had to accommodate eighteen men and officers in the smaller vessels, and thirty-three officers and men in the larger ones. Space was limited and uncomfortable with the ever-present hazard of a fire or explosion due to the use of petrol rather than diesel engines, and the need to store large quantities of fuel on the upper deck. Although cooking facilities were available within a small galley, the meals produced were dependent on the expertise and versatility of a willing non-trained crew member.

Dowsett-Mackay Engineering Construction Company Ltd

Harry Lyttelton Dowsett was the chairman of a number of companies responsible for the construction of a variety of products, including pre-stressed, pre-cast railway sleepers and small craft for the Admiralty. In 1940, he bought control of the company trading in Lowestoft as Brooke Marine Motor Craft Ltd which was later re-named Brooke Marine Ltd. The old shipyard in the relative safety of Dinas in Port Dinorwic (where twenty-nine ships ranging in size between 40 and 860 tons had been built in the period between 1849 and 1897) became the company's new home during the Second World War.

On arrival in about 1943, the name of the company was changed from Brooke Marine Ltd to Dowsett-Mackay Engineering Construction Company Ltd (known locally as Dow-Mac). The works was managed by George Henry McGruor and Dave Mackenzie. Although most of the men employed by the company were recruited locally, some specialists were transferred from the company's headquarters at Lowestoft. The large sheds that were built over the site, including the old slipway, facilitated the assembly and launch of the marine craft.

Pre-fabricated steel sections, manufactured at Lowestoft, were brought

Harry L. Dowsett.

Dowsett-Mackay barges being assembled in Port Dinorwic. [Brooke Archives]

Bottom left: Jim Potter working at Dow-Mac, Port Dinorwic. [Eirwen Potter]
Bottom right: Completed Dow-Mac barge being launched at Port Dinorwic. [Emyr Owen]

by road to Port Dinorwic where they were stored on the seafront (and at Ala Las and St Helens Road in Caernarfon). These were then assembled to form flat-bottomed, all-riveted tugs of approximately fifty-feet in length, powered by a single-screw petrol engine, and a larger version of approximately fifty-five feet, powered by a twin-screw petrol engine. Both had a small, open wheelhouse aft, and were used for towing sixty-foot barges which were also constructed in Port Dinorwic. The completed unicraft, as they were called, undertook sea trials on the Menai Strait against a measured mile between Rowen Bay, Port Dinorwic and Llanfairisgaer.

The tugs and barges were used as supply boats in the Persian Gulf waterways. Some had also been destined for use in the Far East in support of operations against Japan but, as a result of the dramatic ending of the war by the dropping of two atomic bombs in 1945, many of the unicraft became surplus to requirements.

Diamonds

The depression in trade which followed the First World War affected the diamond industry as much as any other and caused many of the highly-skilled workers, whose expertise had been nurtured over generations in Belgium and Holland, to be laid-off, leaving but a handful to run depleted factories. Paradoxically, with the threat of war looming, there was a fresh demand for diamonds because of their negotiating value and transportability. Diamonds, whether gems or industrial, are prized possessions at any time, but in time of war, their value increased considerably.

Since less than 40% of the supply of rough diamonds is suitable for cutting into gem stones, it led to the industry developing ways of using the ever-increasing stock of inferior diamonds. The stones that were free from flaws could either be cut, prior to being set in tools or even in some cases, used in tools without cutting. Those that were flawed could only be used in industry after being crushed to powder.

Diamond cutters and polishers, Bangor, 1941. [Hans Wins].

Antwerp and Amsterdam had figured prominently in the cutting and polishing of diamonds, and London for handling and selling. When war seemed inevitable, a committee appointed by the British Board of Trade had the responsibility of ensuring that diamonds shipped to Antwerp and Amsterdam were stones suitable for gem-cutting only. The British Government effectively placed an embargo on the export of industrial diamonds, thus preventing Germany from acquiring a reserve at a time when they were urgently required by their industry. A report dated November 1939 stated, 'It is suspected that Industrial Diamonds probably from Brazil intended for Germany are being carried by ship's officers and stewards in Dutch and Belgian ships.'

With the invasion of Holland and Belgium by German forces, a few of the diamond-cutters managed to escape to Britain but it left Germany in control of most of the labour force and diamond-cutting tools.

Hubert Huxley Owen, diamond cutter at Bangor, 1941. [Diana Morton].

Directly after the First World War, the Government established a scheme in Brighton to teach disabled servicemen the art of cutting and polishing gems. However, because of the vulnerability of the south coast immediately after Dunkirk, the decision was taken to establish a new diamond industry in Bangor, north Wales by transferring some of the work from Brighton. A. Monnickendam, a Hatton Garden trader who was put in charge of the operation, took some Dutch and Belgian diamond cutters and a few apprentices, with him to Bangor. He was also joined by Henry Lek, a diamond cutter and polisher, who had fled with his family from Antwerp, just prior to the German occupation.

The factory in Bangor was initially set up above the Burton's Tailoring shop in the High Street where the polishing and cutting machines which had been brought from Brighton, were installed and maintained by a local man, Jack Davies. Similar small industrial diamond factories were also established in Farrar Road and near Penrhyn Hall in Bangor.

Some local boys joined the diamond workforce as apprentices straight from school and became very proficient as a result of the tuition provided by their continental tutors. Their wage was 15s a week, reduced to 13s. 6d. after stoppages, and they worked from 8 a.m. to 5 p.m. Because of its contribution to industry generally and to armaments in particular, the diamond industry was a reserved occupation and workers in the trade were not liable to be called up to the forces. The *North Wales Chronicle* for 21 March 1941 reported,

Diamond cutters and polishers, Bangor, 1941. [Hans Wins].

> Diamond Cutting – Bangor's New Industry – Who in Bangor prior to the war would have dared predict that the city would have become a centre of the important diamond cutting industry. But for some time a well known diamond cutting firm which had carried on business in Antwerp and Amsterdam is now operating in High Street, Bangor with a staff of sixty. In the room where they are employed on their precious stones, Dutch, English, Flemish, French and Welsh is spoken – the last language by five young local lads who have been taken on and are now learning the highly skilled trade. The owner of the business is Mr Monnickendam.

Rough diamonds were purchased from the Diamond Trading Company and Monnickendam travelled to London once a month to the diamond syndicate for an allocation of rough diamonds, the allocation being based on the size of the factory. Ninety per cent of the production at Bangor was exported to the USA, as part payment for armaments and other imports into the country under the Lend-Lease agreement.

The town of Colwyn Bay also became involved in the diamond trade at the beginning of the war when Gerrit Wins arrived from Antwerp with his family to live at Clifton House (9 Bay View Road). He, together with Max Frish, formed a company – Frish and Wins Ltd – to cut and polish diamonds in accommodation rented from Bevans the ironmongers, in Princess Drive.

The initial consignment of diamond-cutting and polishing machines made by Slamco of New York was lost when the ship bringing them across the Atlantic was torpedoed, but the second consignment of twenty-five machines arrived safely.

Rough diamonds, which were obtained from the Diamond Trading Company, the selling section of De Beers Consolidated Mines, were described as melee (from the French *melange*) which is a mixture of different quality rough diamonds – crinkled dark melee to describe irregular shaped diamonds or dark when they contain dark impurities (known as *piqué* in French). The size of the diamonds was established by putting them through sieves of various sizes and detailed as +12, +11, etc. When diamonds were required, the purchaser would go to London to inspect 'sights' arranged every month during the war years, but now held ten times a year. Payment for the diamonds was always on a cash before delivery basis.

Mr Monnickendam remained in Bangor for approximately sixteen months until November 1941 when he decided to return to Brighton, accompanied by eight of the apprentices. Mr Gerrit Wins and Mr Aardewerk then took over the Bangor operation and, at the same time, moved the diamond-cutting equipment to the Liberal Club, Llys Gwynedd, Bangor.

At the end of the war, most of the Belgium and Dutch diamond workers returned to their respective countries and the Bangor factory was closed (although Mr M. Coronel, director of Technical Diamonds Ltd had stated that they intended to continue with the industry at Bangor). Mr J. K. Smit, a well-known manufacturer of industrial diamond tools, employed some of the workers trained by Mr Wins, when he took over the Colwyn Bay works. Mr Smit's family had left Holland before the war and had set up a factory at Coventry but, because of the intense bombing of that city, they moved to Colwyn Bay in about 1942. His uncle, Mr Jan Kors, was involved in bringing diamonds from the continent on HMS *Walpole* before the Germans could get hold of them. A film based on this clandestine exercise was made called *Operation Amsterdam*.

Another evacuated industry: staff of the Daimler motor company of Coventry at Penrhyn Castle. [AC]

Notes

1. GAS, XM1301.
2. GAS, X/DQ/1783.
3. Percy Hunting's private diary.
4. GAS, DQ1783.
5. GAS, Q1783.
6. GAS, XM/1301–17.
7. Percy Hunting's private diary.
8. GAS, XB2/417.

Chapter 9
The Armed Forces

The Royal Navy

HMS Thetis

Although not strictly part of the story of north Wales in the Second World War, the loss of the submarine *Thetis* in 1939 is inexorably linked to the region and is worthy of mention here. HMS *Thetis*, a modern T-class submarine of 1,100 tons, left the Cammell Laird shipyard in Birkenhead on the morning of 1 June 1939 for her sea trials which consisted of checking the submarine's diving machinery and adjusting her underwater trim, prior to being handed over to the Navy. She was accompanied by the civilian tug, *Grebecock*, whose role was to ensure that shipping was kept well clear during the trials.

On board the 275-feet long submarine were her full crew of fifty-three officers and men, together with fifty passengers – yard technicians and civilian and naval observers. Prior to the start of the trials, the passengers were given the opportunity of being transferred to the accompanying tug, but they all decided to stay on board the submarine.

The captain, Lieut-Cdr Bolus, gave orders to begin the three-hour trials by taking her down. Despite flooding the ballast-tanks, she remained on the surface. Even after flooding the auxiliary tanks, she was only partially submerged. To establish why this was happening, various tests were undertaken including the checking of the torpedo tubes. The Torpedo Officer, Lieut Woods, methodically checked each tube by lifting the handle of the test-cock fitted on the rear doors. When he came to open the test-cock on tube N$^{o.}$ 5, no water came out, which should have indicated that the tube was empty of water. To inspect the inside of the tube, it was necessary to open the rear door and, as both Woods and another crew member struggled with the opening lever, the door suddenly crashed open and the sea poured in. It was eventually discovered that the tiny hole in the test cock had been blocked by thick enamel paint and this had been overlooked during the course of inspection at the shipyard.

Despite putting the vessel into full-speed astern and at the same time, blowing the ballast tanks to

HMS Thetis *being launched int Birkenhead. 1939. [AC]*

Attempting to rescue the crew of HMS Thetis.
[Roy Sloan Collection]

force the water out, *Thetis* remained 160 feet below the surface. When, after three hours, the officers aboard the *Grebecock* realised that the *Thetis* had not surfaced, naval vessels were ordered into the area. However, due to the lack of an adequate rescue plan and inaccurate information concerning the position of the submarine, hours slipped by while conditions on board steadily deteriorated.

Attempts had been made to make use of the forward escape chamber, but the pressure caused by the depth under water proved too much. Nevertheless, work carried out by the men on board caused the stern to slowly rise towards the surface whilst the bow remained on the bottom. By making use of the aft escape chamber, pressure on those using it would be less since it was nearer the surface. Eventually, the crew of the destroyer *Brazen* spotted the stern of the *Thetis* sticking out of the water and two crewmen, Capt Oram and Lieut Woods, who suddenly appeared on the surface near the vessel. The message that they brought with them described the desperate scene in the submarine. Dr Ramsey Stark, a general practitioner in Holyhead, received a call from the Coastguard station to advise him that a flying boat was in Holyhead harbour to take him out to the scene of the disaster. As an additional precaution, Llandudno lifeboat was asked to stand by in case the sea was too rough for the plane to land. Within fifteen minutes of leaving Holyhead, the plane landed safely about 100 yards from where the *Thetis* was lying. The doctor was transferred by a naval cutter to HMS *Vigilant* so that he could attend to Capt Oram and Lt Wood who had escaped from the submarine. Both showed signs of asphyxia and severe shock. After *Thetis* had been submerged for twenty-hours, two more men escaped – Stoker Walter

The salvaged HMS Thetis *beached October 1939 about 40 yards from the shore at Traeth Bychan on the north coast of Anglesey.*
[John W. Morris]

Arnold and Frank Shaw, a Cammell Laird engine-fitter and Dr Stark was taken by naval pinnace to HMS *Brazon* to see them. Lt Wood was eventually transferred to HMS *Eskimo* and, accompanied by Dr Stark, was taken to Liverpool where he was admitted to the Southern Hospital.

In the meantime, a number of ships had arrived but still there was little that could be done apart from placing a light wire around the stern to prevent it sinking. As soon as a tug arrived from Birkenhead with oxy-acetylene equipment, an attempt was made to cut a hole in the hull but, as work started, the wire holding the vessel in position snapped and the *Thetis* once more sank to the bottom, still with ninety-nine men on board.

The vessel was eventually floated and beached at Traeth Bychan before being towed to Holyhead on the 10 November. Six coal miners from Cannock Chase, Staffordshire, all trained rescue workers and specially

The grave of some of the crew of HMS Thetis *in Holyhead.*
[AC]

engaged by the Admiralty, arrived in Holyhead at the end of the month. Their task was to enter the sealed stern compartments of the *Thetis* and recover the bodies. Apart from private arrangements made by relatives of the deceased members of the crew, most of those who died in the vessel were buried with full military honours at Maeshyfryd cemetery at in Holyhead.

HMS *Thetis* was subsequently taken back to Cammell Laird and was re-launched twelve months later as HMS *Thunderbolt*. She sailed on her first operational patrol on 3 December 1940 and was depth-charged and sunk by the Italian warship *Cicognan* off Cape San Vito, Sicily on 14 March 1943. For the second time she was lost with all hands.

HMS *Glendower*

In the 1930s, Butlin Camps had provided holiday-makers with regimented accommodation, food and entertainment at an affordable price. As far as the Admiralty was concerned, these were ideally located for training camps for naval ratings at the outbreak of the Second World War. When the camp in Skegness was requisitioned in the autumn of 1939, it was re-named HMS *Royal Arthur* and, in common with other training establishments, referred to as a ship. In the early part of the war, when the Admiralty was anxious to establish a new naval training camp in a comparatively safe part of the country, Billy Butlin was asked to find a suitable location. Having visited south Caernarfonshire before hostilities started, with a view of establishing a holiday camp in the area, he suggested a site at Penychain, just outside Pwllheli, to which the Admiralty agreed. With a proven record at Skegness, Butlin was given the task of building the camp which was to be very much in the style of his other holiday camps.

The building project at Penychain included the provision of an adequate water supply, sanitation, land drainage and storage accommodation. In the latter case, a nearby property called Broom Hall and its outbuildings were found to be adequate. Once completed, 100 officers and 5,000 ratings were housed in rows of chalets, whilst 500 Wrens, well-guarded from the remainder of the camp, had their own billets. Bryn Beryl Hospital, built near Fourcrosses in 1924, was extended by the Royal Navy in 1942 to serve the training station.

Having considered the names HMS *Caernarvon* and HMS *Llewellyn* for the new establishment, the name HMS *Glendower* was finally selected as appropriate for the district, although it was pointed out by the Head of N Branch that there was already a paddle minesweeper by the name of HMS *Glengower*, which might cause some confusion. The name *Glendower* was settled upon, believing that 'it would be easier to change the name of the Paddle Minesweeper if necessary.'[1]

HMS *Glendower* was used initially as an overflow camp for HMS *Royal Arthur*, and naval recruits continued to be kitted out at that establishment. Those destined for HMS *Glendower* travelled by train to Pwllheli, where they were met by a fleet of lorries which conveyed them to Penychain where they were confronted by a large building site and regimented rows of tents. These would serve as accommodation for both officers and ratings, offices and stores until permanent buildings had been completed. The Commissioning Order issued by the Lord Commissioner of the Admiralty stated that, 'having directed that His Majesty's Ship *Glendower* is to be commissioned on Tuesday the 1st October 1940 or as soon afterwards as circumstances permit as a Training Establishment, independent command.'[2]

Once HMS *Glendower* became independent of HMS *Royal Arthur*, it was then administered by the Commander-in-Chief Western Approaches. However, according to the Flag Officer-in-Charge, some confusion remained,

> I wonder if you could tell me under whose administration HMS *Glendower* is supposed to be. Actually we have had no official correspondence about her, and the Vice-Admiral rather feels that his jurisdiction extends to coastline (i.e. to Bardsey Island). We unofficially gather that *Glendower* herself seems to think that she is under us, but going from the coastline rule she is undoubtedly under Milford. Could you possibly clear this up for me please?[3]

The camp, under the command of Captain J. Figgins, provided Ordinary Seamen Part I and Part II training, also a gunnery course for Acting Seamen. One hundred and fifty trainees arrived each week for a thirteen-week training programme. Recruits, from both the Royal and Merchant Navy, were also assessed as to their future potential and possible

Photographs of HMS Glendower *are very scarce. The following three pictures show ratings at HMS* Royal Arthur, *another naval training station also located in a Butlins Holiday Camp.*

Boat drill for naval ratings. [Butlins Archives]

Naval ratings being kitted out.
[Butlins Archives]

Naval ratings learning the art of hammock hanging outside the chalets.
[Butlins Archives]

commission according to their ability and the work which they could undertake under war-time conditions.

The chalets for holiday campers were not suitable for naval ratings since their size only allowed one double bed, a single bed and a cupboard. However, to prevent a breach of King's Regulations, it was necessary for the double bed to have a wooden divider! Those ratings that had the misfortune of having to stay in these chalets during winter months, suffered greatly from the cold, as no form of heating was provided (these camps had only been used by holiday-makers during summer months). Even sleeping in their overcoats did little to ease their discomfort and as a result the sickbays became overcrowded with men suffering from colds and influenza. Eventually, the Admiralty relented by installing tubular electric heaters in the chalets, and steam-operated blow-heaters in the dining-halls which were equally as cold in the winter.

Although run on strictly naval lines, the holiday-camp image prevailed. The swimming pool, for instance, was utilised to teach ratings the art of handling a boat and survival techniques. Training films were shown at the camp cinema, as well as health warnings and precautions to be taken against venereal disease. Many ratings fainted as a result of seeing on the screen the unexpectedly large images of the effects of the disease.

The task of inflicting regulation haircuts at the camp was given to Molly Rowntree, who had previously been responsible for hair-cutting at HMS *Royal Arthur*. As a result of her barber shop being destroyed when the camp was bombed, she moved to HMS *Glendower*, only to find that hair-cutting would be performed under canvas. This she endured for a few months until the marquee took off in a storm, at which point she left to work in a fashionable hairdressing salon in London for the remainder of the war.

The HMS *Glendower* football team participated in the Welsh League (North) and managed to win the cup during the 1945–6 season.

Perhaps the best-known resident of HMS *Glendower* was the Duke of Edinburgh, who as Lieut Prince Philip of Greece, RN, served as an Instructor Officer at HMS *Glendower* between 4 June and 6 August 1946. Lieutenant Mountbatten then moved on to set up the Petty Officers' School at HMS *Royal Arthur* in Corsham in September 1946.

A great deal of correspondence and discussions were generated in the 1940s when it was realised that the camp had been built without reference to the local council. This is confirmed in a letter written on 30 August 1940 by Mr T. Owen, County Surveyor, to W. E. Butlin.[4] It stated that although the camp was purported to be outside the provisions of the County Planning Scheme (as a result of being built for Admiralty use during the war), Butlin was reminded that when it became his private property after the war, it would become subject to the Planning Scheme. In an attempt to resolve the *impasse*, plans were sent, on behalf of W. E. Butlin, on 15 November 1940 to the chairman of the Rural District Planning Committee and the Caernarvonshire County Council, seeking their consent under the town planning scheme. In his accompanying letter, Butlin stated that the camp had been built for the Government on the understanding that it could be used as a holiday camp after the war.[5]

Less than two months after the end of the war, a meeting was arranged on 24 October 1945 in Committee Room 16 at the House of Commons, between a deputation consisting of Lady Megan Lloyd George, MP and thirteen other Welsh Members of Parliament, and the First Lord of the Admiralty, the Minister of Town and Country Planning and a number of other officials. Its purpose was to discuss the initial purchase of the land by W. E. Butlin, the contract/arrangement established between him and the Admiralty and, more importantly, its use after the war.

It was pointed out that prior to the Admiralty deciding to use it as a training establishment, Butlin had already completed negotiations for the purchase of the land and for its use as a holiday camp in Pwllheli. Similar 'deals' had been executed in different parts of the country without town planning consideration, such was the urgency for training establishments to be established during the war. Discussions were primarily centred on ways of preventing Butlin proceeding with converting the now defunct training establishment into a holiday camp.

However, the thought of such a scheme taking as long as five years and the possibility of Butlin having to be compensated by as much as half-a-

The extension to Bryn Beryl Hospital built by the Royal Navy to accommodate patients from HMS Glendower. The standard pre-fabricated concrete structure was still in use as a ward in 2008.
[W. Alister Williams Collection]

million pounds from local authority funds, made them realise the futility of even considering it. The Minister of Town and Country Planning was asked whether the camp could be used 'for education or for a convalescent home or something of that sort'. He confirmed that this was possible, but subject to the payment of compensation. The delegates were reminded that the camp had cost £559,375 (as a holiday camp) with an additional £104,625 being spent on 'special equipment for naval requirements), a total of £664,000. If Butlin were to be compensated by as much as half-a-million pounds then this money would have to be paid from local authority funds. It was eventually realised that, short of a special Act of Parliament to deal with the matter, the position could only be regarded as a *fait accompli*. The Minister of Town and Country Planning did however put forward the suggestion,

> At the moment Butlin feels there is an element of doubt about his position. It might be possible by negotiations to get some improvement in the situation. For instance, a number of points have been put to me that it might be possible for him to surrender part of the foreshore and leave that free for walkers or ramblers or passers-by to walk along without interruption. We might be able to get him to plant trees and shut off some of the view from the outside and various other amenities which could cost him money. I think if one tried to negotiate with him he might probably agree to do them. Supposing one had an enquiry which came down on his side, as I think would almost be inevitable, what then? My negotiating powers have gone, and I am wondering which would be better way to proceed.'[6]

Such was the animosity felt against Billy Butlin, and the fact that he had been able to acquire Welsh land for a holiday camp, deviously in their view, that the vociferous delegates, acting in the parochial rather than national interest, resorted to any means to prevent it – even though the local economy would probably benefit from visitors to the camp which would provide employment for local people. In the end, Butlin won the day and the Pwllheli Holiday Camp opened in Pwllheli on 29 March 1947.[7]

Local distinguished serviceman:
Robert Charles Michael Vaughan Wynn, DSC, 7th Baron Bewborough (1917–98)

The Hon. Robert Charles Michael Vaughan Wynn, son of the 6th Baron Newborough, of Glynllifon, generally known as Micky Wynn, served as 2nd Lieutenant (Special Reserve) in cavalry regiments from 1935 until he was invalided in 1940. He subsequently joined the Royal Navy and was given command of a yacht that was responsible for air-sea rescue for HMS Daedalus, *the RN air station at Lee-on-Solent. A day after he arrived, he was ordered to Ramsgate to participate in the Dunkirk evacuation. After five successful trips, his yacht was hit by a shell and only managed to reach Ramsgate with the boat on the point of sinking.*

The threat posed by Hitler's biggest battleship, the Tirpitz, *and the fact that there was only one dock on the western European seaboard large enough to accommodate her – the SS Normandie dry dock at St Nazaire – resulted in the decision to destroy its lock-gates. The Chariot Force that sailed from Falmouth on 26 March 1942 consisted of HMS* Campbeltown *(originally the USS* Buchanan *suitably modified to resemble a German warship), together with two escorting destroyers and eighteen coastal vessels, one of which, Motor Torpedo Boat 74, commanded by Sub Lieut R. C. M. V. Wynn RNVR, was towed by HMS* Campbeltown *due to it being the smallest vessel and only having a limited operational range.*

If HMS Campbeltown *had failed to reach the lock gates, then MTB 74 would have deployed its two torpedoes, each of which contained 1800 lbs of explosives that were fitted with a delayed-action charge, designed to explode after an interval on the seabed. This, however, was not necessary as the lock-gates were successfully rammed and destroyed by the five tonnes of explosives that HMS* Campbeltown *had on board.*

The greater part of the original flotilla was destroyed including Wynn's MTB and, of the 353 sailors and 268 commandos that took part, 169 were killed, five that had been left ashore managed to find their way home by various routes whilst the remainder of the men that survived were taken prisoner including Micky Wynn. After a number of attempts at escaping he was eventually imprisoned in Colditz Castle where he remained until repatriated

Sub-Lieutenant Hon Michael Wynn, RNVR.
[Lady Newborough]

MTB 74 *which Micky Wynn commanded on the St Nazaire Raid of 1942.*

in January 1945 on medical grounds. For his role in the raid he was awarded the Distinguished Service Cross. The Normandie dock remained unused for the duration of the war.

When Micky Wynn succeeded his father as 7th Baron Newborough in 1965, he inherited 20,000 acres in north Wales. In his latter years he lived at Rhug, Corwen.

The Army

North Wales, with its varied terrain and nearness to the sea, was ideally suited for military training bases for all three services, especially as the area was sparsely populated, devoid of industry (at the beginning of the war) and was considered to be comparatively safe from enemy attack. With the threat of war looming during the 1930s, much of the groundwork on where such bases were to be established had already been decided. Although the south coast of England was considered to be the area most at risk from a German invasion, it was not beyond the bounds of possibility for the enemy to land at any point on the British coastline, including north Wales, which was considered at risk of invasion via neutral Éire, if that country was taken over by the Germans. For this reason, army units based in north-west Wales had the dual role of training and guarding the coastline. Even though Éire maintained a state of neutrality throughout the war, thousands of Irishmen served with the British forces with the agreement of both the Irish and British governments (southern Irishmen serving in the British forces were awarded a total of 780 decorations, including eight Victoria Crosses). However, to mitigate the possible repercussions of large numbers of men in British Army uniform being seen on Irish streets, it was stipulated that those returning home on leave should wear civilian clothes. To comply with this ruling, 'civvies' were always made available for returning servicemen at the 'left luggage section' of Holyhead station.

The 46th (Liverpool Welsh) Royal Tank Regiment, formed in the spring of 1939, was stationed at Llandwrog on the outskirts of Caernarfon during the summer and autumn of 1940. As well as training on Matilda tanks at nearby Glynllifon, they were given the task of guarding the southern entrance to the Menai Strait. Other units responsible for patrolling coastal roads were:

    Penmaenmawr–Aber–Llandegai–Bangor: 226th Light Anti-Aircraft Training Regiment, RA, Conwy.
    Beaumaris–Penmon–Llanddona: 6th Bn, Royal Irish Fusiliers, Beaumaris.
    Trearddur Bay–Valley–Benllech: 6th Bn, Royal Irish Fusiliers, Trearddur Bay.
    Trearddur Bay–Valley–Newborough: 6th Bn, Royal Irish Fusiliers, Trearddur Bay.
    Menai Bridge–Caernarvon–Glynllifon: 6th Bn, Royal Irish Fusiliers, Beaumaris.
    Nevin–Llanaelhaiarn–Glynllifon:14th Bn, Royal Welch Fusiliers, Nefyn.
    Nevin–Morfa Nevin–Aberdaron: 14th Bn, Royal Welch Fusiliers, Nefyn.
    Pwllheli–Llanbedrog–Abersoch: 163rd Officer Cadet Training Unit (OCTU), Pwllheli.
    Pwllheli–Cross Road: 163rd Officer Cadet Training Unit (OCTU), Pwllheli.
    Cross Road–Portmadoc–Talsarnau: HMS *Glendower*, Penychain.
    Barmouth–Llanbedr–Harlech–Talsarnau: 164th OCTU, Barmouth.
    Barmouth–Fairbourne: 164th OCTU, Barmouth.
    Towyn–Llangelynin: Anti-Aircraft Practice Camp, RA, Towyn.
    Towyn–Aberdovey: 223rd Heavy Anti-Aircraft Training Regiment, RA, Towyn.

Until March 1943, the duplicate headquarters of the searchlight and anti-aircraft guns for Liverpool, which would have come into action if the main HQ had been put out of action, had been based at the Royal Hotel (now called Plas-y-Brenin), Capel Curig. With the number of air raids on Liverpool gradually reducing, N°· 1 Battle Camp, commanded by Major E. L. Kirby, was given permission to take over the premises, with staff and cadets being accommodated in the main building, whilst the stables and Nissen huts on the other side of the road, housed three Bren Gun Carriers, various machine guns (both British and German) and 'tons of ammunition.' The surrounding mountainous area provided practical experience of firing live ammunition and participating in various exercises for the OCTUs from Sandhurst, who had already learned the theory in the classroom. The cadets, arriving by train at Betws-y-Coed, were met by the station master and the camp commandant, prior to being transported by road to Capel

Trawsfynydd (North Camp) army training camp and artillery range. Opened in 1905 and closed 1958. It was also used to house WW2 Prisoners of War.
[Keith T. O'Brien]

Curig. It was not unusual to find an occasional fishing rod and shot-gun being carried by the cadets. However, any thought of a holiday in the mountains was soon dispelled!

The cadets, who were entirely self-sufficient, would participate in exercises, which sometimes lasted for four or five days in various parts of the mountain area, depending on the area allocated to them by the Officer Commanding, Colonel Ivor Davies, Welch Regiment, based at Llanberis. In order for the cadets to experience realistic battle conditions, an 'ambush' could occur at any time during the course of an exercise, without prior warning, to assess their reactions.

Although there were many other training camps in the area, such as the OCTU battle camp at Barmouth, there was virtually no contact between them, since travelling was governed by the strictly-controlled petrol allowance. The Advance Handling and Fieldcraft School at Llanberis had various sections, including the Lovat Scouts (named after Lord Lovat, who led the raid on Dieppe), considered to be amongst the forerunners of the Special Air Services (SAS). One of the instructors was Lieut Tasker Watkins (Welch Regiment) who was later awarded the Victoria Cross in Normandy.

The Royal Irish Fusiliers were stationed at Baron Hill, Beaumaris until the Royal Artillery arrived to carry out Search and Direction Finding courses. The Welsh Guards were stationed at both Baron Hill and nearby Henllys Hall. Baron Hill was also the base for the Intelligence Corps for a short period.

Officers of the 6th Battalion, Royal Welch Fusiliers in camp at Holyhead, 1944.
[R. T. Jones]

Local distinguished serviceman:
Rt Hon. Sir Tasker Watkins, VC, KGBE, Kt, KSJ, DL (1918–2007)
Born in Nelson, Glamorgan, Tasker Watkins served in the ranks of the Duke of Cornwall's Light Infantry before being granted an Emergency Commission as 2nd Lieutenant in the Welch Regiment in May 1941. He was appointed an instructor at the War Office Battle School, Rifle Wing, Advanced Handling and Fieldcraft School in Llanberis in September 1943. Later that year he was appointed Chief Instructor before being posted to 103rd Reinforcement Group, British Liberation Army on 27 June 1944 and served in Normandy and Northern Europe serving in the 1/5th Welch Regiment. He was appointed a temporary captain on 12 August 1944 and acting major on 22 September 1944. He was awarded the Victoria Cross for his gallantry in Normandy. The citation in the London Gazette for 2 November 1944 reads,

Acting-Major Tasker Watkins, VC, 1/5th Battalion, The Welch Regiment. [W. Alister Williams Collection]

On the evening of 16th August 1944, a Battalion of the Welch Regiment attacked objectives near Bafour. Lieutenant Watkins's company came under murderous machine gun fire while advancing through corn fields set with booby traps. At the head of his men, Lieutenant Watkins, now the only officer left, charged two machine gun posts, personally accounting for the occupants with his Sten gun. Later, his gun jamming, he threw it in the face of a German anti-tank gunner, killing him at the same moment with a pistol shot. His small remnant counter attacked. Lieutenant Watkins led a bayonet charge, destroying the enemy and finally at dusk, their wireless gone and separated from the Battalion which had withdrawn, he ordered his men to scatter, and himself personally charging and silencing an enemy machine gun post, he brought them back safely. The Officer's superb leadership not only saved his men's lives but decisively influenced the course of the battle.

Wounded in Holland, he was appointed OC Royal Engineers' Battle School, Penmaenmawr. After the war, Tasker Watkins qualified as a barrister and went on to become a High Court judge, Deputy Chief Justice for England and Wales and was knighted three times. After retiring, he became the President of the Welsh Rugby Union.

In addition to the regular army units that trained in north-west Wales, 'clandestine' units were also based in the area. When it was decided that a specialist unit would be formed within N° 10 (later N° 3 Troop) Inter-Allied Commando, there was no shortage of volunteers from amongst those men who were keen to play a more useful and active role in the war. To be considered for the special unit, each member had to speak perfect German and to have the ability to operate on his own, whenever and wherever necessary. Some still had families living under German occupation and, since particulars of many of the men were known to the Gestapo, it was decided that each one would forsake his real name and be given a new identity. 'X-Troop', as they were known, was commanded by Brian Hilton Jones who had been born in Harlech then moved at an early age to live in Caernarfon where his father, Dr Hilton Jones had his surgery. After gaining his BA degree with a double first in modern languages at Caius

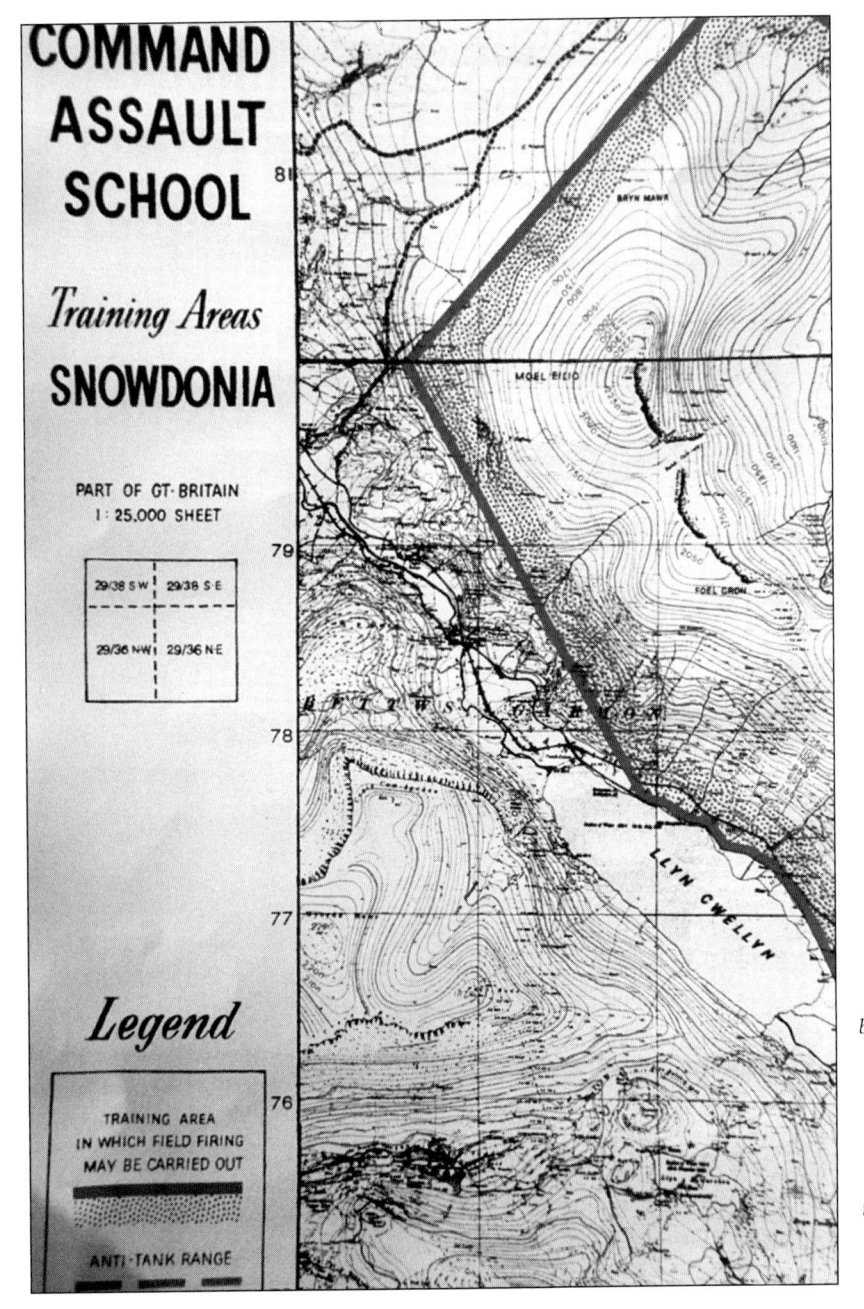

Map showing part of the boundary of the training areas in Snowdonia. Tasker Watkins recalled having access to almost any upland area between Cader Idris and the Conwy Valley. As late as the 1960s, piles of unexploded mortar bombs could still be found in this area. [AC]

College, Cambridge, he was commissioned into the Royal Artillery in 1939. He subsequently volunteered and served with N°· 4 Commando before being transferred to N°· 10 (Inter-Allied) Commando which had been formed by Lord Louis Mountbatten as Chief of Combined Operation. The Inter-Allied Commando was so-named as it was composed of a number of different nationalities including French, Belgium, Dutch, Norwegian, Polish, Yugoslav and British, as well as men who were originally from Germany and Austria. They were commanded by a British officer. Due to the fact that most of them had families still living in countries that were under Nazi control, they adopted 'British' names to conceal their true identities.

In the late 1930s, people anxious to escape persecution from the Nazis had left Germany and Austria, but those who found sanctuary in Britain were interred as enemy aliens at the outbreak of the war. Rather than be incarcerated behind barbed wire for the duration of the war, many of the men volunteered to serve in the British army only to find themselves having to carry out menial tasks in the Pioneer Corps. Capt Hilton Jones' initial task was to interview each candidate who had already been interrogated and cleared by British Security Service MI5. On 23 July 1942, the few who had been accepted, moved to Harlech where N°· 10 Commando was in the process of being formed. On 21 September, N°· 3 Troop went to a new location at Aberdyfi where they trained independently from N°· 10 Commando. Basic training, carried out between October 1942 and September 1943, included night reconnaissance on Cader Idris, an assault march across the Dyfi estuary to Plynlimon and back, and a 'sabotage' attack on RAF Towyn. Several visits were also made to Bethesda for a course on rock-climbing followed by a march, with weapons and full kit, from Bethesda to Pen-y-groes, via the Ogwen Valley, Crib Coch, Snowdon, Rhyd Ddu and the Nantlle range, and then back to base. Further training included the handling of explosives, train-driving and a parachute course at Ringway Airport, Manchester. When the decision was taken to bring N°· 10 Commando under one headquarters, rather than scattered as before along the north Wales coast, the troop left Aberdyfi for Eastbourne on 31 May 1943.

Brian Hilton Jones, who had by now been promoted to major, formed a special unit of men from the troop to carry out pre-invasion reconnaissance raids on the French coast. For these operations, he and one other member of the unit, were awarded the Military Cross and another member received a Mention in Despatches. For the actual invasion on 6 June 1944, the troop was split into small groups and attached to the various Commandos that took part. There were many casualties and, whilst on a night patrol, Maj Hilton Jones was badly wounded and taken prisoner. He was taken to a German army hospital in northern France where he was operated on. Shortly afterwards, the advancing Allied armies reached the hospital and he was brought back to Britain for further treatment.

The monument, unveiled in Penhelyg Park, Towyn in 1999, in the presence of twenty-eight survivors, commemorates the members of the X-Troop and reads,

> For the members of 3 Troop 10 (1A)
> Commando who were
> welcomed in Aberdyfi while training for
> their special duties in battle 1942–1943
> Twenty were killed in action

Members of 'X Troop', N°. 10 Commando, attend the wedding of their officer, Captain Brian Hilton Jones at Aberdyfi in 1943. A careful study of the cap badges shows personnel to have originally come from a wide variety of other units in the British Army and from foreign units. [Edwina Hilton Jones]

The Royal Air Force

Within six years of the First World War ending, 256 British airfields had been abandoned and only twenty-seven military, and seventeen civil airfields remained. However, with the realisation that Germany's military might was increasing rapidly in the 1930s, eighty-nine new airfields were built between 1935 and the outbreak of war.

The few aircraft seen over Gwynedd flying from local airfields during the First World War were the forerunners of those that participated in exhibition flights and flying circuses during the 1920s and 1930s. A flat field or a stretch of flat, firm sand was all that was required to enable planes to land and take off more often than not with eager passengers keen to experience the thrill of flying. During the same period a gliding club was established on the Lleyn peninsula. Such peace-time activities were enjoyed by most people but the news broke in 1936 that the Royal Air Force intended building an airfield at Penrhos, three miles west of Pwllheli. This was objected to strongly by members of the Welsh Nationalist Party even though it was intended that the new airfield would provide work for some 500 local people. Nevertheless, the project went ahead and when RAF Penrhos hosted the Empire Air Day on 20 May 1938, it attracted a great deal of attention and people flocked to see the attractions as described by a local paper. '(The) programme will include squadron formation drill, thrilling aerobatics, converging dive bombing, and formation drill by five Westland Wallace machines. A gas attack, defended by fast planes, will also be staged. Finally there will be a fly-past of various types of aircraft including the new Battle and Hampden types.'[8]

Violation of the Sabbath was also resented by many including the Caernarvonshire County Council and it registered its strong opposition to a proposal by the Air Ministry to amend a regulation to allow Air Gunnery and bombing practice at any time of day or night, including Sundays, throughout the year at the RAF bombing range at Hell's Mouth.[9] However, opinion on the matter varied as expressed in a local paper, 'If the recent deputation to Parliament succeeds in getting gunfire and bombing practice stopped on Sunday wouldn't it be advisable for the deputation to approach the heads of the totalitarian states and ask them in case of war not to bomb us on the Sabbath. Wouldn't that be manifestly unfair if we were not allowed to retaliate on that day.'[10]

RAF Mona
Since the First World War this airfield in the centre of Anglesey has been variously known as Heneglwys, Llangefni and later Airship Station Anglesey (it had been established as a Detached Unit of the Royal Naval Air Station, Malahide near Dublin, for use by non-rigid airships known as SSZ (Submarine Scout Zero) from 1915 to 1918). When it was re-opened in December 1942 as part of N$^{o.}$ 25 (Armament) Group, it was re-named RAF Mona and used by N$^{o.}$ 3 Air Gunnery School, flying Blackburn Bothas, Fairey Battles and Miles Martinets as towing aircraft, followed by Avro Ansons of N$^{o.}$ 8 (Observer) Advance Flying Unit from November 1943 to June 1945.

The concrete runways that were laid in 1943 not only cured the flooding problem that plagued so many grass landing grounds, but also enabled the airfield to handle any type of aircraft. The proximity of Mona to RAF Valley often caused confusion, particularly for American aircraft arriving from overseas; the first unintentional visitor being a B-24 from Marrakech on 14 March 1944.

With the end of the war in sight, and the need for aircrew being greatly reduced, flying training at Mona ceased 19 May 1945. It reopened 26 July 1946 as a relief landing ground for RAF Valley.

RAF Hell's Mouth

Situated two miles west of Abersoch, construction work on RAF Hell's Mouth was started in 1937 as a range for N°· 5 Armament Training Camp at RAF Penrhos some ten miles distant. There were no permanent structures on the airfield, apart from a few Nissen huts which were used as workshops, and accommodation was confined to tents until wooden huts were provided, together with four Bellman hangars in the early 1940s.

Due to the adverse weather that was often experienced in the area, and the consequent irregularity of bombing practice at Hell's Mouth, the airfield's role became that of a Relief Landing Ground for Flying Training Command and for emergency aircraft accommodation when space in nearby airfields was limited. The airfield was closed in July 1945.

RAF Penrhos

Work on the airfield started with 500 men beginning the excavation and levelling of the ground on 21 February 1936. The airfield was opened on 1 February 1937 with an aircraft establishment of six Westland Wallace machines. The first commanding officer, W/Cdr T. V. Lister, was also responsible for the target range located at Hell's Mouth, ten miles from Penrhos. Three miles away at Pwllheli, a marine section (later to be called N°· 51 ASR Marine Craft Unit) comprising five patrol boats, was established

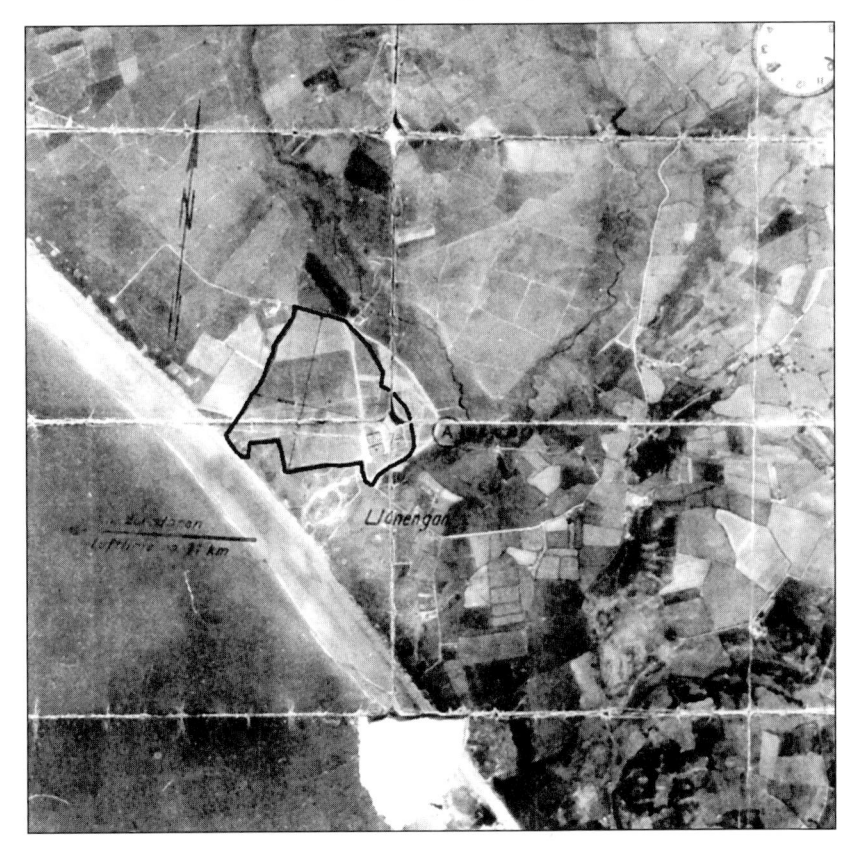

A Luftwaffe aerial reconnaissance photograph of RAF Hell's Mouth, Llanengan. Fears that the building of military airfields in rural south Caernarfonshire would attract bombing raids proved to be well-founded although, because of the range involved, the area was only subjected to a few attacks from single aircraft.
[R. E. Roberts]

RAF Penrhos photographed before the outbreak of war. The concrete roads and buildings and the silver skinned aircraft have not been camouflaged. Hard concrete or tarmac runways were never laid down at Penrhos. [R. E. Roberts]

with personnel accommodated at the Victoria Hotel.

On 1 April 1938, Penrhos was redesignated N°· 5 Armament Training Station, but at the outbreak of the war it became N°· 9 Air Observers School and W/Cdr J. J. Williamson assumed command.

With the knowledge that war was only a matter of months away, the public were given the opportunity of viewing the country's airpower:

Penrhos Air Display – on Saturday 20 May 1939 at nearly all RAF Stations in Great Britain and various Civil Aerodromes an opportunity will be afforded to the general public to see and judge for themselves how our aerial rearmament is progressing. At each station the assembly will be afforded the opportunity of seeing fighters like the Hawker Hurricane in flight at a speed of five miles a minute and bombers like the Bristol Blenheim and the Fairey Battle which fly only a little slower. Those who have seen previous air displays will be enabled to realise the immense development which has taken place in a very short space of time... the programme includes squadron formation drill by nine Audax machines, acrobatics with single-seater Hawker Fury fighters and aerobatics by a formation of three Hawker Furies... after the tea interval a similar varied and breath-taking programme will be provided including converging dive bombing by five Hawker Audax machines.'[11]

RAF Penrhos station became N°· 9 Bombing and Gunnery School (B&GS) on 1 November 1939, but by 14 June 1941 it had reverted to N°· 9 Air Observers School. A special armament course began on 20 October for fifteen air observers (navigators) who had been in the USA under the

Hawker Hurricane fighters against a snowy landscape at RAF Penrhos. [R. E. Roberts]

A detachment from RAF Penrhos begin the march back to camp after Church Parade at Llanbedrog. [R. E. Roberts]

The band from RAF Penrhos. [R. E. Roberts]

Aircrew at RAF Penrhos, c.1941. [R. E. Roberts]

The remains of WAAF quarters at West End Pwllehli, on the site now occupied by part of Ffordd y Mela and Ysgol Glan-y-Môr. [W. Alister Williams Collection]

RAF Marine Detachment at Pwllheli. Their headquarters and slipway was located at Morfa Garreg. The launches were built and maintained in this building now the site of Partington's boat yard.
[R. E. Roberts]

One of the boats belonging to the RAF Marine Detachment at Pwllheli. The large float-like object on the left of the photograph was a bombing target that would be towed out into Cardigan Bay by the launches.
[W. Alister Williams Collection]

One of the RAF launches based at Pwllheli. These were used to tow targets out into Cardigan Bay and to act as an air-sea rescue service.
[R. E. Roberts]

Empire Air Training Scheme. Trainees on the last air gunnery course to be held at Penrhos, had their passing out on 25 November 1944.

The airfield was attacked by enemy aircraft on five occasions. The first time, on 9 July 1940, resulted in two officers receiving fatal wounds from fragmentation bombs. Three blocks of officers' quarters were destroyed, two Hawker Henley aeroplanes (L3290 and L3359) of N[o.] 1 AACU were wrecked and a hangar damaged. Although part of the station was subsequently camouflaged, a further attack occurred five weeks later when a lone plane dropped bombs and machine-gunned the camp from 200 feet, injuring five airmen as well as damaging buildings and vehicles. The raids on 3 and 4 October, with bombs and incendiaries being dropped on the latter day, inflicted considerable damage but no casualties. As a result of further attacks on 9 and 10 October, six Spitfires of N°· 611 Squadron arrived from Tern Hill as a protective measure but no further attacks occurred.

RAF Towyn

The airfield, opened on the Merionethshire coast on 8 September 1940, was a base for Queen Bee and Hawker Henley aircraft of N°· 1 Anti-aircraft Co-operation Unit until its closure in May 1945. It also flew Westland Lysanders for N°· 6 Anti-aircraft Co-operation unit from February 1942 to October 1942.

Since the aircraft only had the benefit of grass for landing and take-offs, aeroplanes were often diverted to Llanbedr airfield, particularly during winter when, due to its low-lying situation, it was prone to mist and had an inclination to flood. The few buildings, including Nissen and Maycrete types, and Bellman, Besonneau and blister hangars, were all built on concrete bases.

Emergency landings took place from time to time including an incident on 16 December 1943 when twelve Lockheed P-38 Lightnings of the 97th Fighter Squadron USAAF made a forced landing on parts of the airfield that were flooded. One aircraft crashed into a gun post, but the remaining eleven survived and three days later, as soon as the airfield was declared operational, took off and continued on their intended flight to North Africa via RAF St Eval in Cornwall.

631 Squadron pose with one of their Hurricanes at RAF Towyn, December 1943. The shell cases indicate the variety fired by the army at targets towed by this squadron. [Roy Sloan Collection]

'U' Flight of N⁰˙ 1 AACU equipped with Queen Bee target aircraft (a radio controlled version of the Tiger Moth) arrived at Towyn in October 1940. They were followed by 'C' Flight from Penrhos, equipped with Hawker Henley aircraft, which provided target towing facilities, until they were replaced by Martinets in February 1945. Norman Giroux, one of the early aviators who gave holiday makers the opportunity of flying in a de Havilland Foxmoth (Giro Aviation) aircraft from the sands at Southport before the war, ferried the Queen Bee to and from Towyn. Although the airfield closed 25 July 1945, the Army Air Corp's DHC Beaver aircraft made periodic use of the facilities until it became an outward-bound school.

RAF Bodorgan
Bodorgan, a grass airfield eight miles west of Menai Bridge in south-west Anglesey, had its original name of Aberffraw changed to Bodorgan on 15 May 1941 to eliminate problems with post and rail communications (especially when aircraft spare parts were required) and related general confusion that had been experienced with nearby airfields. When it was opened 11 September 1940 it was used by 'Z' Flight of N⁰˙ 1 Anti-Aircraft Co-operation Unit (AACU) which flew the Queen Bee for test shoots by anti-aircraft gunners at the Tŷ Croes range. The first radio controlled flight was made on 2 December 1940, with the aircraft eventually crashing on landing after $2^{1}/_{2}$ hours in the air.

The airfield was used for night flying training in March 1941 with a detachment of Westland Lysanders flown in from N⁰˙ 13 Squadron at Hooton Park. The following month it was designated N⁰˙ 15 Satellite Landing Ground (SLG) and adopted the role of a dispersal field for Hawarden's N⁰˙ 48 Maintenance Unit (MU). Thirty Hawker Hurricanes

A Boeing B-17 Flying Fortress (42-31321) at Towyn after over-shooting on 8 July 1944. Dennis Pritchard]

were flown in from Hawarden in May, to be stored on the airfield where they were later joined by Vickers Wellingtons and Fairey Swordfish but, after several accidents, the decision was taken that it would be safer to ferry the aircraft back to Hawarden prior to dispatch.

In the following months de Havilland Dragonflies and Tiger Moths, Westland Lysanders, Hawker Henleys, and Miles Magisters were seen to come and go whilst the radio controlled Queen Bee continued its operation. Many Wellingtons were received in 1942, but the total number of aircraft at any one time was maintained at about thirty to prevent them becoming too tempting a target for enemy aircraft which regularly flew over the area on their way to attack Liverpool and other towns in the north-west of England.

During the winter months, when the muddy conditions precluded locally based planes from operating, other local airfields with improved runways were used. By the end of 1944, the dispersal of aircraft was no longer necessary and RAF Hawarden in Flintshire in order to consolidate its activities Hawarden took over Hooton Park as a sub-storage site and, consequently gave up its SLGs.

The airfield closed for flying on 30 September 1945 and was soon returned to its original agricultural use. The three hangars were dismantled but some of the huts were used by light industry in later years. The airfield never had a control tower, but a bungalow-type building was used as a watch office.

RAF Valley

This airfield was opened 1 February 1941 and became operational on 3 March as RAF Rhosneigr but the name was changed to Valley the following month when it became a Fighter Sector Station under N[o.] 9 Group Fighter Command with the task of providing cover for shipping in the Irish Sea and towns in the north-west of England.

The first aircraft to arrive on 3 March were Hawker Hurricanes of N[o.] 312 (Czech) Squadron which left for Jurby on the Isle of Man on 25 April and was replaced N[o.] 615 (County of Surrey) Squadron, also flying Hurricanes. Bristol Beaufighter aircraft, fitted with AI radar, were used by N[o.] 219 Squadron and, later, N[o.] 68 Squadron, when night operations were started from Valley. A Beaufighter of the latter squadron was responsible for shooting down a Heinkel 111 in November 1941, causing it to crash with a full load of bombs that exploded at Bwlch-y-Fen near Bodorgan. All four members of the crew were killed.

Detachments from both the Royal Australian Air Force and the Royal Canadian Air Force were based for a while at Valley. Other planes that were in service at Valley were Defiant, Spitfire, Beaufighter and Mosquito.

In anticipation of the arrival of heavy bombers from the United States, the runways were extended in 1943, new taxiways were added and fifty hard standings were constructed to accommodate the anticipated increase in transatlantic movements. The USAAF Ferry Terminal became operational in June 1943, with the first B-17 arriving the following month, followed by US Navy aircraft, medium bombers and B-25s and C-47s. When aircraft were unable to locate the Valley airfield, as did happen from time to time, Beaufighters (replaced in January 1944 by Mosquito XVIs) of N⁰· 125 Squadron were sent to guide them in. Other aircraft that sought shelter at Valley, albeit briefly were Bell Airacobras, Lockheed Lightnings, Republic Thunderbolts, Douglas C-54s and a Lockheed Hudson. Having been the recipient of many aircraft during the war, in September 1945 Valley became the last port of call for over 2,500 USAAF bombers passing through on their way back to America, each carrying twenty passengers in addition to the crew. After the war Valley became an important Flying Training Command station.

RAF Llanbedr
This airfield on the Merioneth coast south of Harlech, was opened on 15 June 1941 and came under the control of RAF Valley in Anglesey. Both Llanbedr and Valley undertook a similar role of guarding convoys in the Irish Sea from enemy air operations. In the case of Llanbedr, that task was undertaken by Spitfire aircraft of N⁰· 74 Squadron and later N⁰· 131 Squadron from RAF Atcham. After the Spitfires, Llanbedr played host to a variety of other planes including Lockheed Lightnings (48th Fighter Squadron USAAF), North American Mustangs, Republic Thunderbolts and Hawker Typhoons. The Westland Lysanders in residence in the early part of 1943 were used by the 2025th Gunnery Flight, USAAF, for bombing practice on to a target off the nearby coast.

S/Ldr, William Ross Jones, brought up at Abererch near Pwllheli, joined the RAF in 1929. After training as a wireless operator/navigator, he saw active service in Iraq, Palestine and India. He returned to this country in 1936 to take an air observer's course and, a couple of years later, qualified as a pilot and flew a Spitfire during the Battle of Britain in the summer of

Bristol Beaufighters at RAF Valley.
[Roy Sloan Collection]

Above. Consolidated B-24J Liberator of the 392nd Bomb Group arrives at Valley on Runway 19. Between 17 May and 31 July 1945, Project White handled 2,678 multi-engined U S combat aircraft in transit via the Anglesey airfield to the United States. [Dennis Pritchard]

Top: Consolidated Liberator landing at RAF Valley. [Dennis Pritchard]

Centre: Pilot of Spitfire EN851-D 'Lime Challenger' of 317 Fighter Squadron USAAF preparing for take-off at RAF Valley. [Dennis Pritchard]

Bottom: 1st Lt Richard Steck briefs his crew and passengers at Valley before the Atlantic journey ahead of them. Monotonous Maggie had completed twenty-two combat missions over Nazi Europe. [Dennis Pritchard]

Top left: Westland Lysander used by the Air Sea Rescue unit at RAF Valley to locate aircrew in the sea. [Roy Sloan Collection]

Top right: Miles Master II (DK940), used for target-towing by No. 1486 Gunnery Flight at RAF Valley, June 1942. [Dennis Pritchard]

Centre: C-47B, 43-48770 from the 2nd Air Base Depot at Warton. This aircraft was regularly used on a shuttle service as part of the 'Marble Arch Airline'. During 1944 it carried personnel and mail. Originating at Hendon, near London the route was to American installations at Valley; Nutts Corner, N I; Prestwick, Scotland and subsequent return..

Left: Spitfire VB, piloted by Lieutenant E. R. Cobb, with engineering officer Lieutenant Ellliott, in the foreground, 308th Fighter Squadron, 31st Fighter Group at RAF Valley. [Dennis Pritchard]

Corporal Don Stewart from Mount City, Kansas and Master Sergeant Lawrence McPherson of Parksburg, West Virginia working on the de-icing system of a Liberator bomber at Valley in May 1945. The hangar in the background still exists. [Dennis Pritchard]

Air training at RAF Llandwrog. Lionel Salt, third from the left, back row. [Lionel Salt]

1940. S/Ldr Jones was posted to Llanbedr airfield in 1942 for a tour of duty which involved flying to meet American Consolidated B-24 Liberator bombers off the coast of Ireland, and guiding them on the remainder of their flight from the USA to RAF Valley. His next assignment was to fly unnamed passengers surreptitiously into occupied France by Lysander or Auster, light aircraft capable of landing and taking off in short distances. Sometimes, after delivering one passenger, he or she would be replaced on the homeward flight by another esoteric figure.

On the 12 March 1942, RAF Llanbedr claimed its first aerial victory of the war when, appropriately enough, a Welshman, Flt Lt Ray Harries, a flight commander of N°. 131 Squadron, shot down (in conjunction with another pilot) a Ju88 which was seen to crash into the sea about thirty-five miles west of the airfield. Harries went on to become the top-scoring Welsh fighter pilot of the war with an official score of over twenty confirmed victories.

Sadly, periodic aircraft losses were experienced at Llanbedr including three Spitfires belonging to N°. 41 Squadron that went missing 22 October 1941.

RAF Llandwrog

Work commenced on Llandwrog airfield, four miles south-west of Caernarfon, in September 1940 and material for the work was brought in through Caernarfon harbour, '… part of the Fletcher and Dixon yard at Victoria Dock to be let to the British Asphalt Co… . for the production of asphalt to cover the airodrome [sic] at Dinas Dinlle –10,000 tons required.'[12]

Llandwrog, Llanbedr, Mona and Valley had the benefit of concrete runways whereas Penrhos, Towyn, Hell's Mouth and Bodorgan continued to rely on reasonably flat grass fields.

Airspeed Oxfords, which were the first aeroplanes to arrive at Llandwrog shortly after the airfield opened 7 July 1941, were there in a defensive role, but when the decision was taken that the airfield would be used as N°. 9 Air Gunnery School of the Flying Training Command, the aircraft were replaced by twin-engined Armstrong Whitworth Whitley bombers. Other aircraft that were used on the airfield were the Avro Tutor, Fairey Battle, Gloster Gauntlet and Hawker Audax.

The airfield was described as a 'dispersed' type, with the service personnel accommodated in Nissen huts on the northern end of the main runway so as to be near the aircraft, whilst the trainees lived in huts (N°· 2 Site) on the coast road, close to Dinas Dinlle beach. Their day started at 6.40 a.m. and, after some physical training, they and other airmen from various parts of the airfield, were collected by two old ex-Liverpool Corporation buses which took them, via the coast road and Llandwrog village, to the central communal site which included the officers, sergeants and airmen's messes, as well as the post office. On the other side of the Llandwrog to Saron road, an RAF hospital and a WAAF section were opened on the 12 September 1942. In the same year, a new road was built between the airfield and the communal site which enabled the airmen to cycle between the two places.

Llandwrog's blackest day happened on 10 October 1941 when two Whitley aircraft (K9041 and K7252), returning from an exercise, were coming in to land. The first one had completed its five-mile radius approach and was near the runway when the other plane banked to carry out a similar approach. Its wing cut off the tail of the first aircraft causing it to crash on its nose and burst into flames. Although the second Whitley also crashed, it did not catch fire, nevertheless a total of seventeen airmen were killed including two senior pilots, S/Ldr Barker and Flt Lt Martin. Twelve of those killed were buried in their home town, and five at Llanbeblig churchyard in Caernarfon.

For the early intake of potential air-gunners posted to Llandwrog during the severe winter of 1941–2, the airfield seemed anything but hospitable, especially to those men brought from Bangor station in the back of a cold and draughty RAF lorry. The mixture of days of snow and frost, followed by rain and sleet, together with wild roaring gales, reduced the incomplete airfield to flooded fields and thick mud. Taking off and landing was only possible because of the concrete runways. It was during this same wintry period, that Les Sidwell, a trainee air gunner and pilot officer (later to be involved with the escape by prisoners from *Stalag Luft III* in Germany and mentioned in the book *The Wooden Horse*) described how he and other air-gunnery trainees waiting in the crew-room for the weather to improve 23 January 1942, were taken by surprise: '… a German JU88 flew in at sea level without warning and, before the camp defences could open up their guns, damaged two grounded Whitleys (including P5024) and a beacon with cannon fire. It disappeared seawards just as quickly as it appeared.'

When the weather allowed, three trainee air-gunners, each having been allocated one hundred rounds of ammunition, would be flown in an obsolete Whitley bomber, armed with Vickers machine guns, along the coast to shoot at drogues towed by Lysanders from RAF Valley. Each trainee had ammunition which showed up as a different colour when it hit the drogue enabling the successful strikes to be credited appropriately. Trainees were also taken by bus to Penrhos and to Hell's Mouth to practise on ground turrets by firing at moving targets. Owing to a heavy snowfall during January 1942 the course, which normally ran for six weeks, was extended to ten weeks.

Les Sidwell's first training venture ended in an unexpected manner: '… in January (1942) my first Whitley (Mark V aircraft N1475) flying exercise ended when engine failures out at sea caused the pilot (F/O Watson) to aim for the nearest land, near the golf links by the headland near Morfa Nevin where we crash-landed. We walked to the nearby Linksway Hotel where the splendid Reginald and Dorothy Lane welcomed us and magically whipped up a lovely hot Sunday dinner for us.'

To relieve the monotony of flying up and down Caernarvon Bay on gunnery exercise, the trainees would occasionally get the pilot to fly low over Caernarvon and, whilst passing over Castle Square, take the opportunity to dispose of spent cartridges out of the rear turret which would descend like hail on to the long-suffering inhabitants down below. Inevitably such an incident was reported by the County Constabulary to the Commanding Officer who would reprimand the trainees for their behaviour.

When N°· 9 Air Gunners School was closed at Llandwrog on 13 June 1942, it was transferred to RAF Penrhos. Thereafter, Llandwrog became a satellite to Penrhos and a Relief Landing Ground for N°· 9 (Observers) Advance Flying Unit based at Penrhos. On 11 February 1943 the unit moved to operate from Llandwrog. The Whitley bomber was replaced by twin-engined Blenheim fighter bombers, both long and short nosed types, for training navigators and wireless operators and then, during 1943, by twelve twin-engined Avro Ansons used for training navigators by both day and night. Many of the Royal Air Force observer or navigator air crew had been trained overseas, either under the Empire Air Training or the British Commonwealth Training schemes but, on returning to this country they were given the opportunity to become familiar with local flying conditions at Llandwrog and Penrhos.

The front at Dinas Dinlle was accessible to the public only for a certain distance along the coastal road towards the airfield and sentries and barricades prevented anyone going any further. The public was precluded from most of the seaside by coils of barbed wire which extended all the way from one end of the beach to Fort Belan; only occasional gaps would allow the hardy and the brave access for swimming. The barbed wire served to both inhibit any possible invaders and to protect anyone from straying into the mines laid along the shore and publicised at intervals of twenty yards or so with notices in English and Welsh stating: 'DEATH – HEAVILY MINED'. The occasional dog or rabbit killed by straying through the barbed wire on to the mined area on the shore emphasised the danger.

The coastal sand-dunes bordering the airfield were also defensively mined but when a visiting Mitchell aircraft ran out of tarmac on the main north to south runway and ended up in the minefield it did not cause any

Aerial photograph of the main camp at RAF Llandwrog, taken in 2007. Most of the buildings have survived and many have been converted to light industrial use at Blythe Farm. On the far side of the road which bisects the photograph are further former RAF buildings which now form part of Parc Busnes Llandwrog and Sain record company.
[W. Alister Williams Collection]

Right and below: Two of the original buildings on the airfield at RAF Llandwrog.
[W. Alister Williams Collection]

Right and below: Two of the original RAF buildings at Blythe Farm, Llandwrog.
[W. Alister Williams Collection]

Below: Some of the original RAF buildings at Parc Busnes, Llandwrog which have been converted and enhanced for modern light-industrial use.
[W. Alister Williams Collection]

Left: One of the original RAF buildings at RAF Llandwrog now forms part of the administration block at White Tower caravan park.
[W. Alister Williams Collection]

of the mines to explode. The duty crew, who had the task of towing it and the crew back on to the runway, had to crawl along the tyre marks to attach towing gear. A similar incident occurred when a Wellington bomber overran the runway and landed in the minefield, but again without loss of life.

Entertainment for the airmen usually entailed a visit to one of the three cinemas or a dance at Caernarfon, the journey being accomplished usually on bicycles which were left, with many others, in the safekeeping of Miss Ellis's backyard off Palace Street.

Although the catering on the airfield had a good reputation, hunger and the need for some warmth caused many of the men to visit nearby farms as Les Sidwell described, '… Mrs Williams's farmhouse (Rhydfelen) was unusually placed on an RAF aerodrome and this good lady's kitchen and parlour provided a haven of warmth and good food in the bitter spells that we had. I was one of the regulars who were glad to warm right up before facing the thought of our billets which were often frozen or swimming in water in the floods.' Other eating places were the Harp Inn in Llandwrog which was kept by Miss Griffith (where beer was dispensed from tall enamel jugs) and the Goat Inn and Albert Lloyd's bakery shop at Llanwnda. Because the sand-dunes around the airfield were overrun with rabbits and, since there was a ready market for them to supplement the food supply, Cpl Wilson of the fire section, armed with a borrowed shotgun, would bag a few when other duties allowed.

When the 1,000 bomber raids started 31 May 1942, three pilots and three wireless operator/air gunners from the Llandwrog N°· 9 AGS instructional staff flew in three Whitley bombers from the airfield: N1345 (P/O D. G. Box and Sgt K. Houldcroft), T4155 (F/Sgt. K. R. Rees and Sgt W. H. Orman) and N1428 (P/O J. W. Croudis and Sgt. A. J. Harvey) to RAF Driffield and took part in the operation over Cologne. Whitley N1345 was shot down, but the other two planes returned to Llandwrog.

Apart for the period from the 29 July 1946 when the airfield was under the jurisdiction of the specially formed N°· 277 MU, part of the Bicester based N°· 42 Group, responsible for the storing of gas bombs (see Appendix I), Llandwrog airfield was closed on 29 July 1945 until 1975 when it was reopened as Caernarvon Airport.

Local distinguished serviceman
Dr James Arthur Davies, OBE, MA, BSc, PhD (1923–2007)

Dr Jim Davies was brought up at Blaen-y-Ffos, Pembrokeshire and was educated at Trinity College, Carmarthen and the London School of Economics. He served in the RAF during the war and was shot down in 1944.

When Lancaster DV267 K-King took off from Ludford Magna in Lincolnshire at 23.38 hours on 19 February 1944, it was one of twenty-two similar aircraft from 101 Squadron that had been assigned for 'special duties' and they in turn were part of a combined force of 844 Lancaster and Halifax bomber aircraft that were taking part in a raid on Leipzig.

Warrant Officer J. A. Davies was the eighth crew member of DV267 and his role was that of operating jamming equipment to disrupt radio signals between German fighter aircraft and their controller 'somewhere in Germany.' However, such jamming signals could be counter-productive, especially if they acted as 'homing' beacons for German fighters seeking British aircraft.

The newly-installed radar equipment should have given them warning of an approaching German fighter but it was the sound of bullets ripping through the aircraft fabric and the fire that developed in the port-side engines and wing that caused the pilot to give the order to 'prepare to abandon'. With just sufficient time to clip his parachute on to harness, Jim Davies and other members of the crew left the plane and parachuted to land in the Netherlands.

After a period of nearly six months, during which time he was passed along a chain of Dutch and Belgian people, including those who were involved in the Resistance movements, he was betrayed on 10 August 1944 by a 'double agent' in Belgium. Eventually, he together with other prisoners arrived at Stalag Luft 7, a camp that contained mostly members of the Royal Air Force and Allied air crews.

They remained there until 19 January 1945 when, due to the nearness of the Russian armies, fifteen hundred prisoners were forced to march through appalling winter weather. It took them until 9 February 1945 to reach their destination of **Stalag IIIA**, Luckenwalde, a camp that held some 16,000 men of many nationalities.

As a result of the Western Allies having crossed the Rhine, and the Russian forces about to cross the Elbe, it was a question of which army would reach Berlin first. Despite the fact that the Americans arrived at the camp on 6 May with a convoy of lorries to evacuate Americans, British, Norwegians and French prisoners, in that order, the Russians refused to allow them to leave. VE Day was declared on 8 May but it was another two weeks before they were transported to Leipzig, Jim Davies's original destination.

Post war he served as Director of Education for Montgomeryshire before being appointed Principal of the Normal College in Bangor in 1969. After retiring in 1985 he was chairman of the Wales NSPCC and the Gwynedd Hospice at Home.

W/O Jim Davies. [Nesta Davies]

Jim Davies (climbing into the aircraft) with his fellow crewmen boarding their Lancaster bomber for a mission. [Nesta Davies]

Fuel Supplies

During the period of expansion of the Royal Air Force during the 1930s it became necessary to review the supply and storage of aviation fuel, lubricating oil and tetra-ethyl lead, especially so with the threat of war and the consequent increase in sizes and range of aircraft anticipated. It was imperative that a reserve of fuel be held since there was every chance of the supply from overseas being interrupted.

Initially, the oil companies were obliged to hold 8,000 tons fuel to meet the day-to-day requirements of the RAF which would be sufficient, based on available estimates, for ten days. By 1938, on the assumption that in the event of war America would remain neutral, it had been decided that 800,000 tons of aviation fuel would be held in storage. By 1943, this figure had increased to 2,090,700 tons, held at thirty-six main reserve storage depots, and forty-two distribution depots, located in areas where the demand was expected to be greatest, such as the airfields in the eastern part of England. The supply of steel and construction of storage tanks cost over £12,000,000, a vast sum at that time.

Petrol had been transported to Caernarfon by ship since 24 March 1913 when the first delivery of 450 tons of 'petroleum, oil and spirits' was made by the tanker *Tioga* of the Anglo-American Oil Company. During the Second World War, petrol (the price of which had risen by 2d. to 1s. 8d. per gallon in 1939), including aviation fuel, continued to be brought from Stanlow in ships such as the *Ben Johnson, Ben Read, Nordest II, Rudderman* and *Wheelsman*. But the regular tanker that was familiar to those who lived near the Menai Strait was MV *Shelbrit*. Carrying some 435 tons of spirits, she visited Caernarfon regularly between 1939 and 1945. On arrival at Caernarfon, her cargo was transferred to dockside storage tanks. Since there was always a possibility for these being damaged or destroyed by enemy action, four tanks, each capable of holding 250,000 gallons were installed underground at the old brickworks at Parciau, Griffiths Crossing, between Caernarfon and Port Dinorwic. The first transfer of petrol from Caernarfon to the new Shell depot took place on the 5 August 1941, via a 4-inch pipe laid by the Ministry of Supply alongside the main railway line. The high-octane petrol was then collected by road tankers operated by Pickfords, Cawood Wharton or Harold Wood, for distribution to airfields in north-west Wales. In addition, four-gallon cans assembled at the nearby industrial site, and filled with petrol, were distributed for use by military establishments. Such was the demand for containers that over four hundred and fifty people worked twelve-hour shifts, from seven to seven,

General pass required for entry to the Anglo-American Oil Company Depot at Griffiths Crossing, Caernarfon.
[L. V. Williams]

The MV Shelbrit *at Stanlow refinery.*
[W. L. Hughes]

The outline of the wartime petrol storage tanks at Parciau Brickworks, Caernarfon can be seen in the grassed area on the left of the photograph. [AC]

alternating between day and night shifts, with a fortnight on each. They were allowed twenty minutes break each morning and afternoon, and an hour for lunch. The weekly pay was £3.

Due to the proximity of the underground tanks to the sea, a periodic inspection took place by the Harbour Trust and the Fisheries Patrol Officer for any sign of oil pollution in the Strait.

Air Training Corps

The Air Training Corps (ATC), originally called the Air Defence Cadets Corps, was inaugurated on the 1 February 1941 and within a month over 230 squadrons had been formed in towns and villages throughout Britain. Some 200,000 eventually joined the organisation. A report in the *North Wales Chronicle* on 21 November 1941 stated:

Staff at the Parciau petrol terminal, Caernarfon. [Hugh Howel]

> The Air Training Corps movement was the subject of a discussion at yesterday's meeting of the Caernarvonshire Education Committee. It was decided that a letter be sent to the governing bodies of the Secondary Schools in the county emphasising the importance of the movement and urging them to take the necessary action for setting up an ATC unit in each school. Mr W. George, the chairman, hoped that attention would be given to the expression of hope by the Higher Education Committee and that it would be possible to foster the activities of the Air Training Corps in the county without unduly introducing a militaristic spirit into the Secondary School.

Although the Arvon Union of Congregational Churches deplored the action of the Caernarvonshire Board of Education in allowing schools and colleges to be associated with militarism, pupils aged between sixteen and eighteen readily joined, even if it was only for the glamour of wearing the uniform. The fact that they were given the opportunity of spending weekends and summer camps at a variety of airfields and had the

No. 2183 Squadron ATC, County School Holyhead. [Dr J. Ken Roberts]

opportunity of flying with the Royal Air Force was an added incentive. Youngsters liable to be called-up at the age of eighteen to the forces either during the war or post-war, also benefited from the various forms of training that was provided. By the end of October 1941 squadrons had been formed in many towns in Caernarvonshire and Anglesey.

Weekly lectures at Holyhead County School for members of N°· 1505 Squadron began in November 1940 on a variety of subjects including weather forecasting for the RAF, morse code and mathematics. However, it was not until November 1942 when, jointly with the Beaumaris Squadron, the cadets were fitted with uniforms. On the assumption that at least some of the cadets would endeavour to join the Royal Air Force when enlisting, a special film dealing with the training of RAF pilots was shown to members of the Holyhead Squadron at the Hippodrome Theatre.

On 28 April 1941, the first cadets enrolled with the N°· 1557 Squadron of

N°· 985 Squadron ATC, Caernarvon County School with F/O R. D. Pritchard. [Olive Bocking]

Caernarvon County School & Segontium Higher Grade School, Girls Training Corps. [Nancy Mothersole]

No. 1557 Squadron ATC, Friars School, Bangor. [W. H. Lovelock]

Friars School at Bangor with uniforms being issued the following September. The weekly lectures were primarily aimed towards air-crew training, including signalling, meteorology and aircraft recognition, together with the inevitable drilling (square bashing). An occasional visit to RAF Mona airfield would also be provided in order that the cadets gain experience in rifle shooting on an outdoor range.

Caernarfon cadets had the benefit of two squadrons: N[o.] 1310 inaugurated in February 1941 under the command of F/O C. C. Williams, and which met at the Central School, and the County School N[o.] 985, inaugurated in March 1941, commanded by F/O R. D. Pritchard. When Pritchard took up an appointment in Loughborough, F/O Hubert I. Hughes took over the squadron. A variety of subjects including aircraft recognition, lamp signalling and navigation was provided by their day-time teachers who willingly gave up some of their spare time to improve the proficiency of the cadets.

Air Crashes and Mountain Rescue

The mountainous terrain of Snowdonia was notoriously difficult to fly over, particularly in adverse weather conditions and in the training aircraft used during the early years of the war. Altimeters could often be inaccurate and compasses were prone to fluctuate in the vicinity of the mountains which often resulted in the loss of aeroplanes and their crews. Possibly the only aids to flying in the mountains were devices called 'balloon squeakers' that, late in the war, were placed on mountain summits such as Cwm Silin (generally described as an aircraft graveyard) and Foel Grach to warn aircraft when they were in their vicinity.

Searches for the survivors from aircraft that had crashed in Snowdonia were carried out by inexperienced personnel in remote and virtually inaccessible areas. This 'Crash Party', as it was described, consisted of any personnel that happened to be available at RAF Llandwrog who would have to participate in the rescue attempts in totally inappropriate clothing and footwear, often having to clamber up rocks or attempt to negotiate bogs and streams in rubber-soled shoes. When the crashed aircraft was located, the party would invariably be confronted with the sight of members of the crew having been severely injured or killed. Some of the younger members of the Crash Party, having never before undergone such an experience, would find it distressing to have to carry the dead crew, many of a similar age to themselves, strapped on stretchers down to the nearest road where an RAF vehicle would be waiting. In November 1942, the senior medical officer at Llandwrog wrote:

> During the past five months there have been 10 major crashes in the area from the Conway Valley to the Rival Mountains which this SSQ (Station Sick Quarters) has attended, over an area of 40 by 30 miles.

Time taken varies from one to three days in the mountains, according to the degree of accessibility. Total time away from the station 15 days, total number of dead 40, total number of injured removed to hospital.[13]

At 9 p.m. on 14 January 1943, an Avro Anson (EG110) from Llandwrog crashed while on a night navigating exercise to Shrewsbury and back. Next day a telephone message was received stating that the pilot had made his way to a farmhouse. The Senior Medical Officer (SMO) and a search party then set out to try and locate the aircraft and any other surviving crew while air searches were mounted from both Llandwrog and Valley. The ground search party gave up at 2 a.m. on the 16 January owing to the moon setting and bad conditions on the mountain. After resuming the search at dawn, the wreck was eventually located at 11.00 a.m., thirty-nine hours after the crash. Two of the crew were dead and the New Zealand Air Force navigator, seriously injured.

Air crash memorials:
Top left: Llanberis Pass, 1 February 1945. [AC]

Top right: North Stack, 22 December 1944. [AC]

Bottom left: Rhosneigr, 28 August 1941. [Roy Sloan Collection]

Bottom right: Penmaenmawr, 7 January 1944. [John Lloyd Roberts]

RAF Mountain Rescue Service 1943.
L–R: Cpl. Gregory McTigue, Fl.Lt. Graham, LAC Driver Cummings, LAC Jackson planning their route to a crashed aircraft.
[R. E. Roberts]

RAF Llandwrog Mountain Rescue Service ambulance with canvas extension.
[R. E. Roberts]

This incident together with previous experiences led to a conference on mountain crashes being held at SSQ Llandwrog. It was decided to allocate a Humber ambulance (the roof of which was painted with black and yellow bands as an aid to ground parties to home in on by day, and to indicate its position to co-operating aircraft, and a jeep carrying radio equipment for field trials in the area between Tal-y-Bont, Dyffryn Conwy and the Melynllyn Hut and also on Carnedd Llywelyn.

The Mountain Rescue Service (MRS) was officially started on 6 July 1943, by Flt Lt George Graham, the SMO at Llandwrog and the log entry for that day stated that the field trials, which had started at 4.45 a.m., had proved successful. Thereafter they continued to be called out in all weather conditions and to all sorts of terrain but, the fact that the service was now staffed by trained personnel, wearing more appropriate clothing, and with specialised equipment and vehicles, greatly assisted them in their task. Sometimes their endeavours were successful but, sadly, in many instances they would arrive at the location of the crash only to be confronted with a scene of desolation and to find that the crew of the aircraft had been killed.

In August, W/Cdr Ruffell Smith arrived at Llandwrog from HQ Flying Training Command to ascertain the progress being made with the Mountain Rescue Service (MRS). Accompanying him was F/O Richwaite of the Royal New Zealand Air Force, who hoped to learn how the system worked in order that a similar service could be started in New Zealand.

In many instances the MRS had excellent support from local police and hill farmers whose knowledge of the terrain enabled them to assist in locating the scene of the crash. On the 18 August 1943, following receipt of a crash report by the local police, the MRS team were alerted, '... 23.00 hrs – notified of crash E of Bethesda

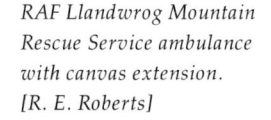

The crew of USAAF B-24 Liberator 'Bachelor Baby' that crashed above Penmaenmawr, 1944. [John Lloyd Roberts]

and N of Llyn Ogwen ... all crew dead... MRS party (F/Lt Graham, Sgt Harvey, LAC Jackson, A/C Ventura [and] 20 men to help remove bodies ... a mountain stretcher fitted with sledge runners was loaned from Ogwen cottage & proved extremely useful in carrying bodies over grass and loose rock.'

In some cases, because of the difficult terrain and poor visibility, it would take a day or two to find the crashed aircraft:

> 29. 8. 43 – 17.00 hrs – ... report of a Botha crashed eastern Carneddi (no trace found after a great deal of searching until 31.8.43 when it was seen from an aircraft five miles from purported crash site) ... crew of 4 killed instantly ... bodies tied to stretchers but the severity of the ground delayed the return ... decided to leave the stretchers where they were as the party was considerably exhausted & return in daylight ... 1.9.43 fresh party sent out at 0900 to retrieve bodies ... Thus ended the longest continuous operation in which the MR unit had been employed. The long delay in finding the crash was due entirely to have been given a grossly inaccurate pin point.[14]

Another example of the excellent cooperation between local people, the police and the rescue service occurred on the 8 June 1944 when at 04.45hrs the flying control officer at Llandwrog was informed that, 'a farmer living at Tŷ Gwyn farm near Bethesda had heard a plane flying fairly low near his house. He heard a thud shortly afterwards and looking out of his window he saw a flash near the summit of a mountain (Mynydd Perfedd) on the opposite side of the Nant Ffrancon Valley. He immediately took steps to inform the police at Bethesda and they in turn informed the FCO at Llandwrog.' The aircraft, an Anson (LT116) from RAF Llandwrog, was found at 06.55 hours, about 300 feet below the summit of Mynydd Perfedd. The five members of the crew had suffered multiple injuries 'from which they must have died instantaneously.' The crewmen were:

F/Sgt Sullivan, Peter Selwood (412855), pilot, aged 21, Australian, buried Chester;

Sgt Pearce, Leonard John (1321554), wireless operator, aged 23, buried Bristol;

F/O Mott, Malcolm James (428745), navigator, aged 20, Australian, buried Chester;

W/O Fletcher. Harold Jackson (405204), wireless operator/air gunner, Australian, buried Chester;

F/O McKessock, William Donald Nelson (J38813), air gunner/bomb aimer, aged 30, Canadian, buried Chester.

Whenever an aircraft ditched in the sea, the MRS co-operated with the Air Sea Rescue service to effect a rescue. At 01.10 hours on the 1 June 1944, when the Medical Officer (MO) and SSQ staff had retired to bed and were trying to sleep through heavy rain and thunder and lightning, reports were received of an aircraft which, having overshot the runway on landing at Llandwrog, had ditched in the sea about one mile off-shore. On being called out, the MO, Flt/Lt Scudmore, together with Sgt Harvey and Cpl Jackson, established from a small group of airmen on the beach that they had seen the aircraft with its lights on. A few red Verey lights had been fired, but the aircraft lights had disappeared after about five minutes. Even the flashes of lightning revealed nothing. The MO had been told that N[o.] 63 Air Sea Rescue Unit at Fort Belan had been duly notified of the crash and that their pinnace had left base. A dinghy was immediately commandeered from the nearest available aircraft and inflated. After paddling for about half an hour, they saw that the Verey lights were being sent up from a dinghy launched from the aircraft. The MO boarded it to check the crew but decided that no immediate medical help was required. The two dinghies were lashed together and the MO's party began to row towards the shore where 'one could now see numerous bright lights and masses of people – reminiscent of Blackpool.' When accommodation became available at Fort Belan as the result of the number of naval ratings manning the 403rd Coast Battery being reduced in December 1941, the opportunity was taken to increase the number of Air Sea Rescue personnel under the charge of F/O G. Strang, from twenty-three to thirty-eight, on the instructions of Hubert Lynes, Resident Naval Officer. (GAS, XD2 2944)

Further lives were saved in August 1944 when the crew of a Wellington aircraft ditched in the sea.

Sea Rescues – I wish you to personally convey my congratulations and thanks to the member concerned with the reporting of A45-N dropping red flares and the tracking of dinghy out to sea in the early hours of Saturday morning 26 August 44. You will be pleased to know that seven airmen were rescued and brought safely to Llandwrog and are recovering in the sick bay at this airfield.[15]

The following incident over the Lleyn peninsula on 1 June 1944 illustrates the speed at which reports were sent by the Royal Observer Corps to the Flying Control Liaison Officer (FCLO). N°· 9 Group at Shrewsbury reported to FCLO that a pilot had baled out from a Thunderbolt. FCLO enquired as to whether he seemed to make a safe landing and the reply from the Observer was 'we will let you know, he is still descending.'[16]

Another joint operation with an Air Sea Rescue launch occurred on the 9 September 1943.

> 17.15 hrs – informed ... that Anson a/c [aircraft] had crashed into sea half a mile off Trevor point ... 3 survivors picked up having been ferried ashore by locals ... suffering from much bruising, lacerations and a fair degree of shock ... restorative measures were taken in Humber Ambulance: blankets, hot water bottles ... hot tea had already been supplied ... 3 of the crew still remained trapped in the Anson ... proceeded to wreck on which ASR [Air Sea Rescue] crew had just landed. A hole was made and 2 bodies were extracted ... no trace of 3rd could be found. RT message ... from ASR launch by MO to Humber for oxygen and artificial respiration was continued with this for over an hour without avail ... 3rd body released at 00.30 hrs 10. 9. 43. Highly satisfactory co-operation was achieved with ASR in this combined operation. Two more might have been saved had a faster launch been available ...[17]

To avoid duplication and time-wasting, all reports of crashes were co-ordinated by the Flying Control Officer (FCO) and he invariably notified the Mountain Rescue Unit whenever a crash occurred,

> 8.11.43. At 20.55 hrs the FCO notified MRU that a crash had occurred and preliminary reports from HQ 9 Group suggested that it had occurred near Snowdon ... at 21.15 the local Observer Corps informed MRS through the FCO that a fire had been seen near Carnedd Dafydd at 20.30. Bethesda police station appeared to have more information so the MO and the crew of MRS left SSQ at 21.40 in Jeep and Humber and called at Bethesda Police Station ... established mountain HQ by the side of a farm near Llyn Ogwen ... a civilian party with police officers and a small contingent from MU RAF Bethesda ... had just descended from the crash where they had found 4 corpses ... MRS crew ascended and found the a/c [aircraft] at 01.00 hrs, 9.11.43 near the summit of Pen-yr-Oleu Wen (3,210 feet) map ref. 121840 ... The a/c was an Anson (9855) from Halfpenny Green ... four dead bodies were found and (later) ... a fifth body ... all five had multiple injuries and must have died instantaneously.[18]

It was always gratifying to the MO attached to the MRS when there were survivors from a plane crash as was the case at 12.30 hours on 1 December 1943 when an Anson aircraft (EF909) from Jurby, Isle of Man crashed the previous evening near the summit of Foel Grach. Two crew members had walked down from the crash site to Bethesda where they were met and questioned by the MO about the location of the crash but they were vague about it. After searching Carnedd Llywelyn, a report stated that the third member of the crew had walked from the crash and arrived at Bethesda police station. Eventually the wreck was found and the fourth crew member was sleeping in the gun-turret compartment at the intact rear part of the fuselage. He had wrapped himself in a few parachutes and, apart from suffering from dehydration, hunger and a fractured foot, the report stated that his spirits were high. On being offered rum by the MO, he refused it, saying 'I never touch the stuff.' He was taken by stretcher down the mountainside in darkness and then to SSQ at Llandwrog.

On 3 January 1944, Flt Lt Graham, who had done a tremendous amount of the work involved in getting the service off the ground, was told to report to Airways Traffic in London for posting overseas. His duties were taken over by F/O Scudamore. Other MOs involved with the MRS were S/Ldr Collins, and F/Lt Lloyd.

There was often a sense of frustration amongst the team if they were not informed quickly of an air crash. This happened on 7 January 1944 when a Liberator aircraft crashed at 13.45 hours between Llanfairfechan and Penmaenmawr, shortly after leaving RAF Valley, Anglesey. The MRS was not notified until 16.00, by which time civilian ambulances had taken six members of the crew of eleven for treatment to the Caernarfonshire and Anglesey Infirmary in Bangor. Two other injured crewmen walked over the mountain, whilst another was picked up by the MRS at Penmaenmawr. The MRS eventually reached the aircraft at 17.30 and found three charred bodies amongst the burning debris which they removed to the mortuary at Bangor.[19]

Fortunately not all aircraft crashes resulted in injuries or death.

14.01.44 – 22.45 – Notified by FCO that an Anson a/c from Llandwrog had crashed in Anglesey … and that a WT message from the a/c had stated that all the crew were alright. No intimation of the position of the a/c had been given … MO & MRS crew set out at 23.59 and after crossing the Menai Bridge, Humber contacted base on WT and a message was received to the effect that the crew had arrived at Parciau Auxiliary Hospital. MRS proceeded immediately to that hospital and picked up 3 of the crew of four. The 4th member had stayed with the a/c in a field to guard it. MRS plus the 3 aircrew personnel proceeded to the a/c, picked up the 4th survivor and proceeded to SSQ. The a/c had been flying in low cloud and had crashed on level ground. The fuselage was relatively intact. The crew of the a/c had received only minor injuries and all were fit for flying duties 24 hrs after admission to SSQ, Llandwrog.[20]

31.3.44. at 14.15, ... a Wellington a/c flew over SSQ with only one engine functioning. The Humber proceeded to the drome and almost encountered the Wellington flying over the airfield towards N[o.] 2 site in great difficulties. The a/c then flew towards the Menai Straits over the sea and the Humber went quickly to the northern end of runway ... parallel to the sea. The Wellington appeared over a hangar and made a skilful belly landing on the runway. Humber and Fordson ambulances proceeded across the airfield to the machine. No one was injured.[21]

Testing of various pieces of equipment, including the 'sledge stretcher' (invented by Dr D. G. Duff of Denbigh) which was designed to assist in bringing casualties off the mountain as quickly and as efficiently as possible, took place on 20 February 1944. The trial was to establish the best method of 'traversing streams, grassy slopes and for negotiating stone walls and vertical rock faces – in fact for general mountain rescue work.' After some modifications further trials of the stretcher took place in June on the scree on the west face of Tryfan with an all-steel, collapsible type with a detachable wheel. The other type tested had a light metal framework designed to clamp over a wooden GS stretcher, thereby converting it to a sledge stretcher. A Bergen rucksack and Mk III Everest cradle were also developed which could carry a casualty bag used to keep a patient warm.

To improve the efficiency of the MRS team still further, a two-week course in mountaineering, rock climbing, cross-country marching and the evacuation of casualties was started on 4 April 1944, under the control of Sgt Pick of the 52nd Mountain Division.

As the result of a crash occurring a crash occurred on Craig Ffynnon in the Conwy Valley on 21 February 1944, MRS Llandwrog was advised of the event at 23.35 p.m.:

MRS left SSQ at 11.42 am and after calling at Conway police station picked up Police Constable Jones (PC 99) at Tynygroes who guided Humber up appropriate mountain track to a farm house where base was established ... Local farmer stated that there were 3 survivors in the a/c and one killed. MO proceeded immediately towards crash with packset, first aid outfit and a Thomas' splint and was followed by PC Jones & 2 civilians carrying 2 GS stretchers with blankets etc. . a few civilians at the crash had kept the survivors warm and one administered tea ... The a/c was an Anson LT433 from RAF Cork ... The pilot, Sgt Grant, was strapped in his seat ... presume that death was instantaneous ... W/O Redman ... taken to Llandudno & District General Hospital ... MO attended to the other two occupants ... They

Top: German airmen Bruno Perzanowski & Lothar Horras. [John Lloyd Roberts]

Above: Former German airmen Kurt Schlender and Lothar Horras with John Lloyd Roberts (middle), a former member of the Home Guard group which captured them in 1941.
[John Lloyd Roberts]

were P/O Byrne, pupil w. op and Sgt Birch, navigator ...[22]

In some cases the role of the MRS was simply to locate aircrew that had baled out of their aircraft as was the case on 29 March 1944:

MRS having collected crew left SSQ at 1435. Conway police station was reached at 15.15 & a civilian then guided the vehicles to a house 2 $\frac{1}{2}$ miles from Conway overlooking the river Conway. From there the crash could be seen on the east bank of the river. The pilot & one other member of the crew were in the house & gave information that the remaining three of the crew had baled out at 9,000 feet three minutes before them. They themselves had baled out at approx. 1,000 feet ... the remaining three had arrived without injury at Conway police station having landed about 4 miles down the road to Talybont near Caerhun ...[23]

On 14 April 1941, a German Heinkel 111 H5 (F4801) of the 1 Staffel KG28 crashed at Llwydmor, a mountain above Llanfairfechan. The engineer/air gunner (*Gefreiter* Josef Brunninghausen) was killed but the pilot (*Leutnant* Lothar Horras), wireless operator/air gunner (Kurt Schlender) and observer/bomb-aimer (*Feldwebel* Bruno Perzanowski) survived and were taken to the Caernarvonshire & Anglesey Infirmary at Bangor. They were eventually transferred to a Prisoner of War Camp at Bury in Lancashire and, eventually, to Camp 132 at Medicine Hat, Albert in Canada. Towards the end of the war, a fellow prisoner of war was murdered at Medicine Hat and, following a lengthy investigation, Bruno Perzanowski, together with three other prisoners, was convicted and executed by hanging in December 1946.

Probably the most dramatic and tragic rescue incident, involving both service personnel and civilians, occurred on 28 August 1941 when at about 11.30 hours, a Blackburn Botha aircraft (L6417) crashed into the sea off Rhosneigr during a south-westerly gale and heavy sea. Some of the crew baled out and two succeeded in reaching the shore, none the worse for their immersion in the sea. The pilot, wearing a 'Mae West' life jacket, was washed ashore unconscious. He revived under artificial respiration, but died later in hospital. Despite the weather, two seventeen-year-old youths, Derrick Baynham of Walton-on-Thames and Stuart Wood of Chester, launched a rowing boat. In an interview with a local paper, Derrick Baynham related their experience:

> We reached the plane and found one of the airmen clinging to the fuselage near the tail. We signalled for him to enter our boat but as he was about to do so the boat was hit by a terrific wave and turned completely over. I scrambled on to the wing of the plane but was immediately washed off and I had to cling to the boat again. During the whole time we were in the water the boat was continually being turned over by the heavy seas. On one occasion I was trapped beneath it but fortunately a wave turned it over and I was released. Neither Wood nor myself are any the worse for our adventure.[24]

Six soldiers, together with Police Constable Arthur and Mr Arthur Owen, a local officer in the Merchant Service, went out in a second boat but this also capsized, and all the occupants were struggling in the sea in full view of those on shore. Even though an aeroplane flying overhead dropped life-saving jackets, the men in the water were unable to secure them. Human chains were formed, but they too were swept back by heavy seas. Shortly afterwards the body of PC Arthur in full uniform, and still wearing his helmet, was washed ashore. A third boat was launched, but to no avail. A fourth boat, which had been brought by lorry the twelve miles from Holyhead, was launched but this too capsized and one oarsman named Evans, a member of the Holyhead life-saving crew was drowned. The three aircrew that lost their lives were – T. A. Dixon, F. C. Glockler and K. S. Rosiewicz. The eleven members of the public who died in the rescue were: G. Arthur, D. W. Bannister, R. Eaton, L. A. Ford, E. Jones, A. W. Moger, A. J. Owen, R. K. Simons, C. H. Thornton, P. T. Whysall and S. Wilkins.

With the disbanding of N°· 9 (O) AFU (Satellite) Llandwrog, Flt Lt Scudamore was posted to RAF Llanbedr, prior to the Mountain Rescue Service being transferred there on 7 June 1945. The following day, an American B-17G Flying Fortress crashed on the mountainside at 1,200 feet near Cader Idris and the MO at Llanbedr was notified. The aircraft was found burnt out and twenty bodies were recovered from the debris; most of them, having received multiple injuries and severe burns, and had been killed instantly.

The people involved with the Mountain Rescue Service of Llandwrog and Llanbedr had given a tremendous service, more often than not in very dangerous places and in dreadful weather. Their task was not made any easier by the inadequate equipment with which they were initially supplied. The general issue clothing was totally unsuited for the task and yet the daunting and often harrowing work was carried out with fortitude, irrespective of time of day or night, and in all weathers. Without the

This rather poor photograph gives some impression of the scale of the military honours accorded by the RAF to Police Constable Arthur at his funeral following the Botha disaster of 28 August 1941. [Roy Sloan Collection]

persistence displayed by the teams led by the station MO, many more crew members would have been lost on the mountains.

The helicopters and equipment now being used by the Air Sea Rescue unit based at RAF Valley and other air bases, have transformed the service completely. Primarily intended for saving service personnel, many civilians also owe their lives to the skill, bravery and fortitude of the RAF's rescue crews.

Development of Radio Direction Finding (RADAR)[25]

The increasing threat of war and the possibility of enemy aircraft being able to fly undetected from bases in Europe, to bomb industrial sites and towns in Britain, perturbed the government greatly. The acoustic mirror system that had been developed as a means of detecting aircraft flying towards Britain had become obsolete by 1934. Even a 'death ray' form of defence had been considered but dismissed as being impractical (and unproven) due to the amount of power that would be required to operate it. Re-radiated radio signals and an account produced by the Post Office in June 1932 confirmed that an aircraft flying in the vicinity of a receiving aerial interfered with the signal. From such interference, it was possible to deduce the distance of the aircraft from the aerial and the height at which it was flying. As far as the Post Office engineers were concerned, the interference was just a nuisance rather than a means of detecting aircraft.

As a result of successful trials in February 1935, Radio Direction Finding (RDF), a combination of RD (radio detection) and DF (direction finding) – the acronym was deliberately chosen to give the impression that experiments being carried out were simply concerned with direction finding – twenty stations were established along the east coast to provide early warning of approaching aircraft. Similar stations were later established along the south coast. This early warning of approaching enemy aircraft became imperative, especially after the German successes in Europe and the additional airfields that became available. Enemy aircraft would then have the capability of flying deeper into Britain from bases such as Brest in northern France.

On the north-west coast of Wales, as part of the 'West Chain' of defences, N°· 9 Group Fighter Command was responsible for the radar stations located at Trewen Sands, South Stack, Wylfa and Bryngwran on Anglesey. However, construction work at Bryngwran was abandoned due to 'the nearness of a proposed airfield.' Three stations were operational on Lleyn – Nefyn (opened 30 September 1940, it was also used in conjunction with the Ministry of Defence missile range at Llanbedr for tracking operations), Pen-y-Bryn (Aberdaron) and Rhiw.

The Radar station on the Great Orme, Llandudno.

In addition to its detection role, the radar station on Great Orme's Head in Llandudno was involved contemporaneously in experimental work with the RAF and Royal Navy. The Rhiw station on the Lleyn peninsular was also involved in similar experimental work. By the end of 1942, the United Kingdom was covered by nearly 200 stations, excluding the many mobiles that were also available.

When the radar stations in north Wales needed servicing, a large Royal Navy vehicle was used as a means of conveying specialists, together with components and spares. For transmission and reception, a seven feet paraboloid aerial was fixed on the outside of the vehicle. However, when it was necessary to visit radar stations on Anglesey, the service vehicle had to be transported across the Menai Strait on a Landing Craft Tank (LCT) since its size precluded it from using the Menai Suspension Bridge.

Flt/Lt A. H. Aynon.

Flt-Lt N. H. Anyon was involved with anti-submarine work and convoy escort duties between September 1943 and August 1944 whilst based in Gibraltar with 202 Squadron. The primitive Anti-Submarine Vision (ASV), then the best radar system available, was used continuously throughout every sortie to assist the visual search in daylight and to initiate the plan of attack at night. During night-time operations, a Leigh light mounted on the underside of the aircraft, provided a powerful searchlight to detect U-boats on the sea surface. Later, with 302 Ferry Training Unit at Oban, he was involved with carrying out tests on ASVs' efficiency in detecting the Schnorkel tube of a captured German U-boat. It was found that in a calm sea, the tube could be detected at a distance of two miles but in anything

210   Anglesey & Gwynedd, the War Years, 1939–45

RAF Nefyn.
The surviving evidence of the radar station that stood alonside the road at Llandudwen. Right: Standby Set House.
[W. Alister Williams Collection]

Above: A concrete base for a leg of one of the radar masts.
[W. Alister Williams Collection]

Above right: Standard pre-fabricated RAF hut from the RAF Nefyn camp at Giat Goch.
[W. Alister Williams Collection]

RAF Pen-y-Bryn, Mynydd Mawr, Aberdaron.

Above and right: Some of the concrete footings of the Chain Home radar station overlooking Bardsey Island.
[W. Alister Williams Collection]

Vehicle arriving at Beaumaris by LCT for servicing Radar equipment on Anglesey.
[Hilary Date]

greater than a stiff breeze, it was lost in the radar 'clutter.'

As a result of the successful testing of ASV's successor, Long Range Anti-Submarine Vision (LRASV) on Catalina DP202 on the west coast of Scotland, the system was specially installed in a Catalina at Saunders Roe, Beaumaris. The aircraft was flown to America to enable the LRASV to be demonstrated to the United States Air Force and Navy. The LRASV significantly increased the success of Coastal Command's anti-submarine work.

N⁰· 31 Maintenance Unit

Storage of high-explosive bombs and similar devices during times of war present many problems, not the least of which is the danger to the public. Before the outbreak of war, the old quarry at Glyn Rhonwy, Llanberis, had been chosen as a suitable place for storing high explosives because of its accessibility by both rail and road, and minimal danger to the public.

The depot, identified as N⁰· 31 Maintenance Unit (MU) and forming part of N⁰· 42 Group, Maintenance Command, was opened in May 1941 with the first consignment of high-explosive 250 lbs and 500 lbs bombs arriving by rail from a munitions factory in Swindon, on 3 June 1941.[26] On arrival, the munitions trains were shunted into a marshalling yard, situated between the main road and Llyn Padarn, before the wagons were taken by diesel-engine, through a tunnel beneath the main road, directly into an underground storage facility. Four engines were used at different times: 0-4-0D, built by John Fowler of Leeds; and N⁰· 186 (4wDM 198324, 1940), N⁰· 187 (4wDM 198325, 1940) and N⁰· 237 (4wDM 210478, 1942), built by Ruston & Hornsby of Lincoln). Specially-constructed sidings, large enough to accommodate eight wagons, allowed the bombs to be manhandled onto nearby platforms, before being stored on two floors within the quarry, each floor being roughly the size of a football field, and interconnected by lifts

N[o.] 31 MU, Llanberis, May 1946, with bomb storage clearly visible. [Ivor Jones]

and stairs. The bombs were stored in pyramid fashion with the heavier bombs kept on the ground floor.

Bombs, both incendiary and high-explosive, were also stored out in the open at Glyn Rhonwy, stacked and grouped in accordance to their size and weight, with each stack seventy-five yards apart and covered with a tarpaulin. These open-air sites were had names such as Piccadilly Circus, Burlington Square, Clapham Common, Hounslow, Olympic and Sevenoaks. Similar open-air sites were located near the villages of Rhiwlas and Clwt-y-Bont on the other side of Llyn Padarn, and in the old lead mines at Holywell which came under the care of N[o.] 31 MSU (Maintenance Satellite Unit). Bomb fins were stored at Marconi's old radio station building at Ceunant near Llanrug.

Orders for bombs or ammunition were usually received by teleprinter and deliveries were made either by rail or by road, depending on the destination, route and possible problems with unloading. When deliveries were taken by Matador or Scammel lorries to various airfields, or to

Liverpool for shipping abroad, two red flags were displayed on each vehicle to indicate the type of load being carried. When sent by rail, bombs weighing up to 500 lbs would be loaded by a gang of men using planks and ropes, but those in excess of that weight were moved with the aid of a crane. The sealed wagons were documented with coded tickets which gave no indication of their eventual destination.

As the number of raids over Germany increased, so too did the demand for bombs from Llanberis. At the time of the first 1,000-bomber raid, there was a considerable movement of bombs to RAF Mildenhall in Suffolk, but the most noticeable demand for high explosives came just prior to D-day. Bombs were still arriving at Llanberis and being dispatched from there to various parts of the country for some five years after the war.

On 25 January 1942, disaster struck when part of the concrete roof over the storage area known as the tunnel, collapsed onto 8,230 tons of high explosive bombs. No attempt was made to extricate the bombs for some time, but when work started, the task took eighteen months to complete. Following the removal of the debris, the bombs were taken initially to Rhiwlas and Clwt-y-Bont, where they were stored in the open and guarded by the RAF.

In a building described as the belting shed near the marshalling yard, women deftly loaded ammunition belts with .303 bullets, and later .35mm cannon shells, for use in fighter aircraft. The loaded belts, containing 1,000 to 1,500 rounds, depending on the size of the bullet or shell, were then placed in metal boxes and sealed prior to being put in wooden boxes. Belt loading also continued for a while after the war ended.

The only known fatality caused by explosives at Glyn Rhonwy occurred on 5 July 1944 when a box of detonators being carried in the proof yard exploded and Ivor David Roberts of Llainwen, Llanberis, died from his

Crane used at Nº 31 MU, Llanberis and with the gas bombs at Llandwrog. [Haydn Holland]

Glyn Rhonwy– Nº 31 MU storage area where the roof collapse occurred 1942. [AC]

Above and below: Staff Nº 31 MU, Llanberis. [Margaret Sheldon]

Staff at Nº 31 MU, Llanberis.
[E. M. Jones]

injuries. Two others, John Parry of Bryngro in Cwmyglo and George Williams of Ty'n Twll in Waenfawr, were injured in the same incident.

Civilian wages were £5 per week in 1945 but an additional 5s. was paid when there was an element of danger, such as checking tins of ammunition for any faults. Although this was an RAF base, most of the duties during the early years were performed by civilians but, gradually after training, RAF personnel took over the handling of bombs.

Bomb clearance at Llanberis

By June 1943, many of the explosives stored at Llanberis had become obsolete or had deteriorated to such an extent that the decision was taken for them to be destroyed. The opportunity arose for Nº 2 MU of the RAF School of Explosives, a unit which dealt with the destruction of explosives by detonating and burning, to be transferred to Llanberis.

Nº 31 MU fire tender.
[Eric Baylis]

Course Nº 41 was started on 27 June 1943 and initially 4 lb and 25 lb incendiaries were burned in a nearby quarry, that had been specially allocated for the purpose. In addition, 571 tons of incendiaries were transferred from various parts of the unit to the burning ground for destruction the following November. 173,000 25 lb incendi-aries, and 88,000 4 lb incendiaries were destroyed between December 1943 and September 1944, and a further 95 tons of incendiary bombs by the end of that year. At the same time, Llanberis was used as a disposal site for obsolete pyrotechnics brought in from various parts of Britain by rail.

The explosives, brought from their storage sites by road, were transferred by gravity-fed rollers through a tunnel to a point where they could be dropped down a chute to the quarry floor. There, in theory at least, they would explode and burn harmlessly and cause sufficient fire to dispose of other pyrotechnics which followed down the chute. Unfortunately, the wind had a habit of changing direction and when that happened, it was not unknown for the summit of Snowdon to disappear behind the resulting black smoke, causing a number of complaints from climbers, walkers and the Snowdon Mountain Railway company. Similar complaints would be received if there was a change in wind direction, resulting in smoke being blown towards Fachwen and Brynrefail. Since disposal of the bombs was totally dependent on the weather, every opportunity was taken to dispose of as many explosives as quickly as possible, since they only had a certain period of time to complete the job, and could only work during daylight hours. If the officer-in-charge thought that the direction of the wind was away from possible objectors, the order would be given to continue with the destruction of various devices.

By 1955, Llanberis had become a maintenance sub unit of RAF Llandwrog and the disposal by exploding and burning of detonators, 750 and 1,000 lbs incendiary clusters, UX bombs, signal cartridges, pyrotechnics and anti-aircraft devices, continued until July 1956. However, although the unit was closed in August 1956, the problem of the remaining explosive devices which had failed to detonate or burn, still remained.

From the outbreak of war, the roads above Llanberis and in the vicinity of storage areas had been controlled by the RAF and the only members of the public who were allowed to use them, and who had been issued with

RAF personnel and civilian staff at Nº 31 MU, Llanberis. [Margaret Sheldon]

Long overdue bomb disposal at Nº 31 MU, Llanberis. Started in 1969, the task was not completed until 1975.
[Aneurin Jones]

Glyn Rhonwy map, 1972

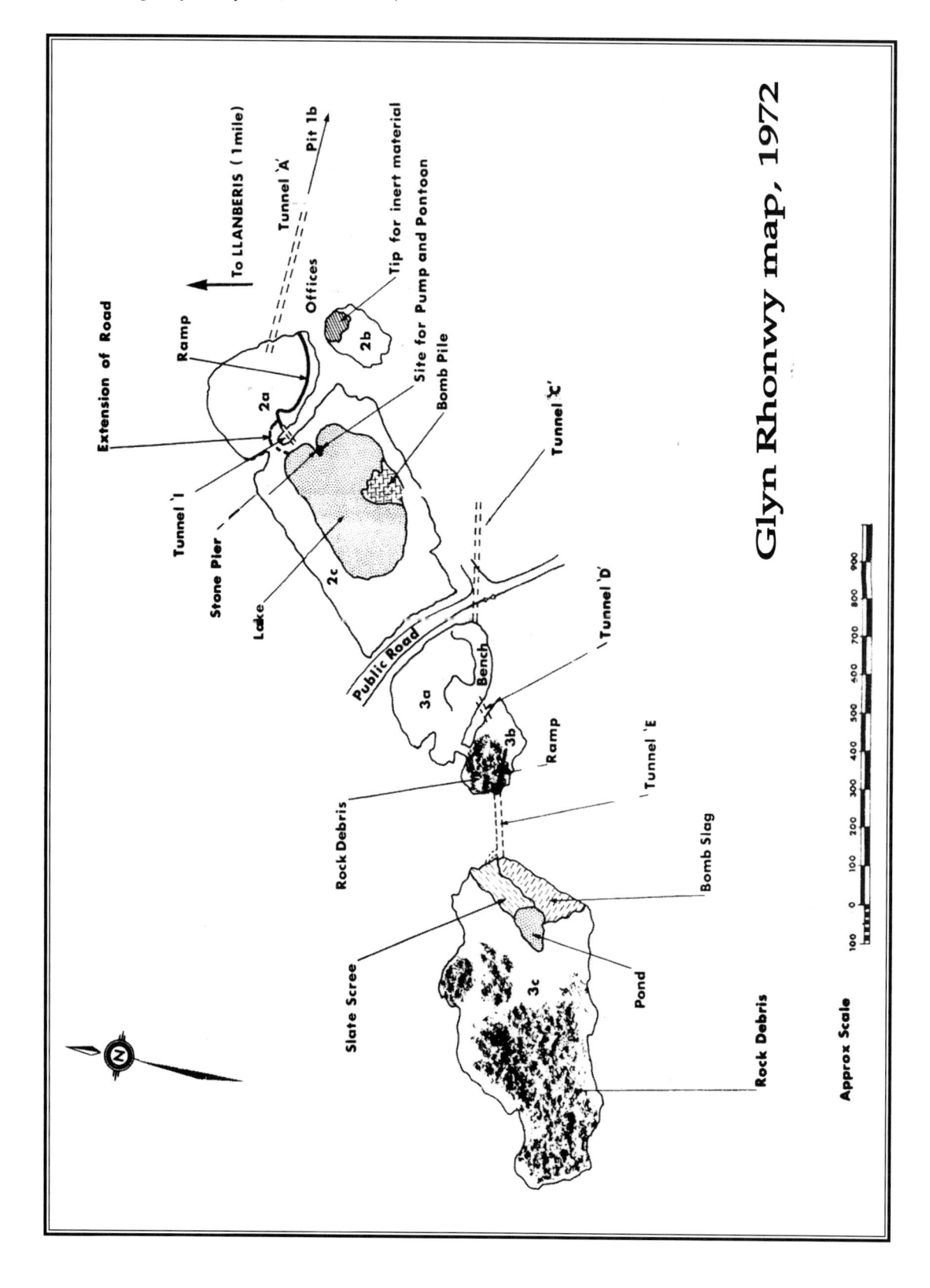

special passes, were those whose property could only be accessed from such roads. When the Air Ministry decided that the roads along the mountain-side and skirting the storage area could be re-opened to the public, suitable fences were erected in an attempt to prevent anyone from entering the potentially dangerous quarries or pits which had been used in the disposal of bombs. In practice however, those of a more determined character found such precautions a mere hindrance and, in the succeeding years, the fence was breached on several occasions. Discussions took place periodically regarding the security of the area and the possibility of clearing the pits of remaining explosives, but this was dismissed as being 'hazardous and uneconomical.' Owing to the presence of explosives and the constant source of anxiety to those responsible for the area, HQ Maintenance Command was given the task of conducting a reconnaissance of the pits area in 1969. No. 71 MU Bomb Disposal Flight, later re-named No. 2 Explosives Ordnance Depot Unit, found evidence of excavation and removal of explosives from Pit Area No. 4. This discovery, and the forthcoming Investiture of the Prince of Wales, prompted the Ministry of Defence to take action.

By May 1970, Pit No. 1 at Glyn Rhonwy, had been declared clear of all dangerous devices and, within two years, a similar clearance was given to Pit No. 4. Similar work continued on Pit No. 3 and interconnecting tunnels. As the result of a survey carried out by naval frogmen, a large quantity of derelict explosives had been found in the lake in Pit 2C. With the assistance of No. 38 Engineering Regiment, Royal Engineers, who were responsible for civil engineering support, including road-building to various pits, twenty million gallons of water had to be pumped out of the lake before work on the removal of the explosives could begin. With the removal of the water, it became apparent that it would take at least two years to dispose of all that had been revealed.

Whilst the quarries were being cleared, and because of the danger involved in such work, a radio link was maintained between Llanberis and RAF Valley from where a Casevac helicopter and medical personnel could be summoned, if an accident occurred.

Although many hazards and difficulties were encountered, the final clearance and handing over of the site to the Property Services Agency was achieved on 31 October 1975.[27]

Gas Bombs Llandwrog – 'Operation Sandcastle'
Allied forces first experienced the effects of chemical warfare in April 1915, when chlorine gas was released by the Germans at Ypres on the Western Front. Five months were to elapse before the Allies were in a position to take retaliatory measures. At the end of the First World War, such was the general revulsion against chemical warfare that it was banned by the Geneva Protocol of 1925. Despite the world's revulsion at the use of chemical weapons, there was a genuine fear that they would be used in the

next war so that, when hostilities broke out in 1939, everyone in Britain, both military and civilian, was issued with a gas mask. Thankfully, no chemical weapons were used against Britain but both sides carried out experiments and tests with a range of chemical weapons during the war years. As far as the civilian population of north-west Wales was concerned, there was a feeling that they were relatively safe from chemical weapon attacks which, if they came, would almost certainly be focussed on the armed forces and the major urban areas of England.

When Allied troops were advancing deep into Germany in April 1945, they discovered a munitions dump with a stock of shells containing mustard gas. When a further stock of shells was discovered at another location, tests carried out by British scientists from Porton Down found that they contained 'a markedly potent and hitherto unknown organophosphorus nerve agent.' In fact, it was found that this agent, named tabun, was ten times more toxic than any other known substance. In 1936, whilst researching for a new insecticide, a German research scientist had discovered an organophosphate chemical that possessed a high degree of toxicity. It was found during tests that even a tiny drop of this substance proved lethal to animals.

Following an agreement with America, Britain was elected to take control of all nerve gas bombs containing tabun while the United States would be responsible for the nerve gas, sarin. The government decided to import the tabun gas bombs into Britain as they 'should be retained for possible use in the Far East.'[28] There followed a period of twelve months of planning before it could be decided how 71,000 of these bombs could be transferred and where they could be stored.

Gas Bombs stacked on the runway at RAF Llandwrog. [AC]

Until 1945, Llandwrog airfield had been the scene of much air activity, but its reversion to a peacetime role at the end of the war was delayed when it was decided that the airfield, four miles south-west of Caernarfon, would be suitable for storing the bombs since it was no longer operational, but still under government control. The site had the benefit of secured boundaries and, since the bombs would be stored in the open, any gas leakage would be dispersed by the prevailing wind. The airfield was taken over on 29 July 1946 by the specially-formed N$^{o.}$ 277 MU (part of the Bicester based N$^{o.}$ 42 Group) which would be responsible for the storing of the bombs.

The bombs, described as 'ex German KC 111 bombs', were initially transported to the port of Hamburg where they were loaded onto vessels, such as the *Empire Condor*, to be shipped to Newport in Monmouthshire. On arrival there, the ship was isolated from all other vessels and, apart from the civilian crane operator, only RAF personnel of N$^{o.}$ 6 Explosives Unit were permitted to be in the vicinity whilst the bombs were being transferred to railway wagons. Even customs officials were not allowed to be involved.

The train, made up of some twenty-four wagons with a similar number of bombs in each wagon, took three days for the journey to Llanberis, since travelling was restricted to night-time. During daylight hours, whilst in railway sidings away from any built-up areas and guarded by RAF personnel, the opportunity was taken for a fresh train crew to take over for the next stage of the journey. It took approximately nine months for all the bombs to be transferred in this way. Llanberis, as a transit point, had the benefit of service personnel (from the nearby maintenance sub-unit) who were well-used to handling a variety of bombs with heavy lifting gear. On arrival at the marshalling yard near Llyn Padarn, the bombs were transferred onto Dodge or Scammel lorries which were formed up into a convoy of eight to ten vehicles, driven by civilians dressed in anti-gas clothing. These convoys, escorted by RAF motor cyclists, travelled three or four times a day to RAF Llandwrog, and were accompanied by a decontamination unit lorry and a fire-tender. When all the railway wagons had been emptied and the bombs transferred to the airfield, the RAF personnel, who had the responsibility of guarding the train on its journey, returned to Newport by passenger train to accompany the next consignment to Llanberis.

The gas bombs were packed in wooden boxes which measured about 6' x 2' x 2' and bearing German identification marks. They were stacked four boxes high on the runways at Llandwrog, which was guarded as a Class A security area by RAF personnel with guard dogs. (Disposal of German Chemical Warfare Stocks.[29] In an attempt to reduce the rate of deterioration and corrosion of the bombs whilst they were being stored in the open at Llandwrog, it was decided that some form of shelter would have to be provided. The arrival and departure register of the Caernarfon Harbour

Gas Bombs from RAF Llandwrog being loaded on to a landing craft at Fort Belan. [AC]

Trust, the body responsible for all maritime movement along the Menai Strait, gives some indication of the extended military activity at the airfield during this period. In the latter part of 1946 and the beginning of 1947, there are references to various craft delivering cargoes described as steel hangars for RAF Llandwrog.[30] A further entry in the register for 7 January 1947 stated, 'two cargoes consisting of airodrome (sic) Hangars for the RAF station at Llandwrog. I am informed that several more of these hangars will be imported in the near future. Some trouble was experienced in getting efficient labour to discharge these vessels but this has now been overcome and quite a good gang of men were engaged on the last ship and can be secured for other ships in the future.' By July 1947, twenty-four Belman hangars had been erected on the runways, with twenty-three of them being used to house the bombs previously stacked on the runway. The remaining hangar was used for servicing and checking.

By the early 1950s, the workforce at Llandwrog comprised eight RAF officers in command of 200 airmen and twelve civilians. The regular checks that were made for leaks meant that personnel had to wear full anti-gas protective clothing and respirators at all times. In addition, medical personnel were given special training for tackling nerve gas incidents should they arise. Special gas detector sets had became available by 1950 and were installed at relevant points on the airfield. Although tabun gas was described as being colourless and odourless in its pure form, another chemical had been introduced during its production stage to increase the bomb's volatility. It was this additional chemical that created the smell of 'ripe fruit' whenever a leak occurred.

The few bombs that were found to be leaking were dealt with by a team of six civilians appropriately trained and supervised by specialists from the Ministry of Supply and the RAF. The leaking bombs were taken to an isolated spot and placed on planks above a pit four feet square and twelve feet deep, into which caustic soda was poured from barrels until three-quarters full. A civilian armourer, dressed in protective clothing, would

L403 about to be loaded with gas bombs at Fort Belan. [AC]

unscrew the plug from the leaking bomb, thus allowing the remaining content to fall into the pit where it would be neutralised by the soda. It is recorded that some fifty leaking gas bombs were dealt with in this manner. Due to the fact that those working in protective clothing perspired profusely, a shift would be restricted to two hours in the morning and a similar length in the afternoon. At the end of the two hours, the men attended the decontamination centre where they showered to remove any possible contamination from the bombs. The protective clothing was then discarded for burning; it was never used a second time. After a further shower, they then had an opportunity to relax until the next shift.

Each member of the squad handling the bombs was examined by a local doctor and given blood tests every six weeks to ensure that there had been no contamination from the gas. If any was detected, it would mean the man being transferred to other duties for six weeks in order that any adverse effects from the gas had time to wear off. For this type of work, they received three shillings a day danger money. Lectures were given periodically to emphasise the care required in handling the bombs and to emphasise possible danger from the gas.

With the war in the Far East having ended abruptly with the use of atomic bombs (long before the arrival of the tabun bombs in Wales) the futility and the stupidity of importing dangerous gas bombs suddenly became apparent. Although described as '250kg CW aircraft bombs', the design would have precluded them from being carried by British aircraft or being adapted for that purpose due to the state of the casing. To further complicate matters, the bombs had been shipped with their fuses still in place. It was eventually decided that the bombs would be disposed of by deep-sea burial and the undertaking was given the code name of 'Operation Sandcastle.' N° 31 MU, commanded by W/Cdr G. Steel, was made responsible for the safe transfer of the bombs from Llandwrog, by naval vessels, to Cairn Ryan, the military port near Stranraer in Scotland. This entailed building a new road in March 1954 from the airfield to a newly-laid concrete apron at nearby Fort Belan. Small flat-topped Bantam lorries transported the bombs to the apron where they were loaded onto Royal Navy Auxiliary Fleet, Landing Craft Transport (LCT) twin-screw vessels of about 180 feet long with front loading ramp. The actual transfer from lorry to ship was accomplished by means of gravity-fed rollers.[31] Up to five of these vessels were used on the run between Belan Fort and Cairn Ryan, and loading at Belan Fort was undertaken immediately after arrival of the LCT, irrespective of the time of day or night. In the latter case, arc lights were used with small portable electric generators supplying the power.

Although there were times when the two beach-masters at Fort Belan would decide against the voyage to Cairn Ryan because of adverse weather, when conditions and tides were favourable, it was feasible to despatch two loaded vessels per day. Stern anchors were used on occasions to assist in getting off the beach, but the power of the LCT engines was usually sufficient. However, as an additional precaution, bearing in mind the dangerous cargo that was being dealt with, an auxiliary naval tug with civilian crew was usually ready to assist each time a craft arrived or departed. If the weather conditions were favourable, the loaded LCT, with a speed of eight to nine knots, could undertake the voyage to Cairn Ryan and return empty in about three days. When loaded, the LCT was obliged to sail around Anglesey but when returning empty, the craft, with a pilot on board, was allowed to sail along the Strait. Most of the voyages took place in the summer months between May and September because the flat-bottomed vessel had difficulty in coping with rough seas in the winter months.

Heading out to sea prior to dumping. [Imperial War Museum]

The first LCT was loaded on 14 June 1955 and sailed with its crew of eight and two airmen personnel around Anglesey to Cairn Ryan on the following day. At Cairn Ryan, the bombs were unloaded onto one side of the military jetty and immediately re-loaded onto an old cargo steamship on the other side. As a result of the thirty-two trips made from Fort Belan to Cairn Ryan with an average of 500 bombs being carried on each trip, 16,088 bombs were loaded on to the hulk SS *Empire Claire* which was scuttled at 10.14 hours on 27 July 1955.

Although there must have been virtually constant movement of these transport vessels through the Strait in 1955 and 1956, very few entries appear in the Caernarvon Harbour Trust's arrival and departure register. One entry notes the arrival of Motor Vessel (MV) ADC 442 on 8 January 1955, under the command of Captain Ross, and its departure a few days later to Cairn Ryan, Stranraer. The cargo was variously described as 'Company RASC' [Royal Army Service Corps], 'OC 99 Coy' and '45 Coy (WT) RASC' although in other entries the cargo was esoterically described as 'confidential matters'.[32] The question of a charge to be levied against Royal Army Service Corps (War Transport) vessels using berthing facilities in the (Victoria) dock was under discussion by the Trust on 5 July 1955 and it was decided that it would be £1 per vessel per berth.[33]

To expedite the disposal of the remaining munitions, it was decided the following year that the length of each bomb (and its wooden case) would be reduced from approximately six feet to four feet by removing the tail-fins with the aid of a guillotine. This was undertaken by the time the LCT arrived on 3 April 1956. As a result, although it was subsequently feasible to increase the quantity being carried to between 700 and 800 bombs on each trip, the actual number loaded was dependent upon weather conditions and the advice of the beach masters. A second hulk, the SS *Vogtland*, loaded with 28,737 bombs, sailed from Cairn Ryan at midday on 29 May 1956 and scuttled two days later.

The final act occurred when a third hulk, the SS *Kotka*, sailed with 25,928 bombs on board and was scuttled on 23 July 1956. In all, 14,000 tons of bombs were disposed of by deep-sea burial, considered to be the most satisfactory method as far as cost, time and safety were concerned. Their final resting place was at a depth of approximately 5,500 feet, at longitude 12 degrees West and latitude 56 degrees 30 minutes North, about 250 miles west of Colonsay in the Inner Hebrides.

Once Llandwrog airfield had been cleared of the munitions, the area was declared free from explosives and chemical contamination and certified accordingly. The airfield was then reduced to 'inactive status' on 21 October 1956. The twenty-four hangars that had become superfluous to requirements, were put up for sale by tender by the Air Ministry in April 1957.[34]

Notes

1. National Archives, ADM 1/10431, Commissioning Order.
2. Ibid.
3. Letter, dated 20 September 1940, from the Flag Officer-in-Charge, Liverpool, HMS *Eaglet*, Royal Liver Buildings, Liverpool to the Head of M Branch, Admiralty, London.
4. GAS, XC2/40/6.
5. GAS, XC2/40/6.
6. National Archives, ADM 1/1910, Notes of deputation to First Lord of the Admiralty.
7. GAS, XM/6615/94; *C&DH*, 9 November 1945.
8. *NWWN*, 26 May 1938; R. E. Roberts.
9. *C&DH*, 2 June 1939.
10. *C&DH*, 7 September 1939.

11. *C&DH*, 5 May 1939.
12. Caernarvon Harbour Trust Minutes, 4 February 1941.
13. RAF Llandwrog Mountain Rescue Log Books via R. E. Roberts.
14. Ibid.
15. BUP, Bangor 31708.
16. BUP, Bangor 31722.
17. RAF Llandwrog Mountain Rescue Log Books via R. E. Roberts.
18. Ibid.
19. GAS, XJ 2366.
20. RAF Llandwrog Mountain Rescue Log Books via R. E. Roberts.
21. Ibid.
22. Ibid.
23. Ibid.
24. Ibid.
25. Although the acronym RADAR (Radio Aid for Detection And Ranging) had been compiled in the USA in 1940, it was not used in Britain until 1943.
26. GAS, X/CA/160–9.
27. National Archives, AIR 29/994, N°· 31 MU, Llanberis.
28. Porton Down, COS (45) 400(0).
29. Porton Down, COS (45) 400(0) and National Archives, WO193/712.
30. GAS, XD15/8/8a.
31. GAS, XD15/39/131 and GAS, XD2/ADD/58.
32. GAS, XD15/6/9.
33. GAS, D/15/2/4.
34. GAS, XD2/ADD/57.

Chapter 10
Social Life

Entertainment

With the threat of air-raids occurring immediately after war was declared, the government, rather hastily, ordered the closure of all places of public entertainment and sports stadia on 4 September 1939, on the assumption that were they to be bombed, there would be many casualties. However, the order was soon rescinded when it was realised that entertainment was considered to be an excellent morale-booster during wartime.

Even though the country was at war, people tried to live as normal a life as possible. At the Castle Hotel in Bangor, a dance was held on Boxing Night, December 1940, with Harold Dobbs and his band and a week later, a New Year's Eve dance with Billy Ternent and his orchestra, with tickets at 21s. which covered a 'Dinner, Supper and Ball.'

Such was the popularity of the cinema that people queued stoically in the dark, whatever the weather, waiting patiently for a vacant seat. Many adults saw at least one film a week during the war. Most war-time films had a morale-boosting theme running through them as well as some propaganda thrown in for good measure. Whenever possible, people still took a seaside holiday during the war even though access to the sea was restricted or even precluded because of anti-invasion measures, as was the case at Dinas Dinlle near Caernarfon.

Majestic Cinema Concert.
[Caroline Jones]

British Broadcasting Corporation

Sound broadcasting in Wales began from a studio at 19 Castle Street, Cardiff on 23 February 1923. Like all other radio stations at that time, it was licensed to broadcast with its call sign of 5WA (London had started its official broadcasting on 14 November 1922 with the call sign 2LO). Since the six-kilowatt Marconi transmitter only had sufficient power to reach a small part of south Wales, north Wales had to wait until 8 November 1935, when David Lloyd George made an election broadcast from the BBC studio at Bryn Meirion in Bangor. Until the 5-kilowatt relay transmitter at Penmon, Beaumaris, with its 250 foot mast, was opened on 1 February 1937, broadcasts from Bangor had to be sent by telephone line to Cardiff.

As a result of the bombing in London, the Variety Department of the BBC was evacuated to Bristol. Because that city was also deemed a prime target for enemy bombing, the BBC moved again, this time to Bangor in October 1940. A

Harold Dobbs & the Marina Band (L–R): Emlyn Jones; Idwal Davies; Harold Dobbs; Harry Parry; Idwal George; Ernie Daniels; Tommy A. Williams. [Caroline Jones]

coded message about a camel being ill at London Zoo, broadcast by the BBC as a news item, was the signal for comedian Tommy Handley, together with a vast army of 'comics, crooners, musicians, producers, actors, writers, spouses, children, bikes, prams, cats, budgies and a parrot', a total of 432 individuals plus seventeen dogs, to depart from London in a special train which arrived in Bangor in February 1941. With this influx of additional artistes and technicians, the original 1935 studio at Bryn Meirion soon proved totally inadequate and it became necessary for the BBC to acquire additional accommodation and Penrhyn Hall, which was rented from the City Council at a cost of £520 *per annum*, in time for the first of the *Music While You Work* series by Billy Ternent's famous dance band. Later Bron Castell (the old St Winifred's School) which housed the administrative staff and canteen, became the hub of its operations in Bangor. The County Theatre (one of three cinemas in Bangor), as well as the vestries of Twrgwyn, Horeb, St Paul's and Tabernacle Chapels, and part of the Free Library, were also taken by the growing army of supporting staff for rehearsals and similar activities. Broadcasts emanating from Bangor were always referred to as 'coming from somewhere in the north-west' for security reasons. One concert, held at the Luxor Cinema in Llanfairfechan on 28 September 1941, intended to raise funds for the evacuees' Christmas fund, unfortunately included a number of 'smutty jokes' cracked by BBC artistes, Horace Perceaval and Jack Train, which were not considered suitable for a Sunday evening concert and the recording was not broadcast.[1]

The shows that were broadcast from Bangor included *Monday Night at Eight*, *Old Town Hall* and *Irish Half Hour*. One of the most popular was, *It's That Man Again,* known by the acronym *ITMA*, which starred Tommy Handley with Dorothy Summers as his charlady, Mrs Mopp. Another character in the show was Sam Fairfechan which, it is said, was based on an Anglesey butcher who, during the days of severe rationing, greeted his customers with the comment 'we have no butter today, it's all under the counter.'

Welsh half-hour programmes were broadcast for the benefit of forces in the Middle East and Africa, with community contributions being made through the outside broadcast sections in Connah's Quay, Rhyl and Llandudno. Many famous artistes, such as the Welsh tenor, David Lloyd, singing at the Pier Pavilion in Llandudno, accompanied by Harold Dobbs, were often heard on the radio. Outside broadcasts were relayed by GPO landline to the Bangor studios where they were recorded.

The theatre organ broadcasts were always popular with listeners and, as a result of an arrangement made in April 1941 between the BBC and Reginald Foorte, his Moller organ was installed at the specially-adapted Grand Theatre in Llandudno. Thereafter, the hire and use of the organ at a cost of £10 per week enabled the BBC to engage any organist for broadcasting. However, if the instrument was used for commercial gramophone recording, then its use would be confined to Reginald Foorte, the first official BBC theatre organist, and Sandy Macpherson. Macpherson was a Canadian who had come to this country in 1928 at the invitation of MGM to open the Empire Cinema in Leicester Square, London. His warm and friendly voice made him very popular, especially during wartime austerity and blitz conditions with his various programmes, including *At Your Request*, *Chapel in the Valley* and *The Twilight Hour*.

By August 1943, the frequency of German air-raids had decreased, and most of the BBC personnel and artistes who had spent the early war years in Bangor, returned to London. As the result of this exodus, it was decided that the theatre organ would be moved from Llandudno to the County Theatre in Bangor. Such was its size, that the console, which weighed two tons, together with the remainder of the organ's paraphernalia, occupied the whole of the ground floor of the theatre. Organists broadcasting from Bangor, were paid £5 5s. per broadcast.

Whether life in Bangor returned to its 1939 pace with the departure of the BBC personnel is debatable. The temporary 'invaders' certainly enlivened the city and many were sad when they departed 'to resume normal service' from London. Ironically, when a parachute mine was dropped on the Maesgeirchen housing estate on 24 October 1941, the only person killed was one of the BBC employees.

BBC Bryn Meirion studios at Bangor.
[Bangor University Archives]

Voluntary Services

The various voluntary organisations that were active during the war created a sense of altruism that was beneficial to both civilians and members of the armed forces. The Women's Institute (WI) and the Women's Voluntary Service (WVS), established in most communities, provided support where need, particularly on the arrival of the refugee children. The WVS also ran small cafés where, in addition to an alternative to 'mess grub', service personnel were provided with reading material in a warm and welcoming atmosphere.

The government's salvage scheme produced a mass of aluminium saucepans, kettles and jelly-moulds for re-cycling as desperately needed raw materials in the manufacture of fighter aircraft. Indeed, the WVS was so well organised that they were quite capable of arranging the collection of any article or material specified by the government as being in short supply. They were also given the task by the Ministry of Works and Planning of visiting some 2,000 farms and derelict sites over a matter of weeks, looking for scrap iron.

Comforts for the Troops committees organised the distribution of wool to individuals who had both the time and the expertise to knit garments for service personnel. These were welcomed by soldiers serving in such units as C Battery, 130th Royal Artillery Regiment at Llanfwrog and the 4th heavy Anti-Aircraft Training Camp at Tŷ Croes,[2] particularly during the winter. Staff and pupils at the County School in Caernarfon were amongst those who contributed to the knitting programme on a regular basis.[3] as did the Port Dinorwic Knitting Class which supplied 3,146 garments during the course of the war.[4]

The British Red Cross Society and St John Ambulance, in addition to their traditional roles of nursing, also arranged and administered the packing of food parcels by volunteers, which contained standard items such as tea, sugar, cigarettes, tinned fruit and corned beef. These were distributed to British prisoners of war held on the continent. By 1944, the weekly output of parcels had reached 102,000. It was also possible for parcels to be addressed individually and incorporated within the Red Cross scheme.[5]

In addition to the weekly house-to-house sale of savings stamps by a band of dedicated collectors, towns and counties were given targets during nationally organised savings schemes such as the *Wings for Victory* or *Warship Week*[6] which were duly acknowledged with the appropriate name being applied to the aeroplane or vessel being 'purchased'.[7] When Caernarvonshire raised the necessary funds, a Mark IIb Spitfire (P8690) was named *Caernarvonshire* and allocated to Nº 12 MU on 25 May 1941 before being taken over by Nº 610 (County of Chester) Squadron on 19 July 1941. Sadly, it failed to return from operations on 21 July 1941. Merioneth was equally successful in raising funds for a Mk 1 Spitfire (R7136) named *Merionethshire*. It was flown by test pilot, George Pickering, on 18 February 1941 before being transferred to Nº 12 MU on 5 March 1941, followed by Nº 124 Squadron on 7 May 1941, Nº 340 Squadron on 20 October 1941 and Nº 52 OTU on 9 December 1941. It was involved in a category B flying accident on 15 April 1942, transferred to AST (Hamble) on 7 November 1942 and 'struck off charge' on 23 November 1942. During the Caernarfon *Wings for Victory* event between 8–15 May 1943, the public was advised that if a figure of £80,000 was reached, then sixteen fighter planes could be built and Llanberis, given a target of £25,000, could fund five fighters.

A similar scheme was organised in September 1941 by the Anglesey National War Savings committee:

> Warship Week – The Plan is to continue a popular appeal for increased savings with the forging of close links between all our cities, towns and Rural Districts and His Majesty's ships. Each Local Committee Area will select as a target the cost of building a certain type of ship. The

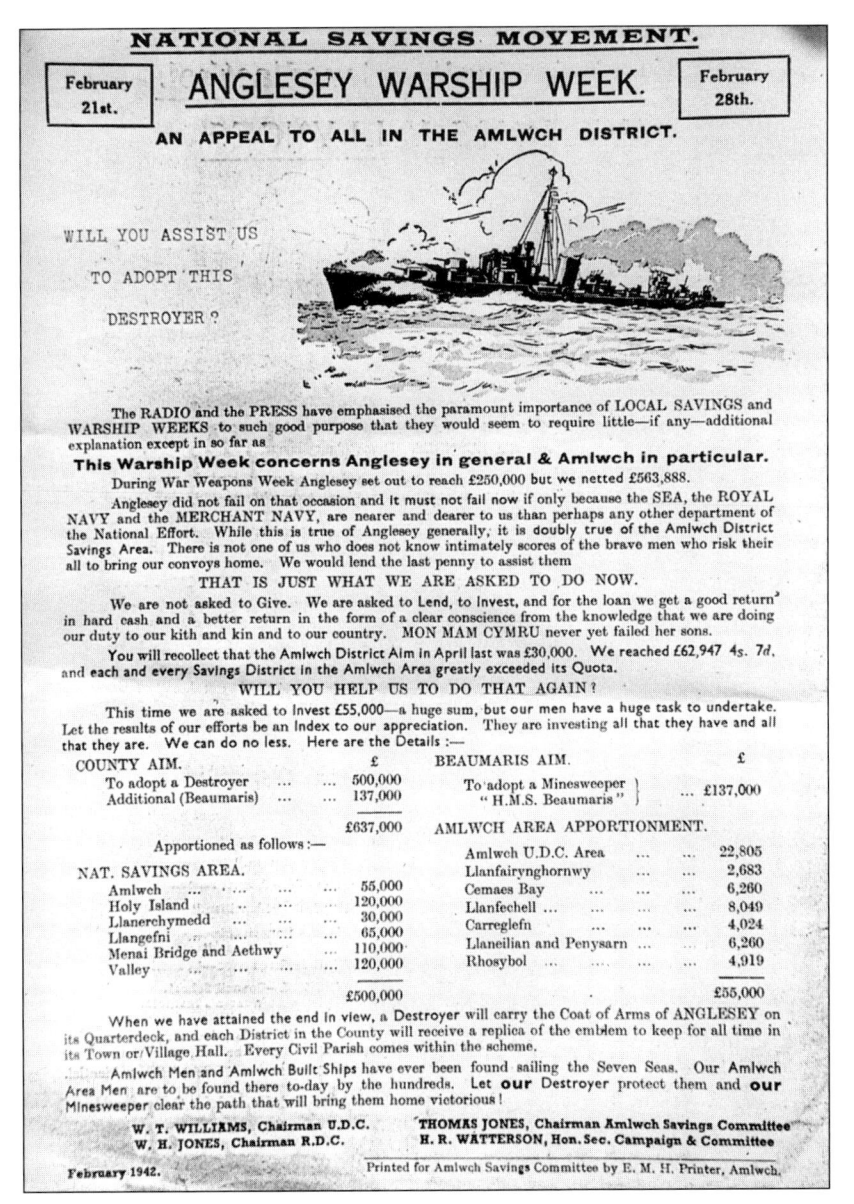

An appeal for support during National Warship Week 1942. [Bangor University Archives]

Weapons Week Parade through Castle Square, Caernarfon, led by the Women's Auxiliary Army Corps followed by a contingent from the British Red Cross. [AC]

Admiralty have gladly agreed that when this target is attained the town (or area) should be allowed to adopt a ship of that class ...'⁸

A further appeal was launched on the 21 February 1942, particularly aimed at 'everyone in the Amlwch district.' They were reminded that a similar appeal in April 1941 raised £62,947 against a target of £30,000. When Anglesey was given a target of £250,000 for *War Weapons Week*, they raised

Red Cross officials and volunteers involved with parcelling food at the Caernarfon Drill Hall for British Prisoners of War in Europe. [Doris Rogers]

Military parades were a regular feature of most county towns during the war years, particularly when a major fund-raising campaign was in progress.

Members of the Royal Observer Corps participating in the 'Salute the Soldier Week'. [D. Meirion Hughes]

Local Army Cadets participating in a 'War Bonds' parade through Castle Square, Caernarfon in 1944. [R. T. Jones]

'Salute the Soldier Week', members of the Women's Royal Naval Service (The Wrens) head a contingent from the Royal Navy in a parade through Castle Square, Caernarfon. [Stuart Whiskin]

£563,888, a very significant sum of money at that time.

During the week of 15–22 November 1941, the *Warship Week* targets set for the Llandudno area, and the type of naval vessel that could be built if the target was attained were:

Targets: Colwyn Bay (a destroyer) £210,000; Llandudno (a fleet minesweeper) £137,000; Conwy (a corvette) £55,000

Monies collected: Colwyn Bay £422,431; Llandudno £222,000; Conwy £125,300.

A concert in the Dolgellau area in January 1943 raised £27 16s. 2d. towards a target of £500 for the *Welcome Home Fund*, which enabled each person within a prescribed area to receive £1 for every six months service in the armed forces. Families of personnel who had been killed during the war were also entitled to the same payment.[9]

Notes
1. GAS, XJ2363.
2. PPP 481.
3. GAS, X/DI/736.
4. *C&DH*, 12 October 1945.
5. PNP 219.
6. GAS, XC2/2/31.
7. GAS, WM/316/9.
8. GAS, XC2-2-31.
9. GAS, ZM/4247/1–9 & 11–16.

Chapter 11
Mulberry Harbour

It was agreed by the Combined Chiefs of Staff in May 1943 that a full-scale attack on Occupied France had to be undertaken across the English Channel within twelve months. Winston Churchill was noted for the brevity of his memoranda and one, dated 30 May 1942, addressed to the Chief of Combined Operations (CCO), Lord Louis Mountbatten, set out his requirements for the intended invasion of Europe, 'Piers for use on Beaches – They must float up and down with the tide. The anchor problem must be mastered. Let me have the best solution worked out. Don't argue the matter. The difficulties will argue for themselves.' Undoubtedly, the Prime Minister had envisaged many of the problems, not least, the vast quantity of stores, including ammunition, petrol and food, that would be required once the beachhead was established. On the assumption that it would be unlikely that the Germans would leave ports in Brittany and Normandy intact for the benefit of invading troops, a way had to be found to ensure that supplies would flow across the Channel and into France unimpeded. Even when it was eventually decided that supplies would be delivered onto open beaches, the possibility of adverse weather, even in the summer-time, curtailing or even preventing deliveries, had to be borne in mind (as it happened, an unseasonable storm did occur). For this reason, the decision was taken to provide an artificial harbour.

Following on from Churchill's memo, Lord Mountbatten asked British engineers to draw up plans for a suitable artificial harbour, which took into consideration the shallow and sandy sea-bed common to the Normandy coast, and the fact that the piers would have to carry the heaviest of tanks and artillery. Of the three schemes submitted, one was by Hugh Iorys Hughes of Bangor, a professional consulting civil engineer, who was in practice in London where he was associated with many notable projects including the Empire Swimming Pool at Wembley and the Piccadilly Underpass at Hyde Park Corner, London. Hughes was instructed by Headquarters Combined Operations in June 1942 to proceed with the construction of prototypes in accordance with his design.

The first intimation that Conwy in north Wales would be involved in the construction of what was to be known as 'Mulberry Harbour' came on 28 October 1942 when H. E. West, a representative of Holloway Brothers, a firm of London builders and contractors, called to see the Town Clerk bringing with him a letter from Iorys Hughes by way of an introduction, and indicated that he intended to make use of a piece of land on the Morfa for constructional purposes which was described as being of a 'vital secret and of Prime Minister priority.' The letter also referred to 'the derelict

Iorys Hughes, one of the leading figures behind the development of the Mulberry Harbours. [Rosemary Hughes]

house known as The Beacons ... and that ... it would be of great use in the proposed works ...' Hughes was given permission for West to make trial borings to examine the subsoil.

Iorys Hughes arrived at Conwy on 30 October 1942, with Captain Coulson of the War Department, and together they produced a plan showing the land required on the Morfa, as well as part of the land leased to the Caernarvonshire Golf Club. Work was to start on the site on 2 November, with the building of a new road by Conway Borough Council on behalf of Holloway Brothers. At the same time, discussion took place on the cost to Holloway Brothers for their vehicles to cross the suspension bridge at Conwy.[1]

A frontage of 1,150 feet of the foreshore was necessary to enable the monoliths to be built and launched into the Afon Conwy (directly opposite Deganwy). Although this was described as 'very sandy and of little agricultural value' it had been agreed with the local council that they would be compensated at £6 per annum. The 850 tons of steel plates used for the pier-heads were pre-assembled by riveting or welding sections at the Joseph Parkes & Son works at Northwich, and transported by articulated lorries to the Morfa. To enable the steelwork to be welded together, it was placed in position at the berths by large cranes. Other construction firms involved included Holloway Brothers, Waring & Co. and Ace Welders Ltd, all from London. The resident engineer was Mr E. W. Etcheles.[2] It was anticipated that the first group of some 200 men would be on site to start work early in November 1942 and that accommodation would be arranged at Bryn Corach, Beechwood Court, Conwy.

A meeting of the workers is held outside The Beacons, Morfa Conwy.
[Rosemary Hughes]

During the busiest period, the men (and women) worked twenty-four hours a day in twelve-hour shifts on the project at Conwy, and such was the pressure to complete the work, that blackout regulations were, more often than not, ignored. This army of workers transformed a quiet and secluded corner of the Morfa, covering about ten acres into a hive of activity whilst the administration staff was housed in The Beacons. To counter the effect of adverse weather on the workers, protective clothing was supplied and the canteens were kept busy providing hot drinks. Although the normal school-leaving age was fifteen, such was the demand for personnel that officials from the site toured local schools inviting youngsters as young as fourteen-years-of-age to

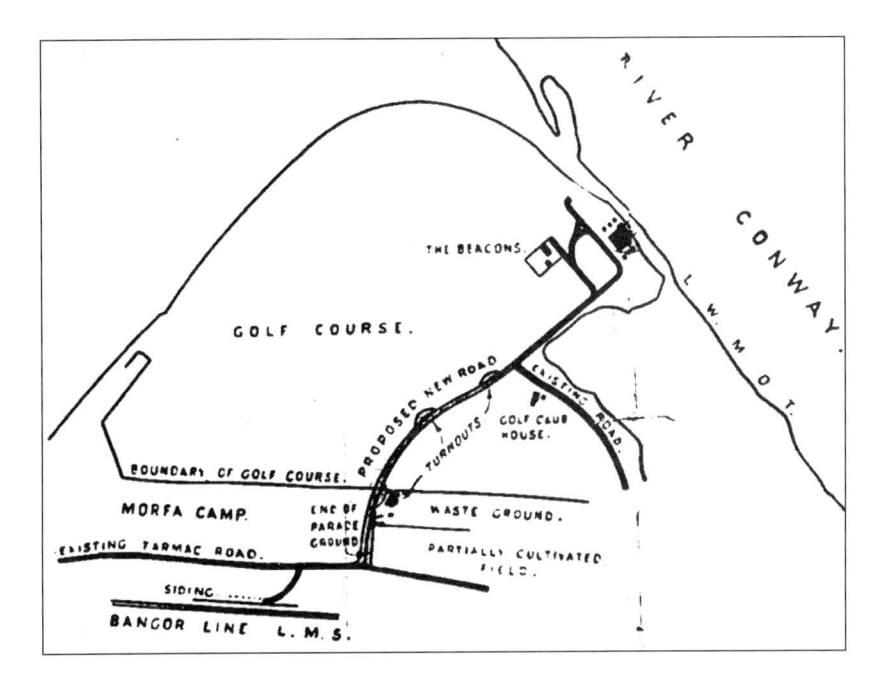

Plan of the area where the floating harbour sections were built at Morfa Conwy.
[Rosemary Hughes]

come and work at the Morfa helping the workmen in various ways, including distributing hot drinks, in order to maintain the momentum of the work.

The workers were housed at hostels, holiday homes and boarding-houses, indeed anywhere where there was a bed to spare. Even convalescent homes were pressed into service when accommodation was required. Buses would tour the various lodging houses to collect the men for work and return them at the end of the shift. One of these men was Olef Kerensky, the son of the former Russian Prime Minister, who served the project as a supervisor (he had fled from Leningrad at the age of ten and entered the UK on a false passport).

The Morfa area, between The Beacons and the golf course, was transformed into a huge construction site where sample units for a floating harbour were constructed. Iorys Hughes later wrote, 'I appointed contractors to build, to my design, three pier units of reinforced concrete, capable of being towed to site and sunk in place, each weighed 6,000 tons (known as Hippo units) and two steel connecting spans (known as 'Croc' units). One Hippo was equipped as a pier-head.' The first concrete barge was launched on Tuesday, 4 May 1943 at 12.10 when the harbour at Conwy was closed to all navigation. After launching, the various components were towed to a site in Rigg Bay near Garlieston, Scotland where the two 'Crocs' were attached to the Hippos and tested in a variety of combinations during different weather and tidal conditions. During the testing, fully laden lorries were driven across the roadway and it was found that the floating piers did not rise and fall with the tide as predicted. Hughes resolved the problem by inserting adjustable spans between the Hippos and the

Above left: Work is well under way on a 'Hippo' section of the floating harbour.
[Rosemary Hughes]

Above right: The reinforced concrete construction of a 'Hippo' caisson is clearly visible in this photograph.
[Rosemary Hughes]

Right: A 'Hippo' on the slipway ready for launching into the River Conwy.
[Rosemary Hughes]

Left: A 'Hippo' floats in the River Conwy for the first time. [Rosemary Hughes]

The 'Hippo' section floats in the Conwy estuary ready to put to sea for testing in Scotland. [Rosemary Hughes]

Three floating 'Hippo' sections linked by a 'Croc' roadway are tested at sea. [Rosemary Hughes]

The view looking along the 'Croc' roadway. [Rosemary Hughes]

A 'Croc' roadway section on the beach at Conwy and (below) being pulled out into mid stream by a tug.
[Rosemary Hughes]

Below: Floating on the river prior (Deganwy in the background) to heading to Scotland.
[Rosemary Hughes]

roadway. A more serious problem, however, was the pitching and yawing of the Hippos which caused Croc roadways to buckle. This was solved when Hughes proposed the construction of Hippos of various sizes on which the roadways would sit. On conclusion of the tests a final design was decided upon.

In August 1943, a mission left Britain for a conference in Quebec to assist in planning the final 'Mulberry Harbours.' It is difficult to assess how far Hughes influenced the final designs for the Mulberry Harbour and certainly others are given significant credit for having helped with the worked, viz Professor J. D. Bernal (whose ideas were expanded upon by Brigadier Bruce White) and Allan Beckett, whose 'Whale' design for the roadway was eventually selected in preference to Hughes' concrete Hippo.

There would be two harbours, each comprising two breakwaters made from hollow reinforced-concrete caissons. In view of Iorys Hughes' commitment to the project and expertise he was invited by Churchill to serve the project as a consultant. Although Iorys Hughes had been asked to accept a temporary senior rank in the Royal Engineers, he made the following observation:

> I would be more useful and my word would carry more weight if I remained a civilian ... I was paid for my services a much reduced professional fee, which scarcely covered the cost of my staff and overheads. I finished the war worse off financially and three stones lighter! When the War Office asked whether I was prepared to accept a reduced fee I accepted the reduction due to my wish not to be thought a 'war profiteer'.[3]

On 27 August, the War Office was instructed to start urgent plans to construct the concrete caissons. Although Iorys Hughes had already made significant progress with his own designs, the War Office decided to use the alternative 'Whale' design. Hughes was asked whether he was prepared to continue advising on the scheme as a whole and modestly declared, 'Being more skilled and experienced than anyone I knew of, and it being a war effort, I agreed and entered into things wholeheartedly.'

In a letter sent which he sent from his Westminster office, dated 28 September 1943 and classified as 'Most Secret', he stated,

> The instructions received are that it is proposed to construct monoliths at points to be selected on the south coast and to float them by launching. The proportions of the monoliths would be up to 5,000 tons displacement, draught from 8 to 18 feet, and some 180 to 200 feet in length ... [and] to side-launch [rather than end-launch] ...[4]

The six sites that he chose were two at Stokes Bay, and one at Southsea, Brighton, Langnay Point (near Eastbourne) and Hastings.

A letter received on 13 September 1943 referred to a new contract on the

The Convoy Pendant Board for one convoy of supply ships heading for Normandy. These ships were to offload their supplies at one of the floating Mulberry Harbours. The third ship in the list is the Dinorwic Quarry ship, Elidir, normally based at Port Dinorwic. [Len V. Williams]

The SS Elidir moored at the Mulberry Harbour off Gold Beach. [AC]

Morfa where some of the chosen 'Whale' designs were to be built although no name was ever given to the components under construction until the 'Whale Project' was mentioned in a letter to the Borough Council on 21 December 1943.

For a few weeks before D-day, Hughes lived with the army in 'the two parking sites – at Selsey Bill and Dungeness, living aboard the accommodation ship and, at times, going to sea. For a few weeks before and after D-day he was at Selsey and Dungeness advising and assisting in the despatch of the Phoenix Units to Normandy.'

There was no reference at Conwy to the project under its code name of 'Mulberry' until 20 September 1945, when the removal of the concrete anchor points, cables and chains was discussed by the Council after complaints had been received from yachtsmen.

Those who were directly involved with the Mulberry Harbour felt that Hughes had not been given sufficient credit for his contribution to the project, notably the floating pier-heads and the towing design for the units. In an attempt to resolve who was responsible for the design of the units, the nebulous reply given to a question asked in the House of Commons on 8 November 1944 made the situation no clearer, 'In a work of such magnitude, many persons were naturally engaged … [including] Civil Engineers and consultants, notably Messrs Gwyther, Iorys Hughes, Lobnitz and Kent, contributed to the design.'[5]

Some 45,000 men throughout the UK were involved in the construction of the various components of the Mulberry Harbour that enabled the landing of 40% of equipment and personnel on the beachhead in Normandy. The enormity of the operation can best be judged by the cost involved – if the same operation had to be undertaken today, the estimated total cost would be £1,000 million.

Notes

1. Private papers, Rosemary Hughes. Conway Borough Council, contract number 294/27/R421.
2. GAS, XB2/454.
3. Private papers, Rosemary Hughes.
4. Ibid.
5. Ibid.

Chapter 12
Peace

With the cessation of hostilities came celebrations which took on many forms, including Victory parades, concerts and street parties for children. However, for the many that had lost relatives and friends in the war, celebratory events merely emphasised a void within a family.

Parts of the country that had not experienced aerial bombardment night after night and the loss of life and property, were unaware of the extent of blitz conditions since little was reported in daily newspapers during the war, due to censorship. Apart from an occasional foray by German bombers, north-west Wales generally escaped the worst of the bombing. However, those who lived in parts of north-west Wales that had been subjected to the sounds of fire-arms and explosions caused by military training during the war were disappointed to learn that it would continue even though hostilities had ended. Much to the consternation of the Portmadoc Urban Council, it was advised that the training camp established in the early years of the war at Harlech would continue to be used for the foreseeable future. The Council complained that 'in the act of firing ... small arms ... and fairly heavy guns ... the resulting vibration ... was so great at times that it may have affected the roofs and brought down the ceilings of some of the houses at Borthygest'. Such on-going training was hardly conducive to re-establishing tourism and the fishing industry which was important to the area. It took a while before life returned to anything resembling peacetime normality.

Although the empty shop shelves began to be filled with stock which had not been seen since early in the war, it would take years before rationing came to an end. The importation of food and material was governed by the number of ships available and home production was controlled by the availability of factories and manpower. Advice on cooking continued to be given by the Ministry of Food which continued to extol the virtues of certain foods, especially potatoes, which were readily available.

Goronwy Roberts, MP for Caernarfon, addressing Clwb y Fenai (the Port Dinorwic Youth Club) in September 1945, stated that the government had in hand the task of turning war industry into peace production, reviving the economy and creating full employment. He prophesied that in a few years there would be, '... more work available than workmen.' Even when employment became available, there was a tendency to pick and choose. Farmers attending the annual hiring fair at Pwllheli in May 1945, found that unemployed skilled farm workers were reluctant to return to their pre-war employment even at a wage of £3 10s. per week.

As an indicator of the revival of tourism in the area, the Snowdon

Mountain Railway resumed operations on 7 May 1945 and charabanc trips, that had been popular before the war, were re-started as soon as buses and staff became available. Caernarvon Football Club was re-formed in October 1945 and, a couple of months later, after six years of inactivity, the Caernarvon Mixed Choir celebrated their first concert under their conductor, Miss Dilys Wynne Williams. The Crosville Male Voice Choir, which had performed regularly during the war under its conductor, Richard Jones, joined other artistes in a concert at the Majestic Cinema in Caernarvon in September 1945, to celebrate the end of the war and in the same month, the senior pupils of Caernarvon Grammar School gave a performance of Oscar Wilde's *The Importance of Being Earnest*, directed by Mrs Nancy Bingley and Mr S. A. Claridge. The London, Midland & Scottish Railway re-introduced its dining-car rolling stock on the north Wales line on 1 October 1945 – 'with cutlery replated.' The North Wales Agricultural Show, suspended since 1938, was resumed at the Oval in Caernarvon on 8 November 1945 when it 'attracted a bumper gate.'

In September 1945, 300 uniformed members of the Land Army marched past the Lord Lieutenant of Caernarfonshire, Brigadier Wynne Finch,[1] who took the salute at the University College of North Wales, Bangor. Later, at the Powis Hall, Hugh Owen, chairman of the Caernarfonshire War Executive Committee, thanked the girls, 'for a difficult job well done.' The following month, the 6th Battalion, Royal Welch Fusiliers were honoured with the Freedom of the Borough of Caernarfon. Those who had served in the forces waited impatiently for their demobilisation from the forces when they were given a free civilian utility suit (in a limited choice of style and colour).

Drifting mines, sometimes dislodged by gales, continued to be a menace along the coast and one caused the residents of Rhosneigr to be evacuated in September 1945 when it drifted onto nearby rocks.[2] Mines, unexploded bombs and other war-time detritus were to be a hazard for many years after the war.

The insularity of the pre-war towns and villages of Anglesey and Gwynedd underwent a dramatic change between 1939 and 1945. Servicemen from the region travelled to all parts of the world to serve against the Axis forces in Europe, Africa and Asia as well as on every ocean. For many, it was a life-changing experience and the men who returned in 1945 and 1946 were very different to those who had gone away a few years earlier.

Guidance from the Archbishop of Wales for those women planning on marrying an American servicemen.

American GIs marching through Castle Square, Caernarfon during 'Salute the Soldier Week'. [Stuart Whiskin]

The many servicemen and civilian industrial workers who spent time in Anglesey and Gwynedd brought with them a taste of the outside world. Perhaps the thousands of children evacuated to the area from the major urban centres of England had the greatest influence and even today, nearly seventy years later, locals still speak with some sympathy about the conditions in which the evacuees had been living, particularly in Liverpool. This influence worked in both directions as children returned home realising that there was another way of life available that was far removed from the squalor of slum living. Some never went back home, while others returned to live in north Wales as soon as they were in a position to control their own destiny. The rock and roll singer Marty Wilde, who lived in Capel Curig during part of the war, credited the Welsh chapels as being responsible for his career in music.

The landscape of the region changed dramatically between 1939 and 1945 as military camps and aerodromes were constructed. Most were abandoned after the war but some remained such as RAF Valley, now the busiest RAF station in Britain and RAF Llandwrog, now Caernarfon Airport, home to the Air Ambulance helicopter and a base for local private aviators.

Notes
1. Later Sir William Heneage Wynne Finch, JP, MC, 1893–1961.
2. GAS, XJ 2366.

Select Bibliography

Beauman, Katherine Bentley, *Greensleeves - WVS/WRVS* (London, 1977).
Beddoe, Deirdre & Leigh Verrill-Rhys, *Parachutes and Petticoats* (Aberystwyth, 1992).
Bridges, Frank, *Saunders Roe Ltd*, 1948.
Brown, Winifred, *Duffers of the Deep* (London, 1939).
Brown, Winifred, *No Distress Signals* (London, 1952).
Carroll, Joseph T, *Ireland in the War Years* (Newton Abbot, 1975).
Cowan, R. J. P., 'Notes on the Construction of Mulberry Harbour in Normandy, June–July 1944'.
Crosland-Taylor, W. J., *Crosville*, Transport Publishing, 1948.
Davies, J. A., *A Leap in the Dark* (London, 1994).
Davies, Martin, The Wartime Storage in Wales of Pictures from the National Gallery.
Davies, Sir William Ll., War-time evacuation to the National Library of Wales.
Doylerush, Edward, *No Landing Place* (Leicester, 1985).
Doylerush, Edward, *Fallen Eagles* (Leicester, 1990).
Fay, Leonard G., 'Career of the Conway', *Sea Breezes*, XX, 1955.
Ferguson, James, *The Vitamin Murders* (London, 2007).
Francis, Dewi B., *Master Mariner, Capt. W. H. Hughes, DSC* (Wrexham, 2006).
Freeman, Roger A., *Britain at War* (London, 1990).
Geary, W., Notes on Farming, 1949.
Graham, Virginia, *The Story of the WVS* (London, 1959).
Harrison, Michael, *Mulberry - The Return in Triumph* (London, 1965).
Hartcup, Guy, *Code Name Mulberry* (Newton Abbot, 1977).
Land at War: The Official Story of British Farming 1939–44 (London, 1945).
Leakey, J. H., *School Errant* (London, 1951).
Mason, David, *U-boat the Secret Menace* (London, 1968).
McCamley, N. J., *The Secret History of Chemical Warfare* (Barnsley, 2006).
Monnickendam, S. A., *Secrets of the Diamond* (London, 1941).
Morgan, Dyfnallt, *Babi Sam Golygydd* (Caernarfon, 1985).
Murray, Keith A H., *Agriculture* (London, 1955).
Ortzen, Len, *Stories of Famous Submarines* (London, 1973).
Pratt, Derrick & Grant, Mike, *Wings Across the Border, a History of Aviation in North Wales and the Northern Marches*, 2 & 3 (Wrexham, 2002 & 2005).
Rowland, Peter, *David Lloyd George - A Biography* (London, 1975).

Sloan, Roy, *The Tale of Tabun* (Llanrwst, 1998).
Smith, David J., *Action Stations 3. Military Airfields of Wales and the North-West* (Leicester, 1981).
Ryder, VC, RN. Commander R. E. D., *The Attack on St Nazaire* (London).
Street, A. G., *Farmer's Glory* (London, 1932).
The Problem of Chemical and Biological Warfare, I (Stockholm, 1971).
Transactions of the Honourable Society of Cymmrodorion, 'National Gallery', 1945 .
Wadsworth, John, *Counter Defensive* (London, 1946).
Williams, W. Alister, *Heart of a Dragon, the VCs of Wales and the Welsh Regiments, 1914–86* (Wrexham, 2008).
Williams, J. Gwynn, *The University College of North Wales 1884–1927* (Cardiff, 1985).
Wood, Keith A., *Echoes and Reflections* (London, 2004).

Brothers Edward Alun Evans & W Glyn Evans (on the left of the photograph) of Machynlleth meet up with Prime Minister Winston Churchill and Field Marshal Sir Bernard Montgomery after the former's crossing of the Rhine in March 1945.
[Y Tabernacl, Machynlleth]